Also by Andrew Podnieks

Silverware (2005)
The Little Book of Hockey Sweaters (with Rob Hynes, 2005)
2005 IIHF World Championship Media Guide (2005)
Lord Stanley's Cup (2004)
The Flames: Celebrating Calgary's Dream Season, 2003-04 (2004)
Players: The Ultimate A-Z Guide of Everyone Who Has Ever Played in the NHL (2003)
Honoured Members of the Hockey Hall of Fame (2003)
The Goal: Bobby Orr and the Most Famous Goal in Stanley Cup History (2003)
A Day in the Life of the Maple Leafs (2002)
Canadian Gold 2002: Making Hockey History (2002)
Kings of the Ice: A History of World Hockey (with others, 2002)
The Essential Blue & White Book: A Toronto Maple Leafs Fact Book (2001)
Hockey's Greatest Teams: Teams, Players, and Plays that Changed the Game (2000)
The NHL All-Star Game: Fifty Years of the Great Tradition (2000)
The Three Stars and Other Selections (with Jefferson Davis, 2000)
The Great One: The Life and Times of Wayne Gretzky (1999)
Hello Hockey Fans From Coast to Coast (with Jefferson Davis, 1999)
Shooting Stars: Photographs from the Portnoy Collection at the Hockey Hall of Fame (1998)
Red, White, and Gold: Canada at the World Junior Championships 1974-1999 (1998)
Portraits of the Game: Classic Photographs from the Turofsky
Collection at the Hockey Hall of Fame (1997)
Canada's Olympic Hockey Teams: The Complete History 1920-1998 (1997)
The Blue and White Book 1997:
The Most Complete Toronto Maple Leafs Fact Book Ever Published (1996)
The Red Wings Fact Book 1997:
The Most Complete Detroit Red Wings Fact Book Ever Published (1996)
The Blue and White Book:
The Most Complete Toronto Maple Leafs Fact Book Ever Published (1995)
Return to Glory: The Leafs From Imlach to Fletcher (1995)

Children's Books

The Spectacular Sidney Crosby (2005)
Hockey Heroes: Paul Kariya (2000)
Hockey Heroes: Patrick Roy (1998)

Printed in Canada

Photo on previous page: Shinny on Lake Louise, Alberta, 2005.

THE
LOST SEASON

A YEAR IN HOCKEY WITHOUT THE NHL

Andrew Podnieks

PHOTO CREDITS

Reuters: p. i, 15, 16, 21, 23, 24, 25, 27, 28, 29, 31, 35, 36, 41, 44, 50, 54, 57, 63, 74, 85, 88, 127, 139, 140, 142 (both), 144, back cover (bottom)

Canadian Press: p. 12, 32, 34, 38, 64, 68, 71, 72, 78, 80, 87, 96, 107, 124, 130, 133

Dave Sandford/Hockey Hall of Fame: p. 8 (both), 9, 10 (both), 13, 14 (both), 17, 18, 19, 20, 33, back cover (top)

Vladimir Bezzubov: p. 77, 90, 93, 95, 100, 114, 119, 144

Brian Smith: p. vi, 22

ACKNOWLEDGEMENTS

The author would like to thank publisher Jordan Fenn for continued support of all things hockey and uber-designer Kathryn Del Borrello for amazing work in the crunch. Additional thanks go to Szymon Szemberg and Kimmo Leinonen at the IIHF, Seva Kukushkin, Danny Braun, Nancy Glowinski, Tammy Egan, Andrea Gordon, Craig Campbell, Phil Pritchard, Darren Boyko, Izak Westgate, Harmony Jagla, Danielle Siciliano, Miragh Addis, Marilyn Robbins, Mike Gouglas, Lucas Aykroyd, and Paul Patskou. To agent Dean Cooke and his associates Samantha North and Suzanne Brandreth. To family and friends, namely Liz, Ian, Emily, Zachary, mom, Jon & Joan, Cathy, and Mary Jane.

LOST SEASON
A YEAR OF HOCKEY WITHOUT THE NHL
A Fenn Publishing Book / First Published in 2005

Fenn Publishing Company Ltd.
Bolton, Ontario, Canada

Library and Archives Canada Cataloguing in Publication

Podnieks, Andrew
        Lost season / Andrew Podnieks.

ISBN 1-55168-298-2

        1. Hockey. 2. Hockey—Canada. I. Title.
GV847.P625 2005   796.962   C2005-904633-3

THE
LOST SEASON

A YEAR IN HOCKEY WITHOUT THE NHL

Andrew Podnieks

Fenn Publishing Company Ltd.

Bolton, Ontario

CONTENTS

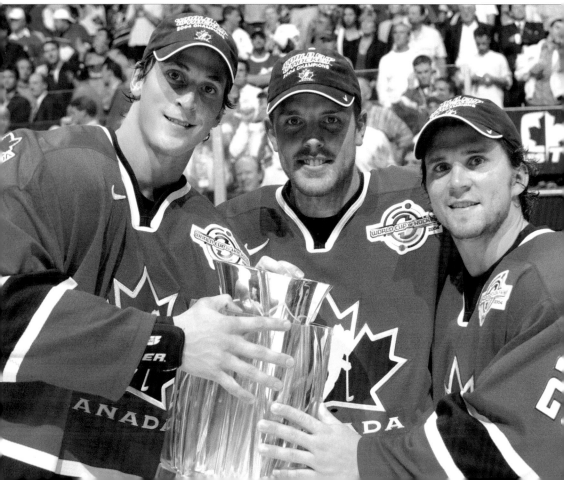

World Cup of Hockey 2004

AUGUST 30-SEPTEMBER 14, 2004

Although this was the first World Cup of Hockey since 1996, the top teams had all played in the same tournament as recently as February 2002 at the Olympic Winter Games in Salt Lake City, Utah. Furthermore, although this was an NHL-organized best-on-best series it was being staged as the darkest days in professional hockey loomed large on the immediate horizon. The day after the World Cup winner was crowned champion, the contract between league and players expired. Thus, there was as much talk about the impending NHL dispute as there was celebration of the game's greatest stars playing together.

To make matters worse, as the summer of 2004 unfolded and the World Cup training camps neared, important players from all countries were pulling out. Canada lost Rob Blake, Chris Pronger, Keith Primeau, Steve Yzerman, and Ed Belfour to injury; Robert Lang and Pavel Kubina pulled out of the Czech entry, but even worse the Czechs lost coach Ivan Hlinka just before the tournament when he was killed in a car crash; Sergei Fedorov, Alexei Zhamnov, Alexei Zhitnik, Nikolai Khabibulin, Evgeni Nabokov, and Valeri Bure all withdrew from Russia; Mathieu Schneider, without a contract, and Jeremy Roenick, because of injury, said no to Team USA; the Slovaks were hit by a rash of injuries and lost Peter Bondra, Ivan Majesky, Michal Handzus, and Zigmund Palffy.

Once the games got under way, the World Cup was a fans' delight. Thirty-eight-year-old captain Mario Lemieux led Team Canada, but the rest of the roster was among the youngest in international hockey history since 1972, featuring some 12 players under the age of 25. The Finns, though, started the tournament with a bang, beating the Czechs 4-0 in Helsinki and limiting their opponents to just 12 shots on goal all game. Miikka Kiprusoff, whose outstanding play took the Calgary Flames to game seven of the Cup playoffs just three months earlier, recorded the shutout.

The night next, as expected, the Swedes, with all of their top players in the lineup, beat Germany 5-2, and the following night Canada opened with a 2-1 win over the USA before a wild and raucous crowd at the Molson Centre in Montreal. It was a tough, nasty, North American game that even had a fight in it (Jeff Halpern of USA and Scott Niedermayer), but Canada, wearing vintage 1920 Winnipeg Falcons sweaters, bettered the much older Americans by the narrowest of margins. The Canadians lost defenceman Ed Jovanovski, though, with a broken rib and tear of a knee ligament.

The final game of the European pool featured a wonderful 4-4 tie between the top teams, Finland and Sweden. The Finns had leads of 2-0 and 3-1 in the first period but Tre Kronor tied the game before the end of the period. The Finns, on a goal by Olli Jokinen, went up 4-3 in the second, but late in the third, with goalie Mikael Tellqvist on the Swedish bench, Tomas Holmstrom tied the game 4-4 with just 45 seconds left in the game.

(opposite, top) Goalie Martin Brodeur holds high the 2004 World Cup trophy; (opposite, bottom) the Tampa Bay trio of (left to right) Vincent Lecavalier, Brad Richards, and Martin St. Louis pose with the trophy; (right) game action from the Canada-Czech Republic semi-finals.

9

In the North American pool, Russia's 3-1 win over the USA showed it still had more skill than the aged Americans, who were going with a lineup eerily similar to what they used eight years earlier for their victorious 1996 World Cup. For Canada, the loss of another defenceman, Wade Redden, later in the round robin, meant the activation of teenager Jay Bouwmeester.

The quarter-finals were anything but predictable. Finland-Germany should have been an obvious Finnish victory, but Marco Sturm tied the game 1-1 midway through the third period for the Germans and only a goal with less than four minutes to play by Mikko Eloranta gave the Finns the win. Meanwhile, the Swedes, who had looked so impressive in the round robin, were trailing the Czechs 5-0 in the third period before they scored their only goal of the game in an embarrassing 6-1 loss in Stockholm to a jeering, sold out crowd.

On the North American side, Canada's expected victory over Slovakia, 5-1, was offset by a significant upset as USA beat Russia, 5-3. It was a game the Russians tied 2-2 early in the third period, but Scott Gomez and Keith Tkachuk scored 22 seconds apart to give the Americans a 4-2 lead they never relinquished. These results set up two unexpected semi-finals: Finland-USA and Canada-Czech Republic.

The first semi-final was the closest-checking game of the tournament. The Americans didn't score the first goal until midway through the game, but in the third period Olli Jokinen tied the score five minutes in and captain Saku Koivu scored the game winner with less than four minutes left to stun a sellout crowd at St. Paul, Minnesota. In the other semi-final, a scoreless first period gave way to three goals in the second. Canada jumped into a 2-0 lead thanks to Eric Brewer and Mario Lemieux, but the Czechs brought the score closer, 2-1, before the second period ended. Martin Havlat tied the game early in the third, and it looked like Kris Draper would be the hero for Canada when he sent his team up 3-2 at 13:47. The packed house of 19,273 at Air Canada Centre was shocked, though, when Patrik Elias tied the game just six seconds later, and the rest of the game was a tense battle that went into overtime. The real hero of the night turned out to be Vincent Lecavalier, Stanley Cup winner with Tampa Bay in June 2004, as he drilled a high shot past Tomas Vokoun from an almost impossible angle to give Canada another berth in the finals.

The gold medal game pitted the experienced Canadian team versus the Finns who were in their first Canada Cup/World Cup finals, playing in Toronto. Both teams scored in each of the first two periods, both times Canada going ahead and the Finns tying the score. The turning point came in the first minute of the third period when Shane Doan, on a give-and-go with Joe Thornton, put Canada ahead to stay. The teams played exciting, even hockey the rest of the way, but the Finns couldn't tie the game and Canada emerged on top of the world again.

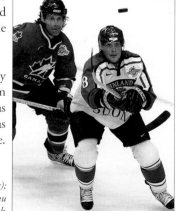

Unfortunately, minutes after leaving the ice with their celebratory trophy (a curious design by Frank Gehry), all the talk switched from World Cup victory to imminent NHL lockout. The real world was upon the euphoric world of hockey, and the World Cup was forgotten, lost, and a thing of the past in almost the blink of an eye.

(top) Joe Thornton (Canada, left) faces off against Pavol Demitra (Czech Republic); (right) Canadian defenceman Scott Niedermayer keeps an eye on Finland's Teemu Selanne who has his eye on the floating puck.

PRELIMINARY ROUND STANDINGS

EUROPEAN POOL

	GP	W	L	T	GF	GA	P
Finland*	3	2	0	1	11	4	5
Sweden	3	2	0	1	13	9	5
Czech Republic	3	1	2	0	10	10	2
Germany	3	0	3	0	4	15	0

*given superior ranking based on goals differential

August 30	Helsinki	Finland 4	Czech Republic 0
August 31	Stockholm	Sweden 5	Germany 2
September 1	Stockholm	Sweden 4	Czech Republic 3
September 2	Cologne	Finland 3	Germany 0
September 3	Prague	Czech Republic 7	Germany 2
September 4	Helsinki	Finland 4	Sweden 4 (5:00 OT)

NORTH AMERICAN POOL

	GP	W	L	T	GF	GA	P
Canada	3	3	0	0	10	3	6
Russia	3	2	1	0	9	6	4
USA	3	1	2	0	5	6	2
Slovakia	3	0	3	0	4	13	0

August 31	Montreal	Canada 2	USA 1
September 1	Montreal	Canada 5	Slovakia 1
September 2	St. Paul	Russia 3	USA 1
September 3	St. Paul	USA 3	Slovakia 1
September 4	Toronto	Canada 3	Russia 1
September 5	Toronto	Russia 5	Slovakia 2

QUARTER-FINALS

September 6	Helsinki	Finland 2	Germany 1
September 7	Stockholm	Czech Republic 6	Sweden 1
September 7	St. Paul	USA 5	Russia 3
September 8	Toronto	Canada 5	Slovakia 1

SEMI-FINALS

September 11	St. Paul	Finland 2	USA 1
September 12	Toronto	Canada 4	Czech Republic 3 (Vincent Lecavalier 3:45 OT)

FINALS

September 14	Toronto	Canada 3	Finland 2

Tournament MVP: Vincent Lecavalier (CAN)
ALL-TOURNAMENT TEAM
Goal: Martin Brodeur (CAN)
Defence: Adam Foote (CAN)
          Kimmo Timonen (FIN)
Forward: Vincent Lecavalier (CAN)
          Fredrik Modin (SWE)
          Saku Koivu (FIN)

Original Stars Hockey League

The day after NHL Commissioner Gary Bettman announced the delay of the 2004-05 NHL season, organizers of the Original Stars Hockey League (OSHL), led by president Randy Gumbley (who also ran the OHA's Streetsville Derbys by day) and commissioner Grant Ledyard, moved into high gear to start a "lockout league" that would provide fans in Canada with high-quality hockey featuring NHL players.

There had been an introductory press conference on August 16 to announce the formation of the league and its six Original Six city names (Toronto, Montreal, Boston, Chicago, Detroit, New York). To make their league more appealing, though, Gumbley and Ledyard modified NHL rules substantially: teams played 4-on-4 and had a game roster of eleven players; games would consist of three, 17-minute periods; penalty shots replaced penalties/power plays; shootouts occurred at the end of each period; no centre red line; players were to be paid based on revenue sharing (every player reaps 1/78 of profits); the championship trophy was named the Assante Cup after a prominent wealth management company.

The first exhibition game, at the Molson Centre in Barrie on September 17, 2004, attracted 2,176 fans who paid from $35 to $60 to watch Toronto beat Detroit 16-13. The second game, in Sarnia, attracted fewer fans, and the third, two nights later at the Brampton Sports Centre, attracted merely a curious few hundred who watched Boston whip Dave Andreychuk and Montreal, 14-11. On September 22, Gumbley tried to downplay reports that the league had already suspended operations, admitting only that, "all we've done is re-schedule some exhibition games for a later date in order to get some time to promote in those markets…we still plan on opening the regular season (October 7)." A few days later, Gumbley admitted that the OSHL was "restructuring."

Sure enough, on October 14, 2004, New York beat Toronto 11-4 before 2,025 fans at the Aitken Centre in Fredericton, New Brunswick. After that, there were more cancellations, player withdrawals, significant monetary losses for Gumbley, and a league that petered out without so much as a whimper. The Original Six Hockey League, like the NHL season itself, was dead and buried.

Goalie Andrew Raycroft of Detroit stops Brian Willsie of Toronto in an Original Stars game in Barrie on September 17, 2004.

Joel Bouchard Night in Canada

In 2000, Joel Bouchard was diagnosed with spinal meningitis, a battle he fought and won. Two years later, doctors suspected he had cancer after they found a tumor in his salivary gland in his neck. Six weeks later, it was removed and found to be benign.

Bouchard's life has been punctuated by physical difficulties, yet he has managed to play more than 300 games in the NHL. In the fall of 2004, the prospects of missing an entire year of NHL hockey inspired Bouchard to do some good with the extra time. He organized a charity hockey tour featuring mostly Quebecois NHLers to raise money for Ronald McDonald House. Called McDonald's Caravan, the tour consisted of a 32-city schedule beginning October 23, 2004, and lasting until February 27, 2005. All profits went to charity, and the fan response was overwhelming. Additional money came from RDS, the French-language arm of TSN (The Sports Network), which gave Quebec fans their Saturday night fix by broadcasting the games to replace *Hockey Night in Canada* games.

"I feel blessed," Bouchard said at the news conference to announce the initiative. "Meningitis may have knocked me out for a while, and it was scary to find out I had a tumor. But I was able to battle those problems. To see a seven-year-old girl fighting cancer isn't right."

Participating players included a who's who of French-Canadian stars: Vincent Damphousse, Jose Theodore, Alexandre Daigle, Pierre Turgeon, Stephane Quintal, Donald Audette, Pierre Dagenais, Pascal Dupuis, Francis Lessard, Patrick Lalime, J-P Dumont, Serge Aubin, Marc Denis, Ian Laperriere, Marc-Andre Bergeron, Donald Brashear, and Bouchard.

In all, Bouchard raised $600,000 for children with cancer.

Joel Bouchard, seen here playing for Nashville (left), put his spare time to charitable use during the year off in 2004-05.

Hockey Hall of Fame 2004 Induction

It was the year of the defenceman at the Hockey Hall of Fame on November 8, 2004, as Paul Coffey, Larry Murphy, and Ray Bourque were honoured as Players, along with Cliff Fletcher in the Builders' category. But while the sold-out ceremony celebrated the careers of four great men, it was also a time to take stock of opinions on the NHL dispute. "Unfortunately," Larry Murphy offered, "both sides were so prepared for a lockout that it became a self-fulfilling prophecy. So, there's not a big push from within the players [to negotiate]. If there is to be a change, it must come from the membership." Among the 1,400 in attendance at the induction ceremonies were Bill Daly and Ted Saskin.

(top) Hall of Fame Chairman Bill Hay (left) poses with inductee Cliff Fletcher; (below) Hay and defenceman Larry Murphy.

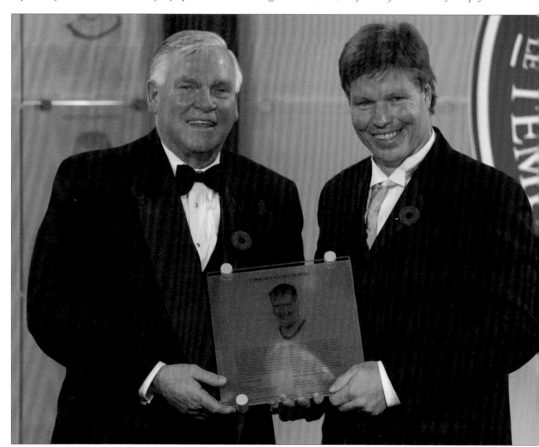

Deutschland Cup

Scott King (#27) celebrates with Chris Herperger (#12) and Francois Bouchard (#7) during the team's 5-2 win over Germany on November 14, 2004, in the final game of the Deutschland Cup. Canada beat the Swiss 3-2 and USA 5-3 and lost to Slovakia 5-3 during the round-robin tournament to finish second to USA. Both teams had identical records but the Americans had superior goal differential (+8/+4) to win.

Spengler Cup

Rick Nash of HC Davos goes to the net where he is checked by defenceman Sergei Gonchar and goalie Evgeny Nabokov of Metallurg Magnitogorsk during Spengler Cup action on December 28, 2004. Nash and teammates Joe Thornton and Martin St. Louis helped Davos beat Sparta Prag 2-0 in the final game to win the 2005 Spengler Cup.

2005 World Junior Championship

GRAND FORKS, NORTH DAKOTA/THIEF RIVER FALLS, MINNESOTA

DECEMBER 25, 2004 – JANUARY 4, 2005

It has been a long time since any major international tournament was as lop-sided and dominated so thoroughly by one team. But the beautiful Ralph Engelstad Arenas in both Grand Forks, North Dakota and Thief River Falls, Minnesota provided just that backdrop for Canada's remarkable display of skill, speed, and scoring.

Going into the tournament, Canada was the favourite to win gold for several reasons. First, there were some 12 returning players from 2004 when Canada lost in the finals to USA 4-3. Never before had Canada sent such an experienced team to the World Juniors. In that 2004 finals Canada led 3-1 after two periods, and the game-winning goal for the Americans came by luck when goalie Marc-Andre Fleury tried to clear the puck from in front of his goal, hit his own defenceman, and watched the puck bounce past him into the open net. It was the third successive gold-medal loss for Canada, which claimed silver in 2002 and 2003 after losing to Russia in both those finals. Furthermore, 2004 saw the introduction of 16-year-old Sidney Crosby to

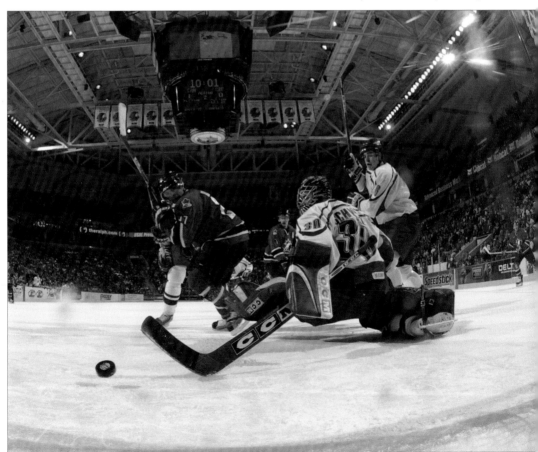

Canadian forward Nigel Dawes watches as the puck slides by Czech goalie Marek Schwartz during semi-final action.

17

Canada's National Junior Team. In the succeeding year, he had grown and matured physically, dominated the Quebec league, and become an even greater young player. The 2005 edition of Crosby was faster, stronger, and quicker. Then there was the NHL dispute which permitted Patrice Bergeron's inclusion with the team. In 2003-04, the 18-year-old made the Boston Bruins at his first training camp, had an excellent year with the team, and then helped Canada win gold at the World Championship in the Czech Republic. In fact, Bergeron made IIHF history in Grand Forks by becoming the first player ever to play in the World Juniors after playing in the more senior World Championship. Nathan Horton, another 18-year-old NHL sensation, was also slated to join the team but a shoulder injury scuppered his participation.

Coach Brent Sutter put Crosby and Bergeron on the same line, the former converting to right wing. He added London Knights star Corey Perry as their left winger, and the trio ended the tournament as the highest-scoring line. The team also featured captain Mike Richards of the Kitchener Rangers on a line with Nigel Dawes and Anthony Stewart, a skilled and hard-hitting threesome coach Sutter kept intact from the 2004 tournament. Other forwards included Jeremy Colliton, Stephen Dixon, Jeff Carter, Colin Fraser, Ryan Getzlaf, Andrew Ladd, and Clarke MacArthur.

The defence featured 19-year-old Dion Phaneuf who, without question, would have been on the blueline of the Calgary Flames had there been NHL hockey at this time. The ferocious hitter was head and shoulders, literally and figuratively, above the rest of the defence at this tournament.

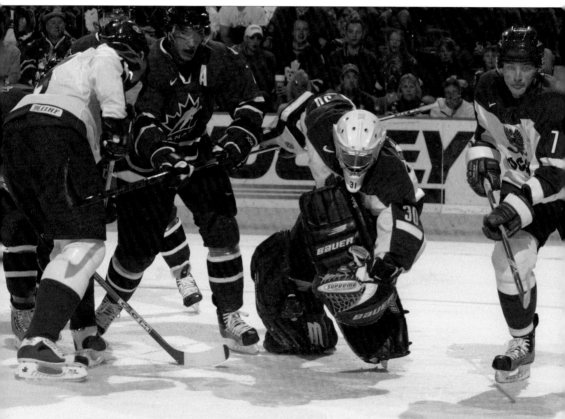

Canada's Corey Perry is checked in front as Czech Republic goalie Marek Schwartz and defender Martin Tuma keep their eye on the puck.

His comrades on the blueline for Canada included Cam Barker, Shawn Belle, Braydon Coburn, Brent Seabrook, Danny Syvret, and Shea Weber. The goalies, who were rarely tested during the tournament, were Jeff Glass and Rejean Beauchemin.

In the preliminary round, Canada won its four games in overwhelming fashion. The Canadians beat Slovakia 7-3 and Sweden 8-1, Germany 9-0 and Finland 8-1. So dominating were the Canadians that even losing Finnish coach Petri Matikainen praised the Canadian players: "That's the way the game should be played," he said with an admiring smile. Sidney Crosby scored two goals in each of the first three games and Bergeron led the tournament in scoring with eight points in those three games. Canada's 4-0-0 record in the preliminary round meant that it advanced directly to the semi-finals where the Czech Republic was the opposition.

Although the score was only 3-1 for the Canadians, they allowed just eleven shots on goal and at no time were the Czechs a threat. It was the lowest score for the team so far, but also their most dominating performance as well. The finals not only featured the greatest international rivalry of them all—Canada vs. Russia—it featured Crosby versus Alexander Ovechkin, the 1st overall draft choice in 2004 by Washington and the player most scouts considered the best in North Dakota. However, after one period of punishment from the Canadian defence, Ovechkin was on the end of the Russian bench nursing a shoulder injury and his mates were being skated into the ice to the tune of 6-1.

Sidney Crosby hopes the puck comes to him as linemate Patrice Bergeron watches from the other side of goalie Marek Schwartz and Lukas Bolf of the Czech Republic.

By the time IIHF president Rene Fasel was dressing Canadian players' necks with gold medals, Team Canada's place in history was already being considered. The team had a perfect 6-0-0 record and outscored the opposition by a cumulative score of 41-7. Most amazing of all, Canada never trailed for even one second during the entire tournament!

If Canada won gold, Canadian fans won double gold. Without them, the tournament would have been an attendance failure, but as always happens with the World Juniors, if it is possible for Canada's fans to be there, they will. The Manitoba border was just a two-hour drive away, and fans poured over the border on game days to cheer on their red-and-white heroes. After one game, a massive snowstorm closed the only highway between Grand Forks and Manitoba, so thousands of fans slept in gymnasiums, arenas, and hotels throughout the city, turning it into a Canadian party zone until it was time to watch the next Team Canada game. Canada had last won gold in 1997, but this victory was particularly important because it meant for the first time in hockey history one country owned every major title available: Olympic gold, men and women, World Championship gold, men and women, and now World Junior gold.

Team Canada gathers near centre ice for the winning portrait after defeating Russia 6-1 to claim its first championship since 1997. It was the most lop-sided victory in World Junior Championship gold medal game history.

Longest Game Ever

On farmland just outside Edmonton, Alberta, Dr. Brent Saik organized forty players into two teams and played hockey for 240 straight hours to set a world record. They stopped playing on February 21, 2005, by which time they had raised nearly $250,000 for cancer research.

World Pond Hockey Championships

PLASTER ROCK, NEW BRUNSWICK

FEBRUARY 18-20, 2005

In only its fourth year, the World Pond Hockey Championships have become perhaps the most quintessentially Canadian representation of hockey in the world. Played in a town of 1,200 souls, the 2005 tournament featured 96 teams from across Canada (every province except, oddly, Alberta) and as far away as Grand Cayman Islands (a group of Canadian ex-pats, of course!), Bermuda, Florida, and California. It was an idea conceived by local community development officer Danny Braun in 2002. In an effort to build an indoor rink for the area, he was able to convince governments to contribute $2 million to the cost of the building if the community could come up with half that amount.

Plaster Rock needs months of preparation for the tournament, from its organization to preparing the 24 rinks necessary for play on Roulston Lake. Locals use farm equipment to clear the snow and water the ice, and a hardware store is the official puck supplier.

The winning team receives a wooden Stanley Cup carved locally. The 2005 winners were the Boston Danglers who defended their title from 2004 successfully. The team included Mark Cornforth, Mark Goble, Cooper Naylor, and Rob Atkinson.

This spectacular aerial view of Roulston Lake, New Brunswick, defines Canada's natural relationship to hockey.

Brad May Raises A Million $ for Charity

A sellout crowd of 16,878 at the Pacific Coliseum in Vancouver came out to watch the Brad May and Friends Hockey Challenge on December 12, 2004. The event raised almost $1 million for charity, notably Canuck Place, a children's hospice. Although the tone of the day was upbeat, the event did spark some controversy in that suspended Canucks forward Todd Bertuzzi took part in the game. He had been banned by NHL commissioner Gary Bettman after assaulting Steve Moore in a game on March 8, 2004, and his criminal trial was pending at the time of this fundraiser. Nonetheless, everyone suspended their feelings for a day in the name of charity. Other players to participate included Markus Naslund, Morris Lukowich, Jarome Iginla, Trevor Linden, Dan Cloutier, Matt Cooke, Bryan Allen, Ed Jovanovski, Mattias Ohlund, Mike Keane, Ryan Smyth, Darcy Tucker, Shane Doan, Todd Simpson, and Claude Lemieux.

(left to right) Todd Bertuzzi, Brad May, and Shane Doan share a laugh in Vancouver on December 12, 2004. They were playing in a charity game organized by May with the WHL's Vancouver Giants to raise a million dollars for a local children's hospice.

23

The Hockey World Bids Adieu to Igor Larionov

After four gold medals at the World Championships, three Stanley Cups, two Olympic gold medals, and one Canada Cup victory in 1981, over a career spanning 27 years and four decades, Igor Larionov finally retired in the summer of 2004 at the age of 43.

To celebrate the end of one of Russia's greatest hockey careers, Larionov was honoured with a farewell game at the Luzhniki Arena in Moscow on December 14, 2004, featuring many of his teammates from his homeland and his adopted hockey home (North America). On the Russian team, Larionov was joined by Slava Fetisov, Slava Kozlov, and Sergei Fedorov. The World Team included Detroit Red Wings teammates and alumni including Steve Yzerman, Brendan Shanahan, Kris Draper, Kirk Maltby, Nicklas Lidstrom, Mathieu Dandenault, Jiri Fischer, Henrik Zetterberg, Chris Chelios, Ray Whitney, and Darren McCarty. The sellout crowd of 10,000 cheered wildly for their hero in his final game.

Igor Larionov, who played half the game for the world team, half for his Russian all-stars, is congratulated by world teammates during his farewell game.

On December 13, 2004, Russian great Igor Larionov played his final game. A group of Russian stars played a group of "world" stars at the Luzhniki Arena to say thank you and adieu to one of the greatest players in that county's hockey history.

WorldStars Tour

DECEMBER 2004

Organized by International Management Group (IMG), this NHLers tour of Europe made its official entrance into the hockey world at Wayne Gretzky's restaurant in downtown Toronto on November 18, 2004. The team consisted mostly of IMG clients and scheduled a ten-game, 14-day tour of Europe playing a selection of all-star and national teams from principle hockey countries overseas. J.P. Barry, manager of hockey for IMG, modeled the trip on Gretzky's successful Ninety-Nine All-Stars tour of Europe a decade earlier during the previous halt in play of the NHL schedule, although attendance in Europe in 2004 varied widely based on sometimes exorbitant ticket prices (unlike Gretzky's tour which was an unqualified success in every way imaginable). The team was guided by head coach Marc Bergevin and his assistants, Petr Svoboda and Marty McSorley. The roster included 27 players, some of whom were already playing in European leagues and who joined the WorldStars for just a game or two:

GOAL   Martin Brodeur, Dominik Hasek, Floyd Whitney

DEFENCE   Rob Blake, Sergei Gonchar, Pavel Kubina, John-Michael Liles, Mattias Norstrom, Sean O'Donnell, Robyn Regehr, Rhett Warrener

FORWARDS   Daniel Alfredsson, Tony Amonte, Daniel Briere, Anson Carter, Alexandre Daigle, Kris Draper, Sergei Fedorov, Robert Lang, Glen Murray, Rick Nash, Petr Nedved, Luke Robitaille, Mats Sundin, Petr Sykora, Joe Thornton, Ray Whitney, Tie Domi

THE SCHEDULE

9 December	WorldStars 4	Riga 2000 2	Sporta Pils Arena, Riga, Latvia
11 December	Russia All-Stars (I) 5	WorldStars 4	Luzhniki Arena, Moscow, Russia
12 December	WorldStars 5	Russia All-Stars (II) 4	St. Petersburg, Russia

WorldStars won shootout 2-1 to decide winner of two-game "series" with Russians

13 December	WorldStars 8	HC Lasselsberger Plzen 3	Plzen, Czech Republic
15 December	WorldStars 7	SC Bern 6	Bern, Switzerland
16 December	Farjestad 6	WorldStars 1	Farjestad, Sweden
17 December	WorldStars 5	HV 71 Jonkoping 1	Kinnarps Arena, Jonkoping, Sweden
19 December	Linkoping 6	WorldStars 4	Cloetta Centre, Linkoping, Sweden
21 December	WorldStars 7	Norwegian All-Stars 6	Spektrum, Oslo, Norway
22 December	WorldStars 4	Poland 3 (SO)	Spodek Arena, Katowice, Poland

Alexandre Daigle of the touring WorldStars floats a pass by Bern's Thomas Rodin during a game in Switzerland on December 15, 2004.

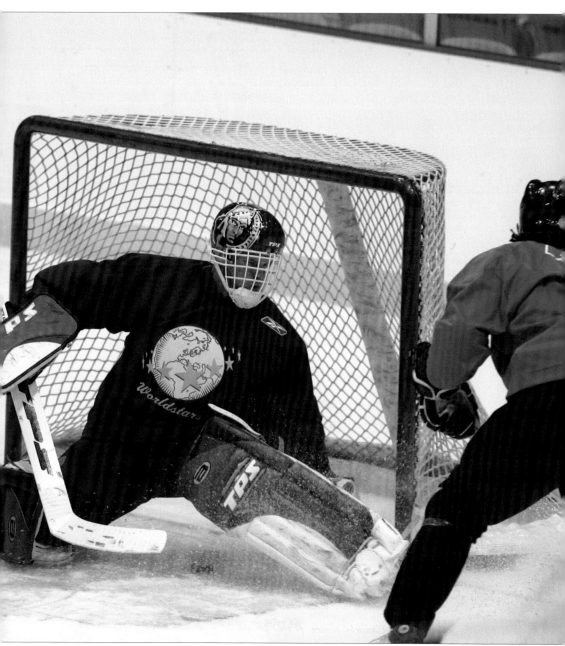

At practice in Toronto on December 7, 2004, forward Anson Carter and goalie Dominik Hasek prepare for the WorldStars tour which began two nights later in Latvia.

Moore v. Bertuzzi

On March 8, 2004, Todd Bertuzzi of the Vancouver Canucks jumped Steve Moore of the Colorado Avalanche late in a lop-sided game won 9-2 by Colorado in Vancouver. Moore did not see the assault and was unable to defend himself. He suffered multiple injuries ranging from a broken neck to post-concussion syndrome that, a year and a half later, had left him incapable of engaging in even basic physical activities. Bertuzzi was suspended by the NHL for the rest of the 2003-04 season, regular season and playoffs, and no date was given for when he would be allowed to return to play. The Canucks organization was fined $250,000 by the league for its culpability in the attack. Vancouver police, meanwhile, charged Bertuzzi with assault, but the case never came to trial. Amid a flurry of behind-the-scenes plea bargaining and very public outrage, Bertuzzi pleaded guilty on December 22, 2004, to a charge of assault causing bodily harm. He received a conditional discharge, thus preventing a trial scheduled for January 2005. He was told by Judge Herb Weitzel that he could not play in a game against Moore for one year and that he must also perform 80 hours of community service.

The outrage caused by the plea bargaining was due in large part because it caught Moore and his lawyers by surprise and thus prevented the injured player from appearing in court to read a victim-impact statement, which he had hoped to do. Because the trial date had been moved up from January 17 to December 22, seemingly at a moment's notice, Moore's statement was read in court by Crown counsel Garth Loeppky prior to Bertuzzi's sentencing, but, of course, it didn't have the same weight it would have had had Moore been in court to read it himself. It read in part:

> The 2003-04 season turned out to be my breakthrough year. It was my third year of pro, I was more prepared and determined than ever, and I felt like my hard work along with my excellent coaching was helping me improve greatly…As the regular season was winding down, the race for first place in our division tightened. We were going back and forth with the Vancouver Canucks for the lead of our division. In the few games that were left to be played in the regular season, three of those games would be played head-to-head with the Canucks, the first of which was played on February 16, 2004, in Denver. It was a close game from start to finish, with Vancouver scoring the only goal in the third period and winning, 1-0. During that game I had a collision with a Canucks player, Mark Naslund, which unfortunately resulted in his leaving the game with an injury. The referees were saying that it had been a clean play. Canucks player Brad May immediately came after me anyway, and received a roughing penalty.

On December 22, 2004, Todd Bertuzzi and his wife Julie arrived at a provincial courthouse in Vancouver where Bertuzzi pleaded guilty to assault on Steve Moore. The plea bargain ensured Bertuzzi received a conditional discharge.

After the game, the Canucks players, the coach Marc Crawford, and the general manager Brian Burke, all were fuming about it. I expressed to the media my respect for Naslund as a player, and that it was unfortunate he was hurt on the play. I also asked a teammate of mine who knew Naslund well to call him and express my well wishes. At the request of the Canucks, the videotape of the play was reviewed again by the NHL head office, and again it was established as a clean play.

I was very surprised and disturbed the next day to hear that public threats were being made against me and my health, by people in the Canucks organization. I was called a "piece of s——" by Todd Bertuzzi. Bertuzzi also said "absolutely" retribution would be exacted upon me. It was said by another Canucks player, Brad May, "It's going to be fun when we get him." There was even a bounty placed on my head. These threats were repeated on news channels across Canada and the United States, and were quite alarming to me and very distressing for my family…

The final regular season's match-up between the two teams was…on March 8, 2004, in Vancouver. It was clear right from the start of the game that the Canucks still had their minds strongly set on going after me. They had now been promising to "get" me for three weeks. Those threats were seemingly all the media wanted to talk about. I thought it best for my team that I try to help put this increasing distraction behind us, and accepted a challenge to fight from Canucks player Matt Cooke. This was my first career fight.

The next thing I knew I was in a dark room, strapped down to a stretcher, with a neck brace on, having medial staff cut my equipment off me…I was bed-ridden in the Vancouver hospital for nearly a week, and was then transferred to a hospital in Denver, where I would remain indefinitely. In the end, I was told my injuries included three spinal fractures in my neck (C3, C4, and T1), a very serious grade three concussion, vertebral ligament damage, stretching of the brachial plexus nerves, along with the stitched up facial cuts I was already well aware of. I spent days confined to my bed in my room, other than for a brief walk up and down the hall twice daily. It was over two weeks before I was even allowed to get outside for a breath of fresh air…

From that moment in the game on March 8, 2004, my reality has been completely altered…I am not able to do the things I normally, and so badly want to do; I do not know if I will ever be able to continue in the sport that I have devoted so much of my life to; and I do not know whether I will ever be even back to the same health again…

This incident has had a severe impact on my financial situation as well. There is no doubt that the Colorado Avalanche Organization was appreciating what I was doing on the ice, and would be anxious to sign me to another contract. It was a bright future, with a great organization and great players that I was really looking forward to…The attack in Vancouver on March 8, however, drastically changed all that. My contractual and financial situation has consequently been drastically compromised, for after playing through comparatively low entry-level contracts of my first few years, this summer was to be my first chance at a contract of even average compensation. That chance has been lost. I now sit, without a contract, without an effort by the Avalanche to sign me, and without any contract offers at all. Even if I am to somehow make a recovery and get back to game-playing condition, I still face the possibility that teams will see me as damaged goods and avoid the perceived risk of signing me…

The Victim Impact Statement Form provided to me by Crown Counsel asked me to comment on how I feel regarding contact with the accused. I have no desire to interact with him in any way. I would respectfully request that should I regain my health and someday be able to get back to playing, that Todd Bertuzzi never be permitted to participate in any sporting activity in which I am competing.

The 6'4", 245-pound Bertuzzi released his own statement after being sentenced: "I crossed a line that a professional hockey player, like anyone else, should never cross. I hit a fellow player from behind with my glove hand when he was not expecting it, was not involved in play, and did not want to fight me. As a result, Steve Moore was injured. I did not intend for him to be hurt as badly as he was, but this is what happened. I had to take responsibility for that. That's why I have apologized to Steve Moore and do so again and continue to wish him a complete recovery. That is also why I have chosen to plead guilty to a crime of assault causing bodily harm. I have spent many months agonizing over this incident—how it happened and how to make sense of it."

One week later, Bertuzzi's agent contacted the league's offices to discuss the re-instatement of Bertuzzi. Despite the ongoing problems between the league and players that prevented the season from being played, Bertuzzi wanted to play in Europe, along with the almost 400 other NHLers who were playing overseas. Until he was cleared to play by the NHL, however, the IIHF balked at giving him a transfer to allow him to play in Europe. The remainder of the European season passed, though, and Bertuzzi did not receive the permission from the NHL for which he had applied and hoped.

On February 15, 2005, Moore went on the offensive, filing a lawsuit in a Denver district court against Todd Bertuzzi of Vancouver accusing the Canucks forward of civil conspiracy, assault, battery, and negligence. The complaint reads in part: "Following the [February 16, 2004] game, but before leaving Denver, defendants Bertuzzi, May, Crawford, and Burke entered into an unlawful plan and agreement to assault, batter, and injure Moore at a future date, in retaliation for the injuries which Naslund had suffered during the game." It continues to allege the plan was aided by coach Marc Crawford and general manager Brian Burke: "Crawford and Burke openly urged the Canucks players, including Bertuzzi and May, to retaliate against Moore, to make physical contact with him, and threaten the same…"

Less than a week later, on February 21, 2005, Markus Naslund, the opponent Moore initially injured to set off the Bertuzzi assault, pilloried Moore for the civil litigation even though Moore's career and even day-to-day health remain in jeopardy a year later. Said Naslund: "He's suing everyone so he can make money. I've got no respect for him at all. This is just a guy who's trying to hit a home run (financially). Someone who wasn't good enough to play…I'm not saying what (Bertuzzi) did was right, but if it was me, I'd be doing everything I could to get back and play and show everyone the character I have." On August 8, 2005, Bettman lifted the suspension and allowed Bertuzzi to resume his NHL career effective immediately. In all, Bertuzzi missed exactly 20 NHL games.

Steve Moore (foreground) and his lawyer Tim Danson met reporters on December 23, 2004, the day after Todd Bertuzzi was given a discharge in his assault case against Moore.

Hamilton's Outdoor Game

Billed as "Our Game to Give," the outdoor game at Hamilton's Ivor Wynne Stadium attracted some 20,000 fans, despite high winds, steady rain, and a sour taste in people's mouths after a year without NHL hockey. The event pitted Team (Doug) Gilmour against Team (Steve) Staios and featured some 26 NHLers as well as former players and special guests.

The evening began with Gordie Howe at centre ice receiving a raucous rendition of Happy Birthday before facing the puck off between the two honourary/playing captains, Gilmour and Staios. Martin Brodeur was in one goal and Curtis Joseph at the other end. Skaters included Mike Comrie, Ryan Smyth, Kris Draper, Bryan McCabe, Rob Blake, Eric Brewer, Darcy Tucker, Michael Peca, Gary Roberts, Joe Nieuwendyk, Wade Redden, and Todd Bertuzzi, again skating in the public eye hoping to have his pro rights restituted in time to play for Canada at the 2005 IIHF World Championship.

All profits after expenses from the $40 per ticket event went to the tsunami relief fund of the Canadian Red Cross and Camp Trillium which cares for children who have cancer.

Todd Bertuzzi (left) and Mike Comrie joke around during Hamilton's outdoor charity game on April 2, 2004.

Diary of A Year Without the NHL

AUGUST 25, 2004 Teen sensation Sidney Crosby rejected an offer by the WHA franchise in Hamilton to join the upstart league for three years and $7.5 million, $2 million of that guaranteed, up-front money from owner Mario Frankovich.

AUGUST 26, 2004 Hamilton police charged Hamilton Bulldogs forward Alexander Perezhogin with assault causing bodily harm from a stick-swinging incident in a playoff game in which Cleveland Barons defenceman Garrett Stafford was left bloody and convulsing on the ice from the vicious attack. Perezhogin was suspended for the rest of the 2004 playoffs and all of the 2004-05 season.

In a Vancouver courtroom, Canucks forward Todd Bertuzzi pleaded not guilty to a charge of assault causing bodily harm in connection with his attack on Steve Moore of Colorado in a game on March 8, 2004, in Vancouver.

SEPTEMBER 7, 2004 A newly-built Oshawa elementary school was named Bobby Orr Public School, and the Hall of Famer was on hand for its christening.

SEPTEMBER 23, 2004 Longtime Chicago Blackhawks coach Billy Reay died in Madison, Wisconsin.

OCTOBER 1, 2004 An arbitrator ruled that referee Mark Faucette and linesman Darren Gibbs had been unjustly fired by the NHL and would receive either compensation or reinstatement.

OCTOBER 2, 2004 Wayne Rutledge, former NHL goalie, died in Huntsville, Ontario.

OCTOBER 4, 2004 Former NHLer Garth Butcher was acquitted of rape charges stemming from an incident involving a woman he met at a bar he co-owned in Mississauga.

OCTOBER 5, 2004 Buffalo forward Adam Mair was charged with assault after a bouncer at a Hamilton bar was punched in the face.

OCTOBER 7, 2004 Phil Housley, Mark Johnson, Paul Coppo, and Mike Ilitch were inducted into the U.S. Hockey Hall of Fame in Eveleth, Minnesota

OCTOBER 10, 2004 Bobby Hull sold 95 personal items and memorabilia at auction, his false teeth and partial plate fetching more than $700.

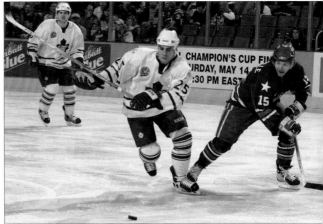

St. John's Maple Leafs (left) played Rochester Americans in one of a few games on blue ice in Buffalo toward the end of the 2004-05 season.

OCTOBER 20, 2004 Jean Perron, former Stanley Cup-winning coach with the Montreal Canadiens in 1986, accepted the position of head coach of the Israeli National Junior team.

Jarome Iginla and his wife, Kara, celebrated the birth of their first child, Jade Grace.

OCTOBER 26, 2004 Gary Roberts was drafted by the Calgary Roughnecks of the National Lacrosse League in the hopes the team could convince the former lacrosse star to play in the NLL should the NHL not start up any time soon.

NOVEMBER 1, 2004 Canada's Sports Hall of Fame inducted six new members including hockey coach Scotty Bowman, player Larry Robinson, and four others—Donovan Bailey, Abby Hoffman, Lori Fung, and Jack Donohue.

NOVEMBER 5, 2004 Mike Gartner and other former NHL players took part in the Hockey for the Homeless tournament in Toronto to raise money for the needy.

NOVEMBER 6, 2004 Former player Pat LaFontaine, whose career ended because of post-concussion syndrome, completed the Ironman Florida Triathlon in 13 hours, 6 minutes, 49 seconds.

NOVEMBER 7, 2004 The Manitoba Moose hosted the Utah Grizzlies in an AHL game at the Winnipeg Arena, the final game in this storied barn that now gave way to the posh MTS Centre in downtown Winnipeg.

NOVEMBER 8, 2004 U.S. District Judge William Stiehl sentenced Mike Danton of the St. Louis Blues to seven and a half years in prison for trying to hire a hit man to kill his agent, David Frost. In an East St. Louis courtroom, Stiehl said, "I do not believe in over 18 years on the bench I have been faced with a case as bizarre as this one."

Four new members were added to the Hockey Hall of Fame's honour roll at a ceremony in Toronto. Three defencemen—Paul Coffey, Larry Murphy, and Ray Bourque—joined Cliff Fletcher (Builder) to celebrate their career achievements.

A memorial service for Sergei Zholtok was held at the House of Blackheads in Riga, Latvia for the national star who died while playing for Riga 2000 in a game against Dynamo Minsk five days earlier.

Johnny Bower, one of the great Original Six goalies and the oldest goalie ever to play in the NHL, celebrated his 80th birthday.

NOVEMBER 16, 2004 Some 15 members of the Stanley Cup champion Tampa Bay Lightning were given their Cup rings by team officials at the Lightning's offices. Each ring contained 138 small diamonds, one for each of the team's 106 regular season points in the standings and two for each of their 16 playoff victories. Each ring also included the player's name and sweater number.

WorldStar players (left to right) Barret Jackman, Robyn Regehr, Glen Murray, Anson Carter, and Dominik Hasek lay wreaths on the grave of Sergei Zholtok on December 9, 2004.

Former NHLer Dale Hawerchuk (left) has a fun moment with Blue Rodeo's Jim Cuddy during the Juno Cup on April 1, 2005.

NOVEMBER 17, 2004 Alexander Ragulin, a 10-time gold medalist at the IIHF World Championship, died in Moscow, Russia.

Francesco Aquilini, a wealthy local businessman, agreed to buy 50% of the Vancouver Canucks and its arena, GM Place, from owner John McCaw.

NOVEMBER 18, 2004 Dolores Claman, composer of the famous theme music for *Hockey Night in Canada*, filed a $2.5 million claim against the CBC alleging the broadcaster violated copyright and broke a contract for its conditions of use.

IMG announced that a WorldStars tour featuring some 25 NHLers would take place in Europe in December, some of the profits going to the NHLPA's "Goals and Dreams" program as well as Garth Brooks's "Teammates for Kids" foundation.

NOVEMBER 28, 2004 Blue Jackets forward Tyler Wright organized a Hats for Heroes charity hockey game at the Chiller North Arena in Columbus, attracting a sellout crowd of 1,200 and raising $25,000 for Wright's charity which benefits pediatric cancer patients. Other players to dress for the game included Luke Richardson, Geoff Sanderson, Trevor Letowski, Todd Marchant, Kevin Dineen, Jean-Luc Grand-Pierre, Mark Recchi, and Robert Esche.

DECEMBER 2004 Michael Payne and Mark Suits of Edmonton launched www.freestanley.com in an effort to ensure that the great hockey trophy be competed for some way, somewhere in Canada if the NHL were to remain dormant for the year.

DECEMBER 3, 2004 Several members of the Detroit Red Wings played the USA U18 national team in a charity exhibition game at Yost Arena in Michigan. Notable participants included captain Steve Yzerman, on skates in game action for the first time since suffering a serious eye injury in the 2004 Stanley Cup playoffs.

DECEMBER 6, 2004 Former players Blair MacDonald, Jyrki Lumme, Tiger Williams, and Manon Rheaume appeared in hockey gear for "A Beachcombers Christmas" TV special.

Peter Worrell, a black, 6'7" player for the Florida Panthers, told police his name was Andreas Lilja (a 6'3" white, Swedish teammate) when he was pulled over in Pompano Beach for driving with an expired tag. He was driving Lilja's car and was charged with driving with a suspended license and resisting arrest without violence.

DECEMBER 7, 2004 Brendan Shanahan hosted a two-day hockey summit in Toronto featuring players and executives trying find ways to improve the on-ice quality of the game. Participants included Bob Gainey, John Tortorella, Dave Tippett, Marc Crawford, Brian Burke, Terry Gregson, Mats Sundin, Curtis Joseph, Alexander Mogilny, James Patrick, Sean Burke, Glen Healy, Al MacInnis, Andy Brickley (broadcaster), Sam Flood (NBC executive), Tom McNeeley (TV executive), and Ron McLean. After the sessions, Shanahan introduced the ten-point recommendations of the group:

1. Create a competition committee comprised of players, officials, general managers, and coaches.
2. Reduce obstruction through rigourous interpretation of the current rules.
3. Institute a shootout if a five-minute overtime in regular season games did not produce a winner.
4. Reduce minor penalties in overtime from two minutes to one minute during the regular season.
5. Streamline goalie equipment.
6. Implement the AHL's experimental rules, namely: tag-up offside; wider blue lines; restricting goalie movement behind the net; narrower width between end boards and goal net.
7. When a team intentionally ices the puck, it can't make a line change prior to the next faceoff.
8. Make all players (not just goalies) subject to a minor penalty when clearing the puck directly over the glass in the defensive zone.
9. Improve arena access points for broadcast rights holders.
10. Improve communication and partnership at all levels.

DECEMBER 10, 2004 The London Knights played to a 0-0 tie with the Guelph Storm, thereby setting a Canadian junior record by going 30 games without a loss (28-0-2).

At the conclusion of the summit organized by Brendan Shanahan on December 7, 2004, members of the committee met the media to discuss what took place behind closed doors (left to right): Ron McLean, Curtis Joseph, Mats Sundin, Shanahan, Terry Gregson.

DECEMBER 15, 2004 Goalie Dominik Hasek was sued for $496,000 US by Twelve Oaks mall in suburban Detroit for allegedly pulling his Dominator Clothing company out of the mall while owing back rent and lease payments for three more years.

DECEMBER 19, 2004 Andrew Brunette of the Minnesota Wild organized a charity game at the University of Minnesota, proceeds going to locally-deployed soldiers overseas, the Herb Brooks Foundation, and the Shjon Podein Children's Foundation. A team of local pros squared off against Governor Tim Pawlenty and others from the National Guard and St. Paul police.

DECEMBER 24, 2004 Former NHLer Pete Palangio died in North Bay, Ontario, at age 96, one of the oldest players of all time.

JANUARY 4, 2005 Bud Poile, former NHLer and longtime executive, died in Vancouver.

JANUARY 11, 2005 CBC cancelled *Hockey Day in Canada*, its all-day tribute to hockey in Canada.

JANUARY 12, 2005 Journeyman Greg Pankewicz scored five goals and added four assists to lead the Northern Conference to a 14-13 win over the Southern Conference at the Central Hockey League's All-Star Game in Laredo, Texas.

JANUARY 16, 2005 Illustrating the broad effects of this NHL-less season, InGlas Co., the official puck supplier for the league, laid off 20 of its 40 employees in Sherbrooke, Quebec, because business had suffered so badly.

JANUARY 20, 2004 Only in Canada, eh? The last words of Archie Bennitz of Ottawa resonated with vitriol against the men in charge of the NHL. Upon passing away, he instructed his sons to include in his obituary that appeared in today's *Ottawa Citizen* the following criticisms: "He asked that Mr. Bettman and Mr. Goodenow know that they are 'skunks' for denying him the pleasure of watching the NHL on TV this year. He also asked that Mr. Bettman step aside and give Wayne Gretzky the job that rightfully belongs to him."

JANUARY 22, 2005 After a three-week feud with Hockey Alberta and Hockey Canada during which time he was ruled ineligible to play because of his ties to the NHL, Theo Fleury finally made his debut with the Horse Lake Thunder of the North Peace Hockey League, his first serious hockey in a year and a half.

JANUARY 25, 2005 Jean Beliveau announced that some 195 personal items and memorabilia would be auctioned, the money going to his grandchildren.

JANUARY 28, 2005 Bill Ruggiero, a goalie with the Rio Grande Valley Killer Bees, played in a Central Hockey League game with his sister, Angela, known as a defenceman for the USA national team, becoming the first brother-sister act to play in the same game in a pro league.

FEBRUARY 1, 2005 Filming got under way for "Waking Up Wally: The Walter Gretzky Story" in Edmonton, chronicling the life of the Great One's father.

FEBRUARY 2, 2005 The New Jersey Devils announced plans to build an 18,000-seat arena in downtown Newark, New Jersey at a cost of $310 million, $210 million of which would be covered by the city of Newark and the rest by the hockey team.

FEBRUARY 4, 2005 Dany Heatley appeared in an Atlanta courtroom and pleaded guilty to four of six charges he faced stemming from a car crash on September 29, 2003, in which the passenger, teammate Dan Snyder, died from injuries suffered in the crash. Prosecutors dropped charges of first-degree vehicular homicide and reckless driving, and Heatley pleaded guilty to second-degree vehicular homicide, driving too fast for conditions, failure to maintain a lane, and speeding. Superior Court Judge Rowland Barnes sentenced Heatley to three years' probation, fined him $3,000, and ordered him to perform community service by making 150 speeches on the importance of driving safely. Barnes also banned Heatley from owning a car that had more than six cylinders and told the player every car he owns must have a mechanism that limits the speed to 112 km/h. Graham and Jake Snyder, the father and brother of Dan, were at the sentencing. "As a parent," Graham said, "it's hard to explain how you feel about losing your son. My pride in Dan was immeasurable. We will all miss him. So, how do we move on from here? Forgiveness in our hearts has helped us move on. Dany has a burden that he will carry for the rest of his life." A spokesman for the attorney's office said that the Snyder support for Heatley contributed greatly to the lightness of the sentence: "Certainly, the family's desires impacted the D.A.'s position and impacted the judge, and the judge made that very clear. That the Snyder family was standing with the defendant certainly said a lot to him." Tragically, Judge Barnes was killed on March 11, 2005, when a man entering his courtroom in a rape trial overpowered a deputy, stole her gun, and murdered Barnes and two others before fleeing the scene.

Goalie Dan Blackburn signed with the Victoria Salmon Kings of the ECHL after missing a year and a half with a serious left shoulder injury that left him unable to lift his catching hand as might a normal goalie. As a result, he became the first goalie to wear two blockers, one for his stick hand, the other to deflect pucks, rather than catch them, with his catching hand. He was released by the team just six weeks later.

FEBRUARY 9, 2005 Frank Mathers, a former NHLer and longtime member of the AHL in many capacities, died in Hershey, Pennsylvania.

The Conn Smythe Sports Celebrities Dinner and Auction for the Easter Seals Society was held at the Metro Convention Centre in Toronto.

Pavel Bure launched a 300-million ruble lawsuit against *Arbat Prestizh Telegid*, a magazine that reported that Bure had boasted of taking Anna Kournikova's virginity and thus "disseminated information inconsistent with reality (and) besmirching my honour and dignity."

FEBRUARY 10, 2005 Louis Sutter, the father of the six, NHL-playing Sutters, passed away in Viking, Alberta. (photo left)

FEBRUARY 12, 2005 A charity game billed as "The Showdown in Hockeytown," pitting alumni from Detroit and Toronto, was played at the Joe Louis Arena, Detroit.

FEBRUARY 14, 2005 Chris Bourque, son of Raymond, scored the overtime winning goal to give his Boston University Terriers the championship in the annual Beanpot tournament in Boston.

Three Swedish players were banned from playing for the national team for the rest of the year and suspended by their club teams after they were accused of rape. They were not charged because police didn't have enough evidence against them. Kristian Huselius, playing for Linkoping and leading the Swedish Elite League in scoring, teammate Henrik Tallinder, and Andreas Lilja of Mora acknowledged having sex with a 22-year-old woman in their hotel room but claimed the act was consensual.

FEBRUARY 15, 2005 Ted Theodore, the father of Montreal goalie, Jose, was fined $30,000 by a Quebec court and ordered not to own a gun for ten years after admitting he ran a loansharking operation.

FEBRUARY 16, 2005 The family of Terence Tootoo, brother of NHLer Jordin, dropped charges against the Brandon (Manitoba) Police Services filed in May 2004 which alleged the police had contributed to Terence's death by failing to put him in the company of a "sober and responsible adult" after he was arrested for drunk driving on August 28, 2002. Shortly after his arrest, Tootoo committed suicide.

FEBRUARY 18, 2005 Gord Downie, lead singer of the band Tragically Hip, auditioned for the part of Ken Dryden in a CBC mini-series on the 1972 Summit Series; Ken Dryden, now Canada's Minister of Social Development, was booed in the House of Commons in Ottawa for his plans to invest $5 billion in a national childcare system.

Former NHLer Bob Probert was found not guilty of three felony charges and one misdemeanour charge as a result of an altercation with police in West Palm Beach, Florida in 2004.

FEBRUARY 19, 2005 To replace the cancelled *Hockey Day in Canada*, The Sports Network aired some 12 hours of hockey coverage across the country to celebrate the game at all levels.

FEBRUARY 22, 2005 Former NHL goon Frank (The Animal) Bialowas announced his plan to become a professional boxer. He had been playing with the Sherbrooke Saints in a senior pro league in Quebec but quit hockey to focus on his ring debut against Jarad Vasquez in Philadelphia on March 24, 2005. He recorded a first-round knockout in his debut.

FEBRUARY 23, 2005 An auction of 195 pieces of Jean Beliveau's memorabilia came to an end as the Hall of Famer profited almost $1 million.

FEBRUARY 25, 2005 Leo Labine, former Boston Bruins great, died in North Bay, Ontario.

A street in Saskatoon was re-named Gordie Howe Lane, and Howe was there for the unveiling.

MARCH 1, 2005 Amidst the turmoil of the season, Wayne Gretzky acknowledged that his mother, Phyllis, had begun treatments to battle lung cancer.

MARCH 4, 2005 Steve Thomas, Doug Gilmour, Eric Lindros, Gary Roberts, and Steve Yzerman took part in a corporate-charity hockey tournament in Markham, Ontario.

MARCH 12, 2005 Jeff O'Neill of the Carolina Hurricanes was charged with drunk driving, failing to stop at a stop sign, and transporting an open container of alcohol near Raleigh. He refused a blood-alcohol test and had his license revoked for 30 days, with a court date set for May 6, 2005.

MARCH 13, 2005 Detroit's Brendan Shanahan acted as Grand Marshal for the St. Patrick's Day parade in Toronto.

Former NHLer Rudy Poeschek was arrested as an habitual traffic offender in Tampa, Florida after crashing into trees near his house. He fled the scene and was arrested after being jolted with a Taser. It was the eighth time he had been arrested since 2002 after a failed comeback with Tampa.

MARCH 14, 2005 Some details for hockey's Bobby Hull Invitational Tournament were unveiled. The putative event would run May 20-June 2, each player receiving $20,000 to play and the winning team receiving an additional $2 million. The six-team tournament would play all games in Vancouver and Hamilton, and an impressive list of interested players apparently included Jarome Iginla, Dany Heatley, Jeremy Roenick, Keith Primeau, and Shane Doan among the 50 or so published names.

MARCH 20, 2005 The Cleveland Barons played the Rochester Americans in an AHL game at HSBC Arena in Buffalo featuring blue ice and orange "bluelines."

MARCH 21, 2005 Former NHL tough guy Dave Morrissette revealed in his French-language book "Memoires d'un dur a cuire" ("Memories of an Enforcer") that steroids and stimulants led to the downfall of his career. "I didn't make the right choices," he said at the book launch, "and I don't want them [his children] to make the same choices. If I save one life, that's one life. By not talking about it, the kids keep doing it."

MARCH 22, 2005 For the second consecutive day, a former NHLer disclosed the use of steroids and stimulants in hockey dressing rooms. Stephane Quintal, who played in the NHL for 17 years, said as many as 40% of players took stimulants. "As for anabolic steroids," he added, "I'd say they were more reserved for fighters and enforcers, even if other players did use them, too."

Ryan Smyth's four-city tour of NHL players began with a charity game in Red Deer, Alberta, before just 800 fans, many of whom jeered and booed Mike Comrie who had forced his old team, Edmonton, to trade him. The second game the following night in Moose Jaw, Saskatchewan, was better attended, as was game three in Regina, Saskatchewan, the next night. But, the last game, scheduled for Winnipeg, Manitoba, on March 25, 2005, was called off because of poor ticket sales—only 400 had been sold by game day. "It's not about the NHL," Smyth said, simply. "It's about the charities and putting smiles on kids' faces."

APRIL 1, 2005 Musicians and former NHLers played in the Juno Cup in Selkirk, Alberta, as part of the Juno Awards festivities (honouring the best in Canadian music).

APRIL 14, 2005 Former Vancouver GM Brian Burke filed a defamation suit against reporter Larry Brooks of the *New York Post* after Brooks refused to retract an article in which he laid part of the blame for Todd Bertuzzi's assault on Steve Moore at Burke's feet.

APRIL 16, 2005 Former NHLer Rick Blight was found dead in his pickup truck just north of Winnipeg.

MAY 15, 2005 The Czech Republic shut out Canada 3-0 to win gold at the 2005 World Championship in Austria.

JUNE 22, 2005 The Stanley Cup kicked off the Silver and Grey Tour, a summer of travel to reunite oldtimers of the game with the trophy they won decades ago but were never allowed to keep for a day or even a few hours. For many players from Cup-winning teams of days gone by, this was the first time they even touched the trophy.

The NHL Diary, 2004-05

SEPTEMBER 15, 2004 Just hours after Canada won the 2004 World Cup of Hockey, NHL commissioner Gary Bettman announced that the start of the NHL season had been postponed indefinitely. He called for "cost certainty" as the only means to bring salaries in line with revenue, to which NHLPA executive director Bob Goodenow responded, "Until he gets off the salary cap issue, there is no chance of getting an agreement." Bettman argued that under a cap, the average salary would drop from $1.8 million USD to $1.3 million USD: "An average salary of $1.3 million may be less than the players are getting now," he rationalized, "but we will not apologize for an average player salary of $1.3 million per season." The average salary in Canada was $31,750 according to a 2001 census.

SEPTEMBER 16, 2004 For the first of many times, a player spoke out contrary to the views of the NHLPA. John Madden, a forward with New Jersey, suggested he would play under a salary cap to save the 2004-05 season: "The only problem I'm having with things is believing whose numbers are right and whose numbers are wrong. Those are the big issues. And if it needs to have a cap, give it a cap, you know?" The next day, he re-phrased his comments: "I was asked if my union decided to go along with a cap, would I accept that and I said, 'yeah, I'd go along with my union.' It obviously has our best interest in mind. That's all I said."

NHLPA senior director Ted Saskin meets the media in Toronto.

SEPTEMBER 21, 2004 Less than a week after the postponement of the season almost 150 NHLers from the previous year began to play in Europe, the Czech Republic leading the way with 47 players, Sweden with 30, and Russia with 23. Most notable was Peter Forsberg with his old club team MoDo (Swedish Elite League) because he committed to the team for the whole season regardless if the NHL started up again at any time. Most other players had a clause in their contract that would permit them to leave at any time. An Ipsos-Reid poll found that 89% of Americans were not interested in the NHL and 67% didn't care if there were an NHL season.

SEPTEMBER 21, 2004 Beginning a two-day town hall meeting on the CBC's Newshour show, The National, Peter Mansbridge hosted Gary Bettman for a full hour, discussing the lockout and fielding questions from a studio and virtual audience. In explaining the need to put fiscal restraints on all teams equally, Bettman explained, "If a player sits out or goes somewhere else, the fans want to know why is it that our team can't be competitive and keep our young stars. It's easy to say, 'the team shouldn't pay the money,' but the media and the fans are screaming, 'keep that player.'"

SEPTEMBER 22, 2004   Peter Mansbridge gave equal time to NHLPA leader Bob Goodenow on The National, the executive director receiving far more criticism than Bettman the previous day. One fan wrote in to Goodenow: "Do the players know the average salary of a National Hockey League fan?" At another point, Goodenow repeated his oft-spoken mantra: "Players are not greedy. They live in a marketplace where salaries can go up or down. If you're skilled enough to be in the NHL, you deserve some of the revenues." He did not define or quantify "some."

SEPTEMBER 30, 2004   Co-founders Allan Howell and Nick Vaccaro of the apparently resurrected World Hockey Association attempted to dispel rumours that the league was on the verge of shutting down for the season after the Dallas Americans had pulled out a few days earlier. A 60-game season featuring teams in Vancouver, Detroit, Halifax, Miami, Toronto, and Hamilton was still a possibility, they said.

OCTOBER 12, 2004   Russian President Vladimir Putin expressed his dismay at the lack of hockey prior to meeting Canada's PM, Paul Martin, to which the latter responded, "Disappointed as you may be, that is nothing to my disappointment and (that) of Canadians at the situation in the NHL. I would very much hope that the parties would sit down and begin negotiations."

OCTOBER 13, 2004   Opening night of the NHL's 2004-05 season was to have featured seven games.

OCTOBER 14, 2004   Phoenix GM, Mike Barnett, indicated that owner Wayne Gretzky might well be the next head coach of the Coyotes. "It's the closest thing to playing, and I do miss being around the team atmosphere," Gretzky said when asked about the rumour.

OCTOBER 27, 2004   Calgary defenceman Mike Commodore, playing in the minors, told a local radio station he'd be willing to return to the NHL under a salary cap. "I don't want to spend however long my career lasts playing here in the American Hockey League," he said. "It's got to be give and take on both sides, so not one side can be making all the money. But if [a salary cap] is what it takes—the sport has to go on—I'm going to say, yeah.'"

OCTOBER 28, 2004   Both sides re-stated their positions as they prepared to meet again. Bettman said, "The union is looking for a leverage point, a critical point where they think the owners are going to give up. It isn't going to happen. The fact that this whole work stoppage is about them waiting for that point will turn out to be a colossal misjudgement." Ted Saskin, the NHLPA's senior director, cut his own version of events: "We've said before that that's an absurd position to take. This has never been about looking for leverage. This is about trying to find a fair deal that works for both sides."

OCTOBER 29, 2004   Daniel Alfredsson, one of six vice presidents with the NHLPA, re-iterated the players' stance: "We won't agree to a cap, no matter what…A salary cap doesn't make any sense for us at all. There are definitely other solutions, but there's nothing to talk about right now."

Goalie Corey Hirsch, a former NHLer now playing in Europe, lost his place with the Langnau Tigers of the Swiss league after Carolina Hurricanes goalie Martin Gerber came to Europe to play and stay in shape during the lockout. Hirsch wrote an article for Sun Media excoriating NHLers for taking positions away from players who needed the money: "NHL players are coming to Europe in droves and are bumping off players that actually need the money, one by one," he wrote. "…the lack of compassion and understanding of what they are doing to many of the players in Europe is extremely unnerving…Where is the logic in not negotiating a Collective Bargaining Agreement that will still pay a player more than he will ever need, but instead he'll come to Europe to play just to stay in shape?…They are scabs over here, replacement players…All these players they are now stepping on over here will now be the first to stand in line if and when the NHL needs replacement players." The next day, retired NHLer Colin Patterson countered Hirsch's claims, saying, "It's no different than the reason he [Hirsch] went over there. When he went, he took someone else's position. No matter if it's a former NHL player, a European player, a North American guy who went over to play—he took someone else's position."

OCTOBER 31, 2004 In the most damning and controversial remarks to date in the NHL-NHLPA standoff, Rob Ray of Ottawa said he'd happily be a replacement player: "I'd cross the line in a second," he said. "Why wouldn't I? The only thing is, I wouldn't be the first one. I know about ten guys who would be ahead of me and these are ten current NHL players. Everybody just wants to get back playing…I went through this whole thing in 1994 when I was making $300,000. They got a deal done and I thought I was going to cash in big time. Well, I went from making $300,000 to $350,000. Big deal."

NOVEMBER 1, 2004 Nolan Baumgartner, a Vancouver Canucks player last year, now playing in the AHL with the farm team, Manitoba Moose, became the latest player to agree to a salary cap from the side of his mouth: "It's hard for me to answer, but if that [cap] is what it takes, obviously we want to get back playing. And that looks like what it's going to take."

NOVEMBER 2, 2004 The NHLPA met in Toronto to update the players and ensure all were on the same philosophical page. Some 74 players representing all 30 teams met for nearly five hours after which Bob Goodenow publicly assured one and all that "there are absolutely no cracks or divisiveness in our membership." Most notable among the attendees was Montreal's Pierre Dagenais who a few days earlier had said, "I'd be curious to see it if they took a poll of the players on the salary cap. They may be surprised to see how many players in my situation would vote in favour of a cap. Do I have a say in this? I'm just a noodle in a bowl of soup." After the day's meeting, Dagenais commented, "I think the union has a good plan and know where they're going. I came here because I didn't want to hide. I think the guys here are really trying to help." One of his leaders, Ottawa's Daniel Alfredsson, was defiant in re-stating the NHLPA's position: "I don't see us getting a deal," he said. "The players are prepared to sit out a whole year, if that's what it takes. We know there are things we can do to help the league, but it's not going to be a salary cap. With Gary's stance, it's take it or leave it. I think it's unlikely there will be a season."

NOVEMBER 3, 2004 Gary Bettman officially cancelled the All-Star Game scheduled for February 13, 2005 in Atlanta.

NOVEMBER 5, 2004 Robert Esche, goalie for the Philadelphia Flyers and vocal opponent to a salary cap, apologized publicly for calling NHL commissioner Gary Bettman a "madman." He had stated after an NHLPA union meeting in Toronto that, "I think there's a lot of great owners out there, but there's a madman leading them down the wrong path."

NOVEMBER 8, 2004 The National Football League signed contract extensions with its television partners that would see the league receive $11.5 billion in the coming seven years. The extensions include coverage by Fox and CBS which extended contracts through 2011. The initial contract paid the NFL $17.6 billion over eight years, ending in 2005, and the sides agreed to an $8 billion extension. Additionally, the NFL extended its deal with DirecTV for five more years and $3.5 billion for its satellite package called Sunday Ticket. (The NHL currently had a one-year deal with ESPN2 for $60 million with an option for two more years at $70 million per season.)

NOVEMBER 9, 2004 From his eponymous restaurant in downtown Toronto, Wayne Gretzky made it clear he would not step into the fray and try to help resolve the dispute. "It does look very bleak," he admitted. "There is a strong possibility now that the whole season will be cancelled. There's no conversation between Gary Bettman and Bob Goodenow, and if there's no talking, there's no hockey...I understand what the players are saying. I was a player. I understand what management and owners are saying. I'm an owner of a team. But this is a complex situation...It's not something I can go into and just fix."

NOVEMBER 12, 2004 Teen sensation Sidney Crosby said through his agent, Pat Brisson, that he would never play in the NHL as a replacement player. "That's not what Sidney is about," Brisson said. "He's about playing with the best and that won't be the best."

NOVEMBER 16, 2004 Friction within the pro ranks in North America heated up as Rob Valicevic, a career minor leaguer, lost his job in the AHL (average salary $62,014) to a locked-out NHLer and was forced down to the UHL (average salary $12,644 plus housing). "If they have replacement players in the NHL," he said, angrily, "I have no qualms about crossing...If my family has to starve because of what you're doing, when the tide turns, I'm going to do everything I can to take your job. It amazes me that these guys [NHL players] have the audacity to say, 'don't cross the line,' when they're pushing guys out that are making $800 a week to support their families."

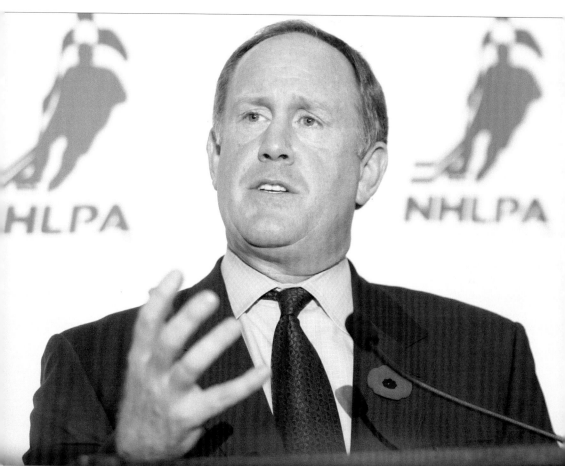

NHLPA executive director Bob Goodenow speaks to the media following a meeting with players in Toronto on November 2, 2004.

NOVEMBER 17, 2004 Bob Goodenow met a select group of player agents at a hotel near O'Hare airport in Chicago. After five hours of communication, the agents praised Goodenow who, of course, represented most of the agents' clients in negotiations with the league. "The people walk out of here today confident and comfortable with the people driving the bus," Don Baizley confirmed. Added Ron Salcer: "If the fans were in that room and heard what went on, I think they would be appalled at how this has gone and they'd know why the players should have a deal right now." Rich Winter was more adamant: "From what I've seen in the [union] presentation, the framework is there and I predict it will ultimately be the framework to get a deal done. I guarantee this will be what they sign."

NOVEMBER 18, 2004 Jeremy Roenick of the Philadelphia Flyers appeared on a U.S. television show called "The Best Damn Sports Show, Period" during which he excoriated both sides for their lax efforts: "Get into a room, lock the door, and don't come out until there's a deal done," he began. "People don't care right now. People are watching football; they're watching basketball. They don't care that hockey's not on TV right now. But I tell you what you should care about, Bob Goodenow and Gary Bettman. You should care about two things: You should care about the fans and the state of the game. And if you don't get this deal done soon, you're going to lose them both."

NOVEMBER 22, 2004 NHLPA vice president Bill Guerin weighed in with his two cents' worth of bargaining rhetoric, rejecting the methods of Gary Bettman to date: "The system that the owners want us to accept crushes everything that we've been working for. I've heard some of the owners say that they're going to lose less money by not playing this year. I guess, in the long run, the same could be said for us by not accepting what they're offering at this point. Everything, up to this point, has been one-sided. We've made proposals and we've been willing to talk about doing some things because we know that there are some franchises that need help financially. All we've heard from Gary is this stance: Salary cap, salary cap, salary cap."

NOVEMBER 23, 2004 Brett Hull criticized the game itself more than either side in particular in offering his views of the dispute: "It's a fantastic game and a great game to watch, but something has happened along the way that has made it very undesirable to TV to want to pick up the NHL, and I think it's because of the level of play, the diluted talent, and poor marketing. I think everyone who has watched the game decline not only in popularity, but the actual game itself has declined in skill and excitement and fan entertainment value."

NOVEMBER 24, 2004 The NHLPA announced that all players would receive monthly payments of $10,000 USD for November and December, and $5,000-$10,000 USD for the rest of the hockey season. "As a result of the ongoing owners' lockout, the NHLPA executive committee has announced a player stipend plan which consists of an initial 24-month schedule and monthly payments for over 730 locked-out players," Ted Saskin said.

It was revealed that talks between the NHL and NHLPA between March 26, 2003 and June 4, 2003, in which revenue sharing and luxury taxes were discussed, collapsed without progress. Dubbed the Blue Fin Project, the NHL believed the NHLPA's proposal was greatly flawed because it never guaranteed that costs would never exceed revenues and also never did anything to reduce the payroll disparities between the highest and lowest teams.

NOVEMBER 30, 2004 Gary Bettman headed to Edmonton for a Chamber of Commerce breakfast followed by a speech: "I believe in the Oilers and all of our Canadian franchises," he said. "Without the Canadian franchises, I believe it is not the National Hockey League."

DECEMBER 2, 2004 The NHLPA invited the NHL to Toronto for meetings on December 9, the first meaningful meetings in nearly three months during which they promised to make "a legitimate offer that can save the season," in the words of Daniel Alfredsson.

DECEMBER 9, 2004 The NHLPA offered the framework of a new deal that included "significant changes," in the words of Goodenow. He stated, "Let me be very clear. This is no grandstand play. This is serious negotiating." The offer featured six parts in a 240-page document: (1) a rollback of 24% on all existing player contracts; (2) a luxury-tax system that would include a 20 cent tax per dollar on team payrolls exceeding $45 million USD, 50 cents on payrolls over $50 million USD and 60 cents on everything over $60 million USD; (3) entry-level contracts would see the cap reduced from $1.295 million USD to $850,000 USD in addition to greater restrictions on bonuses (projected savings of $400 million over the six years); (4) redefining the salary arbitration process such that Group Two free agents making more than $1.5 million could go to arbitration without a qualifying offer (projected savings of $285 million over three years); (5) revenue sharing that would see profitable teams transfer money to less profitable teams; (6) reduced qualifying offers that would ensure that any contract paying $1 million or more would require a team only to match that salary (whereas formerly it had to offer a 10% pay raise). The term of the deal was six years and included player participation in the 2006 and 2010 Olympic Winter games. The NHLPA estimated the deal would save the league $270 million in its first year and $528 million over the next three. In response, Bettman found victory most significantly in the offer of rolling back salaries: "That element is a recognition by the union of our economic condition, but it is a one-time element. We have said consistently the focus must be on the overall systemic issues and the long-term needs and health of our game. The magnitude of the rollback is what you need to get our economics back in line as a starting point. To me, it's an acknowledgement of our economics." In attendance for the league were Bettman, Bill Daly, league counsel David Zimmerman, outside counsel Bob Batterman, and members of the executive committee: Harley Hotchkiss, Jeremy Jacobs, Craig Leopold, Peter Karmanos, Lou Lamoriello. The players were represented by Goodenow, Ted Saskin, John McCambridge, Ian Pulver, Mike Gartner and members of its executive committee: Trevor Linden, Bob Boughner, Vincent Damphousse, Arturs Irbe, and Trent Klatt.

DECEMBER 12, 2004 To prelude the NHL's official response to the NHLPA's proposal, Ottawa Senators' owner Eugene Melnyk rejected the most recent idea out of hand. "It's not a solution," he said. "It's a one-shot deal that doesn't work. Although the 24% rollback is something that we look at seriously, it's not a permanent solution to the problems. The most important thing is to fix the system. What we don't want to do is end up back in the same situation three, four, five years from now…There is one solution, and that's what is being proposed by commissioner Bettman. If we follow that track, we will have hockey that is here to stay."

DECEMBER 13, 2004 Following Eugene Melnyk, Edmonton Oilers' governor Cal Nichols referred to the latest NHLPA proposal only as, "an enticement to carry on doing essentially what we're doing…the Oilers won't be here long term if that's what we're prepared to accept." Furthermore, TSN obtained a letter sent by Bill Daly to the 30 teams rejecting the NHLPA proposal. It read in part: "The union's CBA proposal, while offering necessary and significant short-term financial relief, falls well short of providing the fundamental systemic changes that are required. While the immediate 'rollback' would materially improve league economics for 2004-05, there is virtually nothing in the proposal that would prevent the dollars 'saved' from being redirected right back into the player compensation system (thus re-creating the current imbalance) in only a matter of a couple of years."

DECEMBER 14, 2004 As expected, Gary Bettman rejected the NHLPA's proposal of December 9 and then offered a proposal of his own, a nine-point plan that would move the league's economics in a direction with which the 30 owners would be more comfortable. In rejecting the NHLPA's plan, Bettman said it resembled a jack-in-the-box. "You put the head in. You put the lid down. You get things put away. You crank it twice and it pops back up. We can't live with a system like that." He added, "We demonstrated (to the players) in hard numbers that if we accepted the union's proposal and framework, we would be back in the same position, best case, within two to three years, continuing to struggle the entire time. The unanimous conclusion was that the union's proposal does not work. It is fatally flawed as a system going forward. Of that, I and our thirty clubs have absolutely no doubt." The NHL's counter-proposal included: (1) scaled rollback for all players earning more than $800,000 a season; (2) entry-level contracts capped at $850,000 for four years and no bonus clauses permitted; (3) the total elimination of salary arbitration; (4) players to be paid 54% of hockey-related revenues, clubs paying 51%-57% of hockey-related revenues; (5) revenue sharing between the top-payroll teams and the bottom-payroll teams; (6) reduction of unrestricted free agency from 31 years of age to 30; (7) increase in minimum salary from $185,000 to $300,000; (8) status quo for median salary of $800,000; (9) qualifying offers allowed to be at less than 100% of a player's previous year's salary. Goodenow responded by saying that, "the league took elements they liked from our proposal, changed others in their favour, added new mechanisms skewed against the players, and then slapped a salary cap on top of everything." Said Daniel Alfredsson: "If they think they're going to wait us out, I think they're in for a surprise. I don't know about their side, but unanimity on our side on this issue is so strong."

DECEMBER 15, 2004 Both sides admitted a time out was needed to re-group and that talks might not re-start for "a few weeks" according to Ted Saskin. On radio station Fan 590 in Toronto, former NHLPA executive director Alan Eagleson slammed both sides. "They should have been sitting down since the summer of 2003," he began. "Every day, 20 owners and 20 of the top players hammering out something. Take a year to do it and put it to bed. And I still believe [a deal would be reached] if you got 30 owners and 30 team captains in a room, gave them a week, slid pizza under the door and said, 'Don't come out until you make this deal.' If there are 20 items, sit down and solve the 17 easy ones. There's too much at stake now. In 1994, the owners signed a bad deal, and in 1999, instead of terminating it, they extended it to cover the Olympics. That was going to be the big blossoming of hockey in the U.S. but that was a no-brainer not to happen. So, we got stung for another five years."

DECEMBER 22, 2004 Bryan McCabe, Toronto's player representative, added fuel to the fire with his opinion of Gary Bettman: "Gary's the guy running the ship, and he knows nothing about hockey. He's a basketball guy. If he bumped into me on the street, he wouldn't know me. You could probably say that if he bumped into 95% of the league."

DECEMBER 28, 2004 Rob Ray sued the NHL Players' Association after he discovered that he was not going to receive up to $10,000 a month under the NHLPA's support plan. Ray had come out of retirement toward the end of the 2003-04 season to play again for Ottawa. He commented that he believed he was being blacklisted because he had told a reporter from the *Ottawa Sun* that he would willingly be a replacement player (i.e., scab) if the two sides could not agree on a new CBA. Ray was quoted as saying, "I'd cross the line in a second. Why wouldn't I? I know about ten guys who would be ahead of me, and these guys are ten current NHL players. Everybody just wants to get back to playing." Upon filing the suit in the New York Supreme Court in Buffalo, Ray said, "I was promised something that they're not coming through with, so I've taken the steps that I've needed to take."

JANUARY 6, 2005 Bettman cancelled a board of governors meeting scheduled for January 14, 2005. Said Bill Daly: "I think it's safe to say that at the time the meeting was scheduled, the hope, if not the expectation, was that by this point in time the union would have made a new offer or at least approached us about restarting negotiations. In the absence of the union having done anything, the clubs are of the view that there is no reason to meet."

JANUARY 7, 2005 Bill Daly placed blame for escalating salaries and the financial woes of many of the teams squarely at the feet of the players and NHLPA: "Let's be clear on where the responsibility lies for where we find ourselves today: It lies exclusively at the feet of union leadership who, despite numerous and repeated approaches by the league over many years, utterly ignored—and, in some cases, knowingly exacerbated—the financial distress the league was experiencing. Then, as if to suggest it is the league who must agree to negotiate only on its terms, the union proceeds to hold the game and its fans hostage over its complete and absolute refusal to negotiate any system that is premised on a negotiated—not arbitrary, but negotiated—and rational relationship between player costs and league-wide revenues. I can only hope that the players understand and appreciate the union's chosen strategy in this process: Ignore the economic problems, delay in offering meaningful relief, and refuse to negotiate over an economic system that will ensure that the problems will not be repeated."

JANUARY 11, 2005 In an interview with the *Globe and Mail*, 19-year veteran Kevin Kerr, the all-time goal-scoring leader in the minor leagues with 664 and counting, happily admitted he'd play as a replacement in 2005-06 if he were asked. "Tell the owners in Calgary," he told Eric Duhatschek, "I'll come and play for thirty grand and a jersey and meal money, just to say I had a chance to play in the NHL. That's all I want, to say I played a game in the NHL and that I get to keep my jersey. Maybe they'll realize what it means for some of us guys to play in the NHL."

Carolina owner Peter Karmanos signaled a death knell for the season in a conversation with Canadian Press: "My gut feeling is that the season is gone," he admitted. "I know personally that I'd be willing to risk another season. I'm enough of a hockey fan to realize that once we got it straightened out, the fans will come back. But there's the risk they wouldn't. Even with that in mind, I feel very, very strongly that if we don't get it straightened out, we don't have to worry about the NHL existing anyways."

Mike Modano of the Dallas Stars, one of the league's top-paid players at $9 million US a season, suggested the players will have only so much resolve in the dispute: "It's going to be tough to come back in October and say that we're going to stay tough and stand firm. You're going to have guys who are saying, 'What are we doing?' You're going to have guys chomping at the bit to get a deal done."

JANUARY 12, 2005 Consistent with other players who have spoken out about the feuding sides, Modano back-tracked on his statement of a day previous. "We're still very unified," he told TSN. "Our unity has become much stronger over the past four to five months." Modano admitted that a media frenzy had resulted from his initial comments. "They're coming hot and heavy at me today, so I'm just kind of re-wording the whole 'limit' thing to 'being tested' and that sort of thing."

Walter Gretzky commented on the dispute in his usual paternal, level-headed way: "I don't know how to solve it," he said, "but they're all greedy—the owners and the players…The people would find a solution, but it boils down to two people—Bettman and Goodenow—two people. We're all held hostage by those two people."

JANUARY 19, 2005 In an unprecedented move in a dispute that was now 127 days old, NHLPA player president Trevor Linden met with NHL board of governors chairman Harley Hotchkiss (Calgary Flames owner) mano a mano at an airport lounge in Chicago to try to clear the air, discuss issues, and try to save the season. "There was dialogue and communication, and that's what I set out to accomplish," Linden said. Hotchkiss was equally guarded in his optimism. "We credit Trevor Linden's initiative in requesting this session, which was informal, open, and professional, and which resulted in a constructive exchange of viewpoints." The most important feature of the meeting was that it took place without Bettman and Goodenow. Only Linden, Hotchkiss, Daly, Bob Batterman (NHL), John McCambridge (NHLPA), and Saskin attended the five-hour O'Hare gathering.

JANUARY 20, 2004 Day two of the latest round of meetings took place in Toronto without Hotchkiss, who was back in Calgary attending the funeral of friend and co-owner of the Flames, Bud McCaig. The result of five more hours of talks was discouraging, at the very least. "The window of time we have in terms of playing hockey this season is very short," Daly conceded afterward. Ted Saskin was equally blunt: "The differences of opinion remain and they're differences that are strongly felt between the respective sides. There's certainly enough areas of disagreement between us that's certainly not allowing us to make progress."

JANUARY 21, 2005 Fallout from the latest round of unsuccessful negotiations fuelled Vincent Damphousse, an NHLPA vice president, to predict the worst. "I think the season is done," he said on CBC television. "I don't see how this can be resolved next September. Their strategy is to break the will of the union and impose a salary cap, and I don't think that's going to work. I'm convinced there won't even be a training camp next year."

JANUARY 26, 2005 Another meeting in Toronto with a similar group resulted in nothing more than a terse, "We will meet again this week," comment from Bill Daly. At the meeting were Lou Lamoriello (in attendance for the first time), Hotchkiss, Daly, and Bob Batterman (for the NHL), and Saskin, Linden, and John McCambridge (for the NHLPA).

JANUARY 27, 2005 As the clock ticked toward Zero Hour to save the 2004-05 season, a second day of meetings, this time in New York, with this new configuration of attendees resulted in nothing but a terse rejection by the NHLPA of a new proposal by the NHL which apparently included a salary cap without revenue sharing (the cap had a range of $32 million at the low end and $42 million high end, the figure being predicated by reaching 55% of the league's total revenues). "We continue to have significant philosophical differences. No meetings are scheduled," said Saskin.

FEBRUARY 2, 2005 Daly and Saskin met in Newark, New Jersey at which time the NHL made a 15-point proposal to the players which was rejected. The offer included: (1) a six-year deal; (2) the union has the right to re-open negotiations after the fourth full season; (3) players to receive between 53%-55% of league revenues; (4) a team payroll ranging from $32 million to $42 million, depending on league revenues; (5) guaranteed player contracts will remain; (6) profit-sharing between league and players (50-50) over and above an agreed upon level; (7) a monitored and audited method of tracking team revenues; (8) an owner-player council to discuss business and game-related issues; (9) a shortened 2005 season, players earning 53% of playoff revenues; (10) a four-year entry-level contract cap of $850,000 with permissible bonuses at a maximum of $250,000 a year; (11) revised salary arbitration that allows both players and teams the right to file; (12) age of free agency reduced from 31 to 30, possibly 28; (13) an increase in the league's minimum salary to $300,000; (14) a payroll tax; (15) a 24% rollback on salaries, as proposed by the union earlier. Both parties agreed to meet again the next day.

FEBRUARY 3, 2005 After nine hours of discussions in Manhattan, the only news was that both sides agreed to meet again the next day.

FEBRUARY 4, 2005 Many more hours of meeting in Manhattan yielded nothing but frustration and disappointment as the league stood at the brink of becoming the first professional sport in North America to cancel an entire season of play. "We met the last couple of days and tried to cover some issues to see if there was the possibility of some common ground and getting some traction," said Goodenow. "That isn't the case…The parties agreed to stay in touch but there's really no progress to report of any type." Jeremy Roenick, meanwhile, said he'd play under a salary cap, provided the number was high enough. "Maybe we can survive with a cap, one that's not at a ridiculous level such as what's being offered. I really feel that maybe if there was a bone thrown to us, one that was acceptable, one that the players could gnaw on a little bit, it might be feasible. But we haven't even got that. We haven't even got anything close to something acceptable. I think a lot of players might want to play for a cap, but not for a cap that they're offering."

FEBRUARY 7, 2005 Ken Dryden, now an MP and the federal Minister of Social Development, suggested hockey was more replaceable in Canada than fans at first thought. "I think that there are a number of fans in this country who have sensed over the last number of months that actually maybe it was more habit than it was passion," he said, in reference to the notion that Canadians and Saturday night hockey are intertwined in a cultural relationship of enduring strength.

FEBRUARY 9, 2005 For the first time, Gary Bettman indicated a 'drop-dead date' for the season was at hand. "It's clear to me that if we're not working on a written document memorializing our agreement this weekend, I don't see how we can play any semblance of a season," he said. Additionally, he suggested to Goodenow that the league was prepared to start the season immediately (28 games in the regular season, plus playoffs), accepting the NHLPA's proposal of December 9, 2004, which was highlighted by a 24% rollback of salaries and a luxury tax for teams with payrolls exceeding $45 million. However, if that system hit any one of four "trigger points" then the NHL's proposal of February 2, 2005, would be automatically implemented. The trigger points included: (1) total player salaries exceeding 55% of league revenues; (2) the average of the top three payrolls is 33% greater than the average of the lowest three clubs; (3) if three clubs exceeded payrolls of $42 million; (4) the average team payroll exceeded $36.5 million. "This was a transparent proposal," Goodenow said, swiftly rejecting it. Bettman issued a stern rebuke. "The amount of revenues will obviously decline if we don't have a season,

NHL executive vice-president Bill Daly speaks to the media in Toronto on February 10, 2005.

and therefore whatever the players would expect going forward, it is going to be diminished. I've been telling this to the union for years: The deal can only get worse as a technical matter and as an economic matter the longer we go without a new deal. That's not a threat; that's simply a reality of where we find ourselves."

FEBRUARY 10, 2005 Four hours of heated discussions between the NHL and NHLPA resulted in nothing more than the usual jargon. "The union was as inflexible today as it was six and a half years ago," Daly said. To which Saskin rejoined, "Any time we're not making dramatic concessions, it seems we're wasting their time." "It was a pointless meeting," Daly summarized.

FEBRUARY 13, 2005 The NHL and NHLPA met in Washington along with a U.S. federal mediator, resulting in no progress after five hours of talks. The meeting was requested by Scot Beckenbaugh, acting director of the U.S. Federal Mediation and Conciliation Service. Saskin and John McCambridge represented the NHLPA while Daly and Bob Batterman were there for the league. It was the third time the two sides had met with U.S. mediators, and although nothing seemed to come out of the meeting, Bettman, referring to a letter from Goodenow on February 15, 2005, indicated that for the first time the NHLPA said it might consider discussing a salary cap. Thus, although both sides had said all along mediation was not a solution to the problem, it proved to move discussions along at a remarkable rate.

FEBRUARY 14, 2005 A clandestine, one-on-one meeting between Daly and Saskin in Niagara Falls, New York, lasted until 10:30 pm, after which Daly released the expected statement, "No progress was made…there will be no further comment." However, those talks included discussions of a salary cap, a first in these negotiations, and this in turn led to further last-minute discussions the next day.

FEBRUARY 15, 2005 With a Gary Bettman press conference slated for the following day to cancel the season, both sides actively discussed resolutions to the dispute, each conceding a vital part of their negotiations to date. The NHLPA was willing to discuss playing under a salary cap, and the NHL was willing to discuss a cap without a link to league revenues. The result was a series of four letters between Bettman and Goodenow:

> Dear Bob:
> We attempted to reach out to you with yesterday's offer of a team maximum cap of $42.2 million ($40 million in salary and $2.2 million in benefits) which was not linked to league-wide revenues. As Bill told Ted, "de-linking" a maximum team salary cap from league revenues and total league-wide player compensation has always been problematic for us, especially since we cannot now quantify the damage to the League from the lockout. This presents the risk we will pay out more than we can afford. As you know, if all 30 teams were to spend to the maximum we proposed, and if the damage to our business is as we discussed at our meetings in New York, then the league would continue to lose money.
> I know, as you do, that the "deal" we can make will only get worse for the players if we cancel the season—whatever damage we have suffered to date will pale in comparison to the damage of a cancelled season and we will certainly not be able to afford what is presently on the table. Accordingly, I am making one final effort to reach out and make a deal that will let us play this season.
> We are increasing our offer of yesterday by increasing the maximum individual team cap to $44.7 million ($42.5 million in salary and $2.2 million in benefits). This offer is not an invitation to begin negotiations—it's too late for that.

This is our last effort to make a deal that's fair to the players and one that the clubs (hopefully) can afford. We have no more flexibility and there is no time for further negotiation.

If this offer is acceptable, please let me know by 11:00 am tomorrow, in advance of my scheduled press conference. Hopefully, the press conference will not be necessary.

Sincerely,
Gary B. Bettman
Commissioner

Dear Gary:

Yesterday afternoon, Bill Daly presented us with an offer from the League that, for the first time, was not linked to League-wide revenues. We appreciated your willingness to adjust your position and we worked to respond in kind. By evening, we had fashioned and reached out to you with an offer from the PA that included, for the first time, a team maximum cap. This offer built upon the 24% rollback and other changes in favour of clubs, which were presented by the Players on December 9, 2004.

As you know, and as Ted told Bill, our offer of a team cap represented a radical step for the PA. We took this step because we too believe that our sport will be damaged greatly by the cancellation of this season and the continuation of the lockout through next season.

We wish that the NHL had offered a "no linkage" proposal before yesterday so that negotiations in that arena could have commenced sooner. However, we recognize that they did not and we agree that time is short.

In that spirit, and in a final attempt to reach an agreement, we are adjusting our offer of yesterday in two respects. First, we are reducing the maximum individual team cap to $49 million in salary, which does not include the $2.2 million per team in benefits due.

Second, we will adjust our exception provision so that it is available to teams only twice during the six year term and for up to only 10% over the limit of $49 million (to $53.9 million), at the tax rate of 150%. The exception provision is important so that a successful team does not have to arbitrarily dismantle its roster after it has achieved particular success or is in a unique phase of its player roster cycle.

I can be reached at the usual phone numbers.

Regards,
Robert W. Goodenow
Executive Director & General Counsel

Dear Bob:

It was disappointing to receive the fax of your "final" offer.

We would have been prepared to propose and negotiate over a "de-linked" maximum team salary sooner, but the NHLPA had been consistent in stating that the players would never accept a salary cap. We only learned in the mediation process on Sunday that you would entertain such an offer, which is why we asked for a meeting yesterday and made the "de-linked" proposal.

If every team spent to the $49 million level you have proposed, total player compensation would exceed what we spent last season and, assuming for discussion purposes, there was no damage to the game, our player compensation costs would exceed 75 per cent of revenues. We cannot afford your proposal.

Our offer of earlier today was a $75 million increase over the offer we made yesterday. I hope you will accept it, and that we can move forward and negotiate the myriad of other issues that need to be addressed.

Sincerely,
Gary B. Bettman
Commissioner

Dear Gary:
This is in reply to your most recent letter.

Your claim that the Clubs cannot afford our proposal is based on your hypothetical fear of what would happen if every team spent to the $49 million level the Players have proposed. The notion that every Club will spend at the $49 million level is contradicted by years of actual payroll experience under the old CBA system and by Exhibit 12 of your December 14 document (attached for your recollection), in which you projected 24 teams well below the $49 million level after the rollback. Further, this experience is based on an environment without revenue sharing, taxes on team payrolls and the numerous new system restrictions.

Based on your own calculations from Exhibit 12, over 21 Clubs are spending significantly less than your team payroll limit number of $42.5 million. I am at a loss to understand how you suggest your offer earlier today represents a $75 million increase when it only impacts the spending of nine teams!

You will receive nothing further from us.

Regards,
Robert W. Goodenow
Executive Director & General Counsel

Jay McKee of the Buffalo Sabres summarized the stunning developments of the previous two days succinctly when he said, "It's not so much that I'm angry [the NHLPA] offered a salary cap. I'm angry that, why now? Why not last June, last July?...I'd be awfully surprised if we can't put something together [now]. We're at the point now where it's got to get done, and it's got to get done quick. But I think we can get it done."

FEBRUARY 16, 2005 "When I stood before you last September," Bettman began from the podium at a press conference in a Manhattan hotel, "I said NHL teams will not play again until our economic problems had been solved. As I stand before you today, it is my sad duty to announce that because the solution has not yet been attained, it is no longer practical to conduct even an abbreviated season... I have no choice but to announce the formal cancellation of play for 2004-05. This is a sad, regrettable day that all of us wish could have been avoided." Bettman concluded, much to the

NHL commissioner Gary Bettman holds a press conference in New York on February 16, 2005 to formally cancel the 2004-05 NHL season.

dismay of hockey fans who had hoped for a last-minute negotiating goal to win the day. This represented the first time a pro sports league in North America cancelled an entire season, and doubling this ignominy was the fact that the Stanley Cup, which had been contested for every year since 1893, would not have any competition this year. "Everyone associated with the NHL owes our fans an apology…If you want to know how I feel, I'll summarize it in one word—terrible," he went on. Bob Goodenow responded later in the afternoon: "The league's threats, ultimatums, take-it-or-leave-it tactics, and refusals to negotiate ultimately prevented a deal here. At some point, concessions end, and they end here today." During Bettman's press conference, the commissioner was asked why the two sides couldn't reach an agreement in the middle at, say, $45 million, after one side (the NHL) had offered $42.5 million and the other side (the NHLPA) offered $49. "If they wanted $45 million," he answered, "and I'm not saying we would have gone there, but they sure should have told us. It would have been incumbent upon them to tell us if that's where they would have made a deal." Goodenow's response was only that, "Gary Bettman told us he was not negotiating off his proposal and that was what happened."

FEBRUARY 17, 2005 Just one day after the season was cancelled, it appeared it wasn't 100% cancelled just yet! Bettman told ESPN, "I'm not telling you I would take $45 million because we had to stretch to get to $42.5 million, but if someone is trying to reach out to me in a meaningful way, I wouldn't slam the door on it." Compounding the post-mortem optimism was rumour that Wayne Gretzky and Mario Lemieux had finally become part of the possible negotiations to save the season after the fact. Said Gretzky on radio station the Fan 590 in Toronto: "I did talk to Mario today. I had a brief conversation about pretty much what everyone else is talking about—can we believe we're in the situation we're in?"

FEBRUARY 18, 2005 Fan and media frenzy was at its greatest height since September 15, 2004, as new meetings between the league and players' association were scheduled for the following day in Manhattan. "Late Thursday night the NHL requested a meeting with NHLPA representatives in New York," began a press release from the NHLPA. "Today, the NHLPA accepted the invitation and a meeting has been scheduled for Saturday [February 19]." What made this particularly important was that Wayne Gretzky and Mario Lemieux were to be in attendance, at the behest of Trevor Linden, and even before the two had arrived in New York, *The Hockey News* and ESPN were reporting that the two sides were on their way to striking a new deal. Incredibly, both sides now seemed to think that a 28-game regular season was feasible. Said Ryan Smyth from his home in Edmonton: "To resume talks after the season was just cancelled is a little weird, but, hey, we want to play." Mike Modano also revealed that there had been "a lot of arguing" within the players' ranks over the last-minute capitulation to a salary cap. "There were a lot of people who really couldn't understand how we could go so long not talking about a cap, and then just change over to a cap like that. And a lot of people didn't like it."

FEBRUARY 19, 2005 Even the Great One and the Magnificent One couldn't save hockey from its own suicide. After several hours' worth of meetings at the St. Regis Hotel in Manhattan, the NHL and NHLPA emerged with the final, horrible news that they were nowhere near a twelfth-hour agreement. "It became evident as we got into the meeting that the parties were, in fact, much further apart than everybody thought we were on Tuesday. No progress was made, and no further meetings will be scheduled," Saskin said. He was accompanied to the talks by Vincent Damphousse and Trevor Linden, and director of business relations, Mike Gartner. With Gretzky and Lemieux were Daly and Bob Batterman. It took a few days before details of the meeting were revealed, but Lemieux indicated that he and Gretzky were in New York to help the negotiations, which never happened. "The only way Wayne and I would have gotten involved is because we believed there was a new proposal coming from the players' association," he said a few days later. "We were told by some of the players we were talking to that there would be a new proposal on the table at the $45-million level." That, of course, never materialized, rendering their presence a moot point. Said Gretzky: "I felt, okay, maybe Mario and I don't have the answers, but maybe we can be part of bridging the gap between owners and players. Quite frankly, I expected maybe something a little different. But maybe there was a lack of communication. I don't know. I don't know what to say. It's three days later and I'm not sure what happened. I just feel disappointed and, quite frankly, I'm a little embarrassed."

FEBRUARY 27, 2005 Mario Lemieux, player and owner, put things simply and plainly when he said the time was at hand to get an agreement for 2005-06 if the sides were to maximize their potential for a full year. "The players really have to understand that the ability to maximize revenues next year is dependent on reaching an agreement as soon as possible," he said. "Hopefully they understand that so we can go out and have our marketing plan and season tickets and sell our sponsorships. Have the draft and all the things that need to be in place to maximize revenue. The longer we wait, the more challenging it's going to be for us to generate enough revenues...I think a deal has to be reached in a couple of months. After that, you start losing sponsorships. People start spending money elsewhere. People find other things to do."

FEBRUARY 28, 2005 Philadelphia Flyers' GM Bobby Clarke waded into the storm by unleashing a small torrent of abuse at Goodenow. Said the feisty Clarke: "Someone has to grab Goodenow by the throat and tell him, 'Look after the Canadian cities.' The majority of the players still come from Canada. It's our sport and to me Goodenow has shown no interest in helping build the game. He has done nothing but take from the game, and now he's fighting for power."

MARCH 1, 2005 At the NHL's board of governors meetings, an American business group presented a spectacularly absurd bid to buy the NHL and its 30 teams for a collective $3.5 billion, an offer the governors rejected immediately. Bettman assured everyone that the league would shortly start preparations for the 2005-06 season, signaling hypotheses that it would recruit replacement players to do so. Quote of the day went to Flyers' owner Ed Snider who was asked if he might take part in future talks with the NHLPA: "I don't need aggravation from Bob Goodenow," he began. "I might jump over the table and try and choke him to death. That wouldn't be good. That's why they keep me out of the negotiations." Meanwhile, in Toronto, some 150 players held their own post-cancellation meetings. "Sometimes you're not happy with the team's performance," Brendan Shanahan offered by way of explanation, "and you might get in the dressing room and argue a bit about it and discuss what you can do better. But when you come out for the next game, you are a team again. And that's what has happened over these two days."

MARCH 2, 2005 Goodenow held another four-hour meeting with player agents in Toronto, the latter group emerging, as before, supportive of the NHLPA's executive director. Said Rich Winter: "It's clear that everybody in that room is on the same page as Bob Goodenow because Gary Bettman's proposal will kill the game of hockey and he doesn't understand. And Bob's brilliant approach to negotiations—historically and at present—will save our game."

MARCH 11, 2005 After taking some time to collect their thoughts, both sides met in Toronto for less than two hours and emerged with nothing concrete to report save that more meetings, of greater substance, were planned.

MARCH 17, 2005 The NHL met with the NHLPA in Manhattan for about three hours, and Gary Bettman, as he had promised, delivered two offers to the players that were inferior to the one the players rejected prior to the cancellation of the season. The first was based on last-minute negotiations, but the number was smaller: a $37.5 million hard cap for all teams, without linkage to revenues; the other, with linkage, offered the players 54% of league revenues, down 1% from the previous offer. Said Goodenow: "Both proposals were very similar to ones that we previously rejected several times. We will be determining our next steps and be responding at the appropriate time." The first offer also contained a guaranteed minimum of $22.5 million as well as the chance to move the maximum upward if league revenues increased. But Bettman assured the players this was an offer available only in the short term, before further damage was done to the league's ability to generate income. He gave the NHLPA a deadline of April 8 to accept this offer, vowing that if rejected, the succeeding one would likely be even less attractive.

MARCH 22, 2005 Under cloak of secrecy, the NHLPA began three days of meetings at a Pebble Beach resort in California to consider its options following the NHL's most recent offers. In attendance were the full core of the union: Goodenow, Saskin, associate counsels Ian Pulver and Ian Penny,

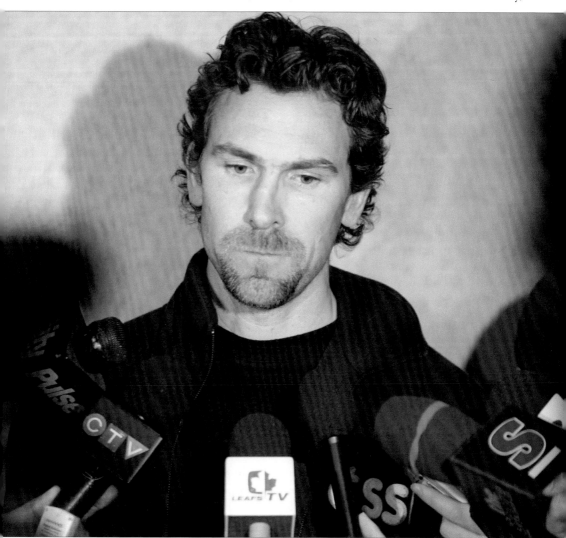

NHLPA president Trevor Linden meets with reporters after a session with players and their executive committee in Toronto on March 1, 2005.

director of business relations, Mike Gartner, outside counsel John McCambridge, and the players: president, Trevor Linden and vice presidents Vincent Damphousse, Trent Klatt, Bob Boughner, Arturs Irbe, and Bill Guerin.

MARCH 24, 2005 The NHL officially cancelled the Entry Draft scheduled for Ottawa on June 25-26 because Ottawa hotels needed a commitment to pay for the many reserved rooms or cancel those reservations. The league promised a draft would be held before any further hockey would be played but speculated a best-case scenario in which the first two rounds were conducted live, with the top prospects present, and the remaining rounds done by conference call.

MARCH 25, 2005 In the first legal move of this dispute, the NHL filed a formal challenge with the National Labor Relations Board in the U.S. because the league felt the NHLPA used a "coercive" policy that violated "the players' rights under the labour laws to decide individually whether to be represented by a union." More specifically, the NHLPA apparently had a rule whereby any player who became a replacement player would have to return payments he received during the lockout, which had been estimated to be $5,000-$10,000 per month.

APRIL 4, 2005 The NHL and the NHLPA met for the first time in nearly three weeks, but the only thing that was accomplished was a formal rejection by the PA of the NHL's offer from March 17 and no counter-proposal in hand. Causing further friction, the NHL filed a second formal grievance with the National Labor Relations Board in the U.S. citing unfair labour practices on the PA's part. The league suggested the PA intended to decertify any player agent representing a player who would become a replacement player for the upcoming season.

APRIL 6, 2005 The NHL and ESPN delayed discussions about the network commiting to their $60-million contract to cover games for the coming season. Each side agreed a six-week extension would be beneficial in determining the hockey climate for the coming season, at which time the network could either commit to or back out of their arrangement.

APRIL 7, 2005 Bettman and Goodenow met for an hour and a half and although they didn't discuss specifics there was a sense of optimism, as Bill Daly acknowledged. "We had more traction on a common concept than we've had in the past," he said. "But again, that could go away in the first five minutes of the next meeting."

APRIL 14, 2005 Using the death of Pope John Paul II as an analogy, New Jersey Devils' GM Lou Lamoriello said, "All we've got to do to solve [the problem] is do what the cardinals are doing to get a new pope. They are not leaving the room until there is white smoke. We can't be allowing two weeks to go between meetings."

APRIL 19, 2005 The league and players met for nearly seven hours, but after little progress Bettman seemed to move toward the use of replacement players. "What I have said," he began afterward, "is that we are going to start the season on time." The meeting ended with Boston owner, Jeremy Jacobs, declaring that the PA's ideas were not good enough and were not going to work unless the union could guarantee the NHL would not spend more than 54% of its revenues on players' salaries.

APRIL 20, 2005 After meeting with the board of governors for four hours, Bettman made clear that replacement players would not be used to start the 2005-06 season. "If we don't have a new CBA so that our players can start the season with us in October, we will not open on time," he stated.

APRIL 24, 2005   Bobby Orr had his views published in the *Sunday Eagle Tribune* in Lawrence, Massachusetts, outside Boston. He wrote in part, "With the unacceptable lack of progress and the continued bickering, I am no longer convinced that there was a genuine interest in getting a fair deal done. The win-at-all-costs attitude of both sides in this process has been disastrous. Both NHL Commissioner Gary Bettman and players association executive director Bob Goodenow have wasted time and squandered goodwill. They now have a responsibility to either lead or get out of the way. Because of what has happened, our sport is in danger of becoming irrelevant unless both sides immediately put an end to this nonsense…The collateral damage caused by their refusal to compromise is a disgrace. Our fans have been used and abused…Enough is enough."

APRIL 28, 2005   The NHLPA applied for union certification in Quebec and British Columbia as a way of ensuring those provinces do not allow NHL teams to use replacement players.

MAY 6, 2005   The two sides met for four hours during which time the NHL proposed an agreement based on a team-by-team salary cap with a low limit and high limit and a payroll tax in the middle.

MAY 10, 2005   The two sides met in New York for more than three hours, agreeing to talk more over the next two days and putting off plans to attend the World Championship in Austria. Later, both the NHL and NHLPA agreed this was a turning point in negotiations.

MAY 11, 2005   Members of the NHL and NHLPA met in New York to start discussions regarding methods to determine revenue and club payrolls for each team.

MAY 19, 2005   After a marathon meeting that lasted 14 hours in New York, both sides said goodnight with the intention of continuing to talk, even though little progress had been made.

MAY 20, 2005   Eight more hours of meetings yielded results that were so positive that Bill Daly suggested a deal might "get done by early June." Bettman added that, "we are on our way home," by far his most optimistic statement on negotiations to date.

MAY 25, 2005   The two sides met in Chicago for six and a half hours without Bettman and Goodenow.

MAY 26, 2005   The NHL and NHLPA met for the second straight day in Chicago with more progress made. "We…focused on revenue measurement and reporting issues," Ted Saskin said of the discussions. Brendan Shanahan, not a member of the NHL executive, nonetheless continued to be a part of the negotiations as he had been for more than three weeks now.

MAY 27, 2005   ESPN formally cancelled its contract with the NHL for the coming season, thus removing $60 million in revenue for the league (or, $2 million per team.)

JUNE 2, 2005   Renewed effort and more precise negotiating continued in Toronto as the two sides worked on defining revenue toward an agreement based largely on a salary cap and revenue-sharing.

JUNE 7, 2005   The league holds a practice in Toronto to experiment with potential new rules, most significantly larger nets and the elimination of the centre-red line as an offside line.

JUNE 8, 2005   Reports start leaking that an agreement has been reached and will soon be finalized.

JUNE 30, 2005 Detroit goalie Manny Legace lashed out at Bob Goodenow: "The whole thing is a farce," he said of the lost season. "We basically sat out for nothing, wasted a lot of money for nothing. It makes no sense to me."

JULY 6, 2005 L.A. Kings forward Sean Avery voiced his extreme displeasure with the way the negotiations had been conducted: "We burned a year for nothing," he told the *Los Angeles Times.* "We didn't win anything. We didn't prove anything. We didn't get anything. We wasted an entire season."

JULY 13, 2005 The NHL and NHLPA reached a new agreement in principle on a six-year contract.

JULY 14, 2005 Buffalo defenceman Jay McKee articulated his opinion of events over the past year: "From Day One, I was behind them in saying we won't accept a salary cap, and I stand behind them today in accepting a cap…I have no regrets."

JULY 21, 2005 Players voted overwhelmingly to accept the new CBA as 464 said yea to the vote and just 68 said nay. The agreement included a salary cap, revenue sharing, and a universal 24% pay cut to all existing contracts. "It's the type of agreement that we think a professional sports league like ours can thrive under to everybody's benefit because we are true and honest partners," Bettman said at the press conference announcing the agreement. Said Goodenow, "The most important aspect, from my perspective, is making sure that the product is revenue driven." The agreement included a cap of $39 million, a floor of $21.5 million and a minimum salary of $450,000. Other highlights included: unrestricted free agency after seven full years in the NHL or at age 29 (2006), 28 (2007), and 27 (2008); entry-level salary capped at $850,000 plus restricted bonuses; stricter drug testing; cancellation of the 2006 All-Star Game set for Phoenix and instead participation in the 2006 Olympics; Entry Draft reduced to seven rounds. Also announced were significant rule changes: removal of the centre-red line for offsides; reduced size of goalie equipment; re-instatement of the tag-up offside rule; another attempt at cracking down on obstruction; shootouts after overtime in the regular season; a skater who shoots the puck over the glass in the defensive end will incur a minor penalty. The NHL also announced that the draft lottery and Entry Draft would not be televised, but after heavy lobbying from TSN the league permitted these events from being broadcast in rudimentary form.

JULY 22, 2005 The NHL owners ratified the new CBA approved the previous day by the players. The first draft lottery in NHL history ended as Pittsburgh won first overall selection with which they chose Sidney Crosby a week later.

JULY 28, 2005 One week after the new agreement was reached, Bob Goodenow resigned as executive director of the NHLPA. "After talking to the players and knowing what the set-up was going to be going forward for six years, I said, 'It makes a lot of sense to make the change now rather than wait 18 months or something like that and then say okay, now we're going to do a handoff,'" Goodenow said. Reaction was mixed among the players. Said Sean Avery: "To be honest with you, most of us didn't know what was going on [during the lockout]…Guys were out there giving interviews, and we didn't know the real story." Sami Kapanen of the Philadelphia Flyers offered this: "The players decided to accept the cap and get back on the ice, but I don't think that's what Bob was looking for. I know that not all the players are happy with the negotiations." Vincent Damphousse said that, "We [the players] owe him a lot because he's done so much for us." Michael Peca agreed. "Bob has done a tremendous job for the players in the game today. But I think moving forward, it's a new system and a new era, and I think everybody feels that maybe there are some other people to lead that charge." Ted Saskin, Goodenow's right-hand man, took over as the new executive director effective immediately.

Alumni Quotes

MIKE BOSSY (September 30, 2004): "I played ten years in the National Hockey League, and I'll admit to the fact that during one's professional hockey career you lose touch with reality, not only because of the money that you're making compared to what you would be making if you weren't a professional hockey player, but also because of the adulation that you receive. In a sense, I know where [the players] are coming from. They're coming from unrealistic behaviour and expectations...In today's market, I don't think that a team could have paid for our team...If Bobby Holik is making $9 million [with the Rangers], in my eyes that means Bobby Nystrom should have been making $9 million. If you put Bobby Nystrom at $9 million, what are the rest of us making?...I don't think that any hockey player is being taken advantage of now.

MARCEL DIONNE (October 20, 2004): "Why should you pay a kid, coming out of junior who hasn't done anything, a million bucks?"

JEAN BELIVEAU (November 9, 2004): "I've always sided with the players in the past, but this time I really believe they're completely wrong. They are making a big mistake, a terrible mistake. I'm sad to see that players don't seem to believe that 20 or 22 franchises are in deep financial trouble. No business can operate with 75% of its total revenue going toward the salary budget. Some players say they want to give back to those who follow them. I can speak for players of my generation, who really had the game in mind. When we left hockey, it was in great shape. Those who follow today's players will face a very serious situation because the game will be in very bad shape, financially and otherwise…The luckiest players are those of the last ten years because all of them were paid too much."

BRIAN KILREA told the *Hockey News* in December 2004: "I was voted a player rep in Los Angeles when we started (in 1967). That was when we had expansion and had trouble with Eddie Shore. When we first started, it was to see what gains and inroads we could make. It was a lot different from today because today the players have the pendulum swung so far to one side. The owners can't make any money. Right now a lot of owners are losing money, and that's a proven fact no matter what they [the players] want to say…Why are we so different from the players who play other professional sports that we are above a cap?"

PHIL ESPOSITO (January 18, 2005): "Well, for the first time in my lifetime, I don't agree with the players. I think they're wrong this time. It's the first time, ever, that I ever thought the players were wrong. And this time I just do not understand what the big deal is with a salary cap. I just don't understand it. (It's) not going to affect anybody, but it might take away the $10-$11 million player which there is no room for anyway in the National Hockey League because the revenues just don't justify it."

DARRYL SITTLER (February 8, 2005): "It's hard as a player to buy it, but at the same time if somebody's guaranteeing a salary cap of $42-$45 million, there's still lots of money to split up amongst the guys to make a good living at something they love doing."

GUY LAFLEUR (February 16, 2005); I have no respect for the mentality of some of the players. They say I'm frustrated I didn't make their type of money. Well, I don't give a s——. We played with passion, for the love of the game. If today's players are so smart, why don't they buy a [bleep] franchise and they'll see what's going on…What hurts me most is that fans have suffered, and people have lost their jobs because of this."

What They Did in 2004-05

A complete list of every player who appeared in at least one NHL game in 2003-04 and what they did during the 2004-05 season.

PLAYER					
YEAR	GP	G	A	P	Pim

GOALIE						
YEAR	GP	W-L-T	Mins	GA	SO	GAA

ABID, RAMZI
b. Montreal, Quebec, March 24, 1980

	GP	G	A	P	Pim
2003-04 PIT	16	3	2	5	27
NHL Totals	49	13	10	23	59

–signed September 24, 2004 by Wilkes-Barre/Scranton Penguins, Pittsburgh's AHL affiliate

ADAMS, CRAIG
b. Seria, Brunei (Malaysia), April 26, 1977

	GP	G	A	P	Pim
2003-04 CAR	80	7	10	17	69
NHL Totals	238	14	23	37	198

–signed July 28, 2004 by Milano (Serie A, Italy)

ADAMS, KEVYN
b. Washington, D.C., October 8, 1974

	GP	G	A	P	Pim
2003-04 CAR	73	10	12	22	43
NHL Totals	363	41	58	99	243

–signed February 13, 2005 by Dusseldorf (Deutsche Eishockey Liga, Germany)
–played for USA at 2005 World Championship

AEBISCHER, DAVID
b. Fribourg, Switzerland, February 7, 1978

	GP	W-L-T	Mins	GA	SO	GAA
2003-04 COL	62	32-19-9	3,703	129	4	2.09
NHL Totals	131	64-44-12	7,515	268	10	2.14

–signed September 17, 2004 by Lugano (Swiss league)
–played for Switzerland at Deutschland Cup (November 2004)
–played for Sparta Praha (Extraleague, Czech Republic); played for Sparta Praha at 2005 Spengler Cup (December 26-31, 2004)
–played for Switzerland at 2005 World Championship

AFANASENKOV, DMITRY
b. Arkhangelsk, Soviet Union (Russia), May 12, 1980

	GP	G	A	P	Pim
2003-04 TB	71	6	10	16	12
NHL Totals	85	7	11	18	16

–signed September 28, 2004 by Lada Togliatti (Super League, Russia)

AFINOGENOV, MAXIM
b. Moscow, Soviet Union (Russia), September 4, 1979

	GP	G	A	P	Pim
2003-04 BUF	73	17	14	31	57
NHL Totals	332	73	79	152	228

–played 2004-05 with Moscow Dynamo (Super League, Russia)
–played for Russia at 2005 World Championship (bronze medal)

AITKEN, JOHNATHAN
b. Edmonton, Alberta, May 24, 1978

	GP	G	A	P	Pim
2003-04 CHI	41	0	1	1	70
NHL Totals	44	0	1	1	70

–played part of 2004-05 with Manitoba Moose, Vancouver's AHL affiliate

ALBELIN, TOMMY
b. Stockholm, Sweden, May 21, 1964

	GP	G	A	P	Pim
2003-04 NJ	45	1	3	4	4
NHL Totals	916	44	205	249	415

announced retirement July 29, 2004

ALFREDSSON, DANIEL
b. Goteborg, Sweden, December 11, 1972

	GP	G	A	P	Pim
2003-04 OTT	77	32	48	80	24
NHL Totals	629	219	349	568	259

–signed November 10, 2004 by Frolunda (Swedish Elite League)
–played for IMG WorldStars tour of Europe in December 2004
–one of six NHLPA vice presidents, he also worked closely with Bob Goodenow to inform players worldwide of goings-on in meetings with the NHL
–played for Sweden at 2005 World Championship

ALLEN, BRYAN
b. Kingston, Ontario, August 21, 1980

	GP	G	A	P	Pim
2003-04 VAN	74	2	5	7	94
NHL Totals	139	7	8	15	173

–signed December 20, 2004 by Khimik Voskresensk (Super League, Russia)

ALLISON, JAMIE
b. Lindsay, Ontario, May 13, 1975

	GP	G	A	P	Pim
2003-04 NAS	47	0	3	3	76
NHL Totals	345	7	22	29	583

–lived and trained in Toronto for most of the season
–did not play professionally in 2004-05

AMONTE, TONY
b. Hingham, Massachusetts, August 2, 1970

	GP	G	A	P	Pim
2003-04 PHI	80	20	33	53	38
NHL Totals	1,013	392	436	828	669

–played for IMG WorldStars tour of Europe in December 2004

ANDERSON, CRAIG
b. Park Ridge, Illinois, May 21, 1981

	GP	W-L-T	Mins	GA	SO	GAA
2003-04 CHI	21	6-14-0	1,205	57	1	2.84
NHL Totals	27	6-17-2	1,475	75	1	3.05

–played part of 2004-05 with Norfolk Admirals, Chicago's AHL affiliate

ANDREYCHUK, DAVE
b. Hamilton, Ontario, September 29, 1963

	GP	G	A	P	Pim
2003-04 TB	82	21	18	39	42
NHL Totals	1,597	634	686	1,320	1,109

–began 2004-05 playing with Montreal in Original Stars Hockey League

Goalie David Aebischer, playing for Sparta Praha, sits on the bench during his team's game against Metallurg Magnitogorsk on December 27, 2004 at the Spengler Cup.

One of the NHLPA's six vice presidents, Daniel Alfredsson spent the last half of 2004-05 with Frolunda after trying to resolve the lockout for the first six months of the season.

ANGELSTAD, MEL
b. Saskatoon, Saskatchewan, October 31, 1972

2003-04 WAS	2	0	0	0	2
NHL Totals	2	0	0	0	2

–played all of 2004-05 with Belfast Giants (Elite Ice Hockey League, UK)

ANTROPOV, NIK
b. Vost, Soviet Union (Kazakhstan), February 18, 1980

2003-04 TML	62	13	18	31	62
NHL Totals	263	48	77	125	261

–signed October 27, 2004 by AK Bars Kazan (Super League, Russia); released by AK Bars Kazan on December 16, 2004
–signed December 20, 2004 by Lokomotiv Yaroslavl (Super League, Russia)

ARKHIPOV, DENIS
b. Kazan, Soviet Union (Russia), May 19, 1979

2003-04 NAS	72	9	12	21	22
NHL Totals	273	46	65	111	74

–signed July 27, 2004 by AK Bars Kazan (Super League, Russia)

ARMSTRONG, CHRIS
b. Regina, Saskatchewan, June 26, 1975

2003-04 ANA	4	0	1	1	0
NHL Totals	7	0	1	1	0

–played 2004-05 with Ingolstadt (Deutsche Eishockey Liga, Germany)

ARMSTRONG, DEREK
b. Ottawa, Ontario, April 23, 1973

2003-04 LA	57	14	21	35	33
NHL Totals	209	35	57	92	119

–signed October 12, 2004 by Geneve-Servette (Swiss league); left team after a disagreement with coach Chris McSorley
–signed February 13, 2005 by Rapperswil-Jona (Swiss league); left Rapperswil-Jona on February 24, 2005

ARNASON, TYLER
b. Oklahoma City, Oklahoma, March 16, 1979

2003-04 CHI	82	22	33	55	16
NHL Totals	185	44	54	98	40

–signed October 29, 2004 by Brynas (Swedish Elite League); released November 27, 2004 by Brynas because he was out of shape

ARNOTT, JASON
b. Collingwood, Ontario, October 11, 1974

2003-04 DAL	73	21	36	57	66
NHL Totals	743	244	324	568	897

–remained in Dallas most of the season; did not play professionally in 2004-05

ARVEDSON, MAGNUS
b. Karlstad, Sweden, November 25, 1971

2003-04 VAN	41	8	7	15	12
NHL Totals	434	100	125	225	241

–signed August 6, 2004 with Farjestad (Swedish Elite League); retired October 11, 2004

ASHAM, ARRON
b. Portage La Prairie, Manitoba, April 13, 1978

2003-04 NYI	79	12	12	24	92
NHL Totals	278	38	40	78	287

–signed January 19, 2005 by Visp (Swiss league)

AUBIN, JEAN-SEBASTIEN
b. Montreal, Quebec, July 19, 1977

2003-04 PIT	22	7-9-0	1,067	53	1	2.98
NHL Totals	168	63-72-11	8,888	432	6	2.92

–played 2004-05 with St. John's Maple Leafs (AHL)

AUBIN, SERGE
b. Val d'Or, Quebec, February 15, 1975

2003-04 ATL	66	10	15	25	73
NHL Totals	300	37	47	84	282

–signed January 5, 2005 by Geneve-Servette (Swiss league)

AUCOIN, ADRIAN
b. Ottawa, Ontario, July 3, 1973

2003-04 NYI	81	13	31	44	54
NHL Totals	602	83	162	245	456

–signed December 21, 2004 by MoDo (Swedish Elite League)

AUDETTE, DONALD
b. Laval, Quebec, September 23, 1969

2003-04 MTL/FLO	51	9	12	21	38
NHL Totals	735	260	249	509	584

–did not play professionally in 2004-05

AULD, ALEX
b. Cold Lake, Alberta, January 7, 1981

2003-04 VAN	6	2-2-2	349	12	0	2.06
NHL Totals	14	6-5-2	791	24	1	1.82

–played 2004-05 with Manitoba Moose, Vancouver's AHL affiliate
–loaned to Team Canada for 2005 Spengler Cup (December 26-31, 2004)

AVERY, SEAN
b. Pickering, Ontario, April 10, 1980

2003-04 LA	76	9	19	28	261
NHL Totals	163	17	30	47	482

–signed November 24, 2004 by Pelicans (SM-Liiga, Finland); left team after just two games
–signed February 11, 2005 by Motor City Mechanics (UHL)

AXELSSON, P-J
b. Kungalv, Sweden, February 26, 1975

2003-04 BOS	68	6	14	20	42
NHL Totals	533	63	110	173	189

–played 2004-05 with Frolunda (Swedish Elite League)
–played for Sweden at 2005 World Championship

BABCHUK, ANTON
b. Kiev, Soviet Union (Ukraine), May 6, 1984

2003-04 CHI	5	0	2	2	2
NHL Totals	5	0	2	2	2

–played 2004-05 with Norfolk Admirals, Chicago's AHL affiliate

BACKMAN, CHRISTIAN
b. Alingsas, Sweden, April 28, 1980

2003-04 STL	66	5	13	18	16
NHL Totals	70	5	13	18	16

–played 2004-05 with Frolunda (Swedish Elite League)
–played for Sweden at 2005 World Championship

BALEJ, JOSEF
b. Myjava, Czechoslovakia (Slovakia), February 22, 1982

2003-04 MTL/NYR	17	1	4	5	4
NHL Totals	17	1	4	5	4

–played 2004-05 with Hartford Wolf Pack, New York Rangers' AHL affiliate

BARINKA, MICHAL
b. Vyskov, Czechoslovakia (Czech Republic), June 12, 1984

2003-04 CHI	9	0	1	1	6
NHL Totals	9	0	1	1	6

–played 2004-05 with Norfolk Admirals, Chicago's AHL affiliate

BARNABY, MATTHEW
b. Ottawa, Ontario, May 4, 1973

2003-04 NYR/COL	82	16	25	41	157
NHL Totals	713	104	161	265	2,257

–did not play professionally in 2004-05

BARNES, RYAN
b. Dunnville, Ontario, January 30, 1980

2003-04 DET	2	0	0	0	0
NHL Totals	2	0	0	0	0

–played 2004-05 with Grand Rapids Griffins, Detroit's AHL affiliate

BARNES, STU
b. Spruce Grove, Alberta, December 25, 1970

2003-04 DAL	77	11	18	29	18
NHL Totals	897	221	292	513	328

–recuperated from off-season shoulder surgery and did not play professionally in 2004-05

BARNEY, SCOTT
b. Oshawa, Ontario, March 27, 1979

2003-04 LA	19	5	6	11	4
NHL Totals	24	5	6	11	4

–played 2004-05 with Manchester Monarchs, Los Angeles's AHL affiliate

BARON, MURRAY
b. Prince George, British Columbia, June 1, 1967

2003-04 STL	80	1	5	6	61
NHL Totals	988	35	94	129	1,309

–did not play professionally in 2004-05

BARTOVIC, MILAN
b.Trencin, Czechoslovakia (Slovakia), April 9, 1981

2003-04 BUF	23	1	8	9	18
NHL Totals	26	2	8	10	18

–played 2004-05 with Rochester Americans, Buffalo's AHL affiliate

BATES, SHAWN
b. Melrose, Massachusetts, April 3, 1975

2003-04 NYI	69	9	23	32	46
NHL Totals	349	53	101	154	172

–played in a charity game with Boston University on October 24, 2004

BATTAGLIA, BATES
b. Chicago, Illinois, December 13, 1975

2003-04 COL/WAS	70	4	7	11	42
NHL Totals	485	68	99	167	408

–played part of 2004-05 with Mississippi Sea Wolves (ECHL)

BAUMGARTNER, NOLAN
b. Calgary, Alberta, March 23, 1976

2003-04 PIT/VAN	14	0	3	3	4
NHL Totals	48	1	7	8	16

–played 2004-05 with Manitoba Moose, Vancouver's AHL affiliate

BAYDA, RYAN
b. Saskatoon, Saskatchewan, December 9, 1980

2003-04 CAR	44	3	3	6	22
NHL Totals	69	7	13	20	38

–played 2004-05 with Lowell Lock Monsters, Carolina's AHL affiliate

BEAUDOIN, ERIC
b. Ottawa, Ontario, May 3, 1980

2003-04 FLO	30	2	4	6	12
NHL Totals	53	3	8	11	41

–loaned January 3, 2005 to Edmonton Road Runners (AHL)
–also played part of 2004-05 with San Antonio Rampage (AHL)

BEDNAR, JAROSLAV
b. Prague, Czechoslovakia (Czech Republic), November 8, 1976

2003-04 FLO	13	1	1	2	4
NHL Totals	102	10	25	35	3

–played 2004-05 with Avangard Omsk (Super League, Russia); won European Champions Cup with Avangard Omsk

BEECH, KRIS
b. Salmon Arm, British Columbia, February 5, 1981

2003-04 PIT	4	0	1	1	6
NHL Totals	99	10	17	27	59

–played 2004-05 with Wilkes-Barre/Scranton Penguins, Pittsburgh's AHL affiliate

BEGIN, STEVE
b. Trois-Rivieres, Quebec, June 14, 1978

2003-04 MON	52	10	5	15	41
NHL Totals	175	21	12	33	233

–signed February 17, 2005 by Hamilton Bulldogs, Montreal's AHL affiliate

BEKAR, DEREK
b. Burnaby, British Columbia, September 15, 1975

2003-04 NYI	4	0	0	0	2
NHL Totals	11	0	0	0	6

–signed November 4, 2004 by Dundee Stars (British Ice Hockey League, UK)
–signed November 22, 2004 by Springfield Falcons (AHL)

BELAK, WADE
b. Saskatoon, Saskatchewan, July 3, 1976

2003-04 TML	34	1	1	2	109
NHL Totals	275	7	15	22	811

–started season playing for Toronto in Original Stars Hockey League
–signed November 8, 2004 by Coventry Blaze (Elite Ice Hockey League, UK)

BELANGER, ERIC
b. Sherbrooke, Quebec, December 16, 1977

2003-04 LA	81	13	20	33	44
NHL Totals	258	46	67	113	107

–signed December 22, 2004 by Bolzano (Serie A, Italy)

BELFOUR, ED
b. Carman, Manitoba, April 21, 1965

2003-04 TML	59	34-19-6	3,444	122	10	2.13
NHL Totals	856	435-281-111	49,509	2,006	75	2.43

–began season on disabled list and did not play the rest of the season

BELL, MARK
b. St. Paul's, Ontario, August 5, 1980

2003-04 CHI	82	21	24	45	106
NHL Totals	257	47	56	103	347

–signed November 6, 2004 by Trondheim IK (Norwegian league)

BERARD, BRYAN
b. Woonsocket, Rhode Island, March 5, 1977

2003-04 CHI	58	13	34	47	53
NHL Totals	510	59	207	266	412

–signed October 2, 2004 by Amsterdam (Dutch league)

BEREHOWSKY, DRAKE
b. Toronto, Ontario, January 3, 1972

2003-04 PIT/TML	56	6	18	24	67
NHL Totals	549	37	112	149	848

–signed December 22, 2004 by Skelleftea (Swedish league, Division 2)

BERG, AKI
b. Turku, Finland, July 28, 1977

	GP	G	A	Pts	PIM
2003-04 TML	79	2	7	9	40
NHL Totals	531	15	62	77	318

–signed September 22, 2004 by Timra (Swedish Elite League)

BERGENHEIM, SEAN
b. Helsinki, Finland, February 8, 1984

	GP	G	A	Pts	PIM
2003-04 NYI	18	1	1	2	4
NHL Totals	18	1	1	2	4

–played 2004-05 with Bridgeport Sound Tigers, New York Islanders' AHL affiliate

BERGERON, MARC-ANDRE
b. St. Louis de France, Quebec, October 13, 1980

	GP	G	A	Pts	PIM
2003-04 EDM	54	9	17	26	26
NHL Totals	59	10	18	28	35

–started 2004-05 with Trois-Rivieres (NAHL, Quebec)
–signed January 23, 2005 by Brynas (Swedish Elite League)

BERGERON, PATRICE
b. Ancienne-Lorette, Quebec, July 24, 1985

	GP	G	A	Pts	PIM
2003-04 BOS	71	16	23	39	22
NHL Totals	71	16	23	39	22

–played 2004-05 with Providence Bruins, Boston's AHL affiliate
–loaned to Canada's National Junior Team for 2005 World Junior Championships in Grand Forks, North Dakota (gold medal)

BERGEVIN, MARC
b. Montreal, Quebec, August 11, 1965

	GP	G	A	Pts	PIM
2003-04 PIT/VAN	61	1	10	11	29
NHL Totals	1,191	36	145	181	1,090

–moved to San Diego where he surfed every day; did not play professionally in 2004-05

BERGLUND, CHRISTIAN
b. Orebro, Sweden, March 12, 1980

	GP	G	A	Pts	PIM
2003-04 NJ/FLO	33	5	4	9	14
NHL Totals	86	11	16	27	42

–played 2004-05 with Farjestad (Swedish Elite League)

BERRY, RICK
b. Birtle, Manitoba, November 4, 1978

	GP	G	A	Pts	PIM
2003-04 WAS	65	0	6	6	108
NHL Totals	197	2	13	15	314

–played 2004-05 with Utah Grizzlies (AHL)

BERTUZZI, TODD
b. Sudbury, Ontario, February 2, 1975

	GP	G	A	Pts	PIM
2003-04 VAN	69	17	43	60	122
NHL Totals	628	198	260	458	911

–suspended during 2003-04 season for vicious attack on Steve Moore (Colorado), a suspension that remained active when the NHL shut down. As a result, after attempting to play in Europe, the IIHF refused to sign his transfer papers and he never played all season. Later in the year, Moore filed a civil suit against Bertuzzi who had earlier pleaded guilty to assault and received a discharge.

BETTS, BLAIR
b. Edmonton, Alberta, February 16, 1980

	GP	G	A	Pts	PIM
2003-04 CAL/NYR	20	1	2	3	10
NHL Totals	35	3	5	8	12

–played 2004-05 with Hartford Wolf Pack, New York Rangers' AHL affiliate

BEZINA, GORAN
b. Split, Yugoslavia (Croatia), March 21, 1980

	GP	G	A	Pts	PIM
2003-04 PHO	3	0	0	0	2
NHL Totals	3	0	0	0	2

–signed May 18, 2004 by Geneve-Servette (Swiss league)

BICEK, JIRI
b. Kosice, Czechoslovakia (Slovakia), December 3, 1978

	GP	G	A	Pts	PIM
2003-04 NJ	12	0	1	1	0
NHL Totals	62	6	7	13	29

–signed September 17, 2004 by Kosice (Extraleague, Slovakia)

BIERK, ZAC
b. Peterborough, Ontario, September 17, 1976

	GP	W-L-T	Min	GA	SO	GAA
2003-04 PHO	4	0-1-2	190	12	0	3.79
NHL Totals	47	9-20-5	2,135	113	1	3.18

–did not play professionally in 2004-05

BIRON, MARTIN
b. Lac St. Charles, Quebec, August 15, 1977

	GP	W-L-T	Min	GA	SO	GAA
2003-04 BUF	52	26-18-5	2,972	125	2	2.52
NHL Totals	246	101-103-25	13,774	560	17	2.44

–remained in the Buffalo area and skated with other Sabres players; did not play professionally in 2004-05

BIRON, MATHIEU
b. Lac St. Charles, Quebec, April 29, 1980

	GP	G	A	Pts	PIM
2003-04 FLO	57	3	10	13	51
NHL Totals	201	8	23	31	127

–played part of 2004-05 with Thetford Mines (NAHL, Quebec))

BISHAI, MIKE
b. Edmonton, Alberta, May 30, 1979

	GP	G	A	Pts	PIM
2003-04 EDM	14	0	2	2	19
NHL Totals	14	0	2	2	19

–played 2004-05 with Edmonton Road Runners, Edmonton Oilers' AHL affiliate

BLAKE, JASON
b. Moorhead, Minnesota, September 2, 1973

	GP	G	A	Pts	PIM
2003-04 NYI	75	22	25	47	56
NHL Totals	350	66	94	160	210

–won gold medal with Team USA at Deutschland Cup in November 2004
–signed December 1, 2004 by Lugano (Swiss league)

BLAKE, ROB
b. Simcoe, Ontario, December 10, 1969

	GP	G	A	Pts	PIM
2003-04 COL	74	13	33	46	61
NHL Totals	903	186	400	586	1,235

–played for IMG WorldStars tour of Europe in December 2004

BLATNY, ZDENEK
b. Brno, Czechoslovakia (Czech Republic), January 14, 1981

	GP	G	A	Pts	PIM
2003-04 ATL	16	3	0	3	6
NHL Totals	20	3	0	3	6

–signed November 19, 2004 by Pelicans (SM-Liiga, Finland)
–signed January 6, 2005 by Znojemsti Orli (Extraleague, Slovakia)

BOGUNIECKI, ERIC
b. New Haven, Connecticut, May 6, 1975

	GP	G	A	Pts	PIM
2003-04 STL	27	6	4	10	20
NHL Totals	120	28	32	60	64

–signed October 4, 2004 by Langenthal (Swiss league, Division 2); later released by team
–signed November 4, 2004 by Nurnberg (Deutsche Eishockey Liga, Germany); later released by team
–signed December 17, 2004 by Worcester IceCats, St. Louis' AHL affiliate

BOILEAU, PATRICK
b. Montreal, Quebec, February 22, 1975

	GP	G	A	Pts	PIM
2003-04 PIT	16	4	3	7	8
NHL Totals	48	5	11	16	26

–signed May 13, 2004 by Lausanne (Swiss league)

Dan Boyle in his Djurgarden togs from the Swedish Elite League.

BOMBARDIR, BRAD
b. Powell River, British Columbia, May 5, 1972

2003-04 MIN/NAS	69	1	2	3	25
NHL Totals	356	8	46	54	127

–did not play professionally in 2004-05

BONDRA, PETER
b. Luck, Soviet Union (Ukraine), February 7, 1968

2003-04 WAS/OTT	77	26	23	49	38
NHL Totals	984	477	362	839	695

–signed January 17, 2005 by HK Poprad (Extraleague, Slovakia)

BONK, RADEK
b. Krnov, Czechoslovakia (Czech Republic), January 9, 1976

2003-04 OTT	66	12	32	44	66
NHL Totals	689	152	247	399	401

–signed September 17, 2004 by Ocelari Trinec (Extraleague, Czech Republic)
–signed January 31, 2005 by Zlin (Extraleague, Czech Republic)

BONVIE, DENNIS
b. Antigonish, Nova Scotia, July 23, 1973

2003-04 OTT/COL	1	0	0	0	0
NHL Totals	92	1	2	3	311

–played 2004-05 with Hershey Bears, Colorado's AHL affiliate

BOOTLAND, DARRYL
b. Toronto, Ontario, November 2, 1981

2003-04 DET	22	1	1	2	74
NHL Totals	22	1	1	2	74

–played 2004-05 with Grand Rapids Griffins, Detroit's AHL affiliate

BOTTERILL, JASON
b. Edmonton, Alberta, May 19, 1976

2003-04 BUF	19	2	1	3	14
NHL Totals	88	5	9	14	89

–started 2004-05 with Rochester Americans, Buffalo's AHL affiliate, but suffered a concussion in early October 2004 and announced his retirement on February 24, 2005

BOUCHARD, JOEL
b. Montreal, Quebec, January 23, 1974

2003-04 NYR	28	1	7	8	10
NHL Totals	339	21	45	66	241

–missed much of 2003-04 with suspected post-concussion syndrome which turned out to be mercury poisoning
–organized McDonald's Caravan, a tour by NHLers throughout Quebec in support of Ronald McDonald House, October 2004-February 2005
–signed March 17, 2005 by Hartford Wolf Pack (AHL)

BOUCHARD, PIERRE-MARC
b. Sherbrooke, Quebec, April 27, 1984

2003-04 MIN	61	4	18	22	22
NHL Totals	111	11	31	42	40

–played 2004-05 with Houston Aeros, Minnesota's AHL affiliate

BOUCHER, BRIAN
b. Woonsocket, Rhode Island, January 2, 1977

2003-04 PHO	40	10-19-10	2,354	108	5	2.74
NHL Totals	188	71-77-30	10,711	473	12	2.65

–signed October 20, 2004 by HV 71 Jonkoping (Swedish Elite League); released December 12, 2004 and replaced by Stefan Liv

BOUCHER, PHILIPPE
b. Ste. Apollinaire, Quebec, March 24, 1973

2003-04 DAL	70	8	16	24	64
NHL Totals	527	54	129	183	456

–played 2004-05 with St. Georges-de-Beauce (NAHL, Quebec)

BOUCK, TYLER
b. Camrose, Alberta, January 13, 1980

2003-04 VAN	18	1	2	3	23
NHL Totals	73	3	7	10	56

–signed October 22, 2004 by TPS Turku (SM-Liiga, Finland)

BOUGHNER, BOB
b. Windsor, Ontario, March 8, 1971

2003-04 CAR/COL	54	0	5	5	88
NHL Totals	589	14	51	65	1,328

–NHLPA vice president did not play professionally in 2004-05; remained with his family and took correspondence courses

BOUILLON, FRANCIS
b. New York, New York, October 17, 1975

2003-04 MON	73	2	16	18	70
NHL Totals	228	8	41	49	171

–signed November 15, 2004 by Leksand (Swedish league, Division 2)

BOULERICE, JESSE
b. Plattsburgh, New York, August 10, 1978

2003-04 CAR	76	6	1	7	127
NHL Totals	127	8	2	10	240

–remained in Raleigh and did not play professionally in 2004-05

BOULTON, ERIC
b. Halifax, Nova Scotia, August 17, 1976

2003-04 BUF	44	1	2	3	110
NHL Totals	172	5	12	17	511

–began 2004-05 playing for Detroit in Original Stars Hockey League
–played most of 2004-05 with Columbia Inferno (ECHL)

BOUMEDIENNE, JOSEF
b. Stockholm, Sweden, January 12, 1978

2003-04 WAS	37	2	12	14	30
NHL Totals	47	4	12	16	36

–signed September 25, 2004 by Brynas (Swedish Elite League)
–signed November 10, 2004 by Karpat Oulu (SM-Liiga, Finland)

BOUWMEESTER, JAY
b. Edmonton, Alberta, September 27, 1983

2003-04 FLO	61	2	18	20	30
NHL Totals	143	6	30	36	44

–played 2004-05 with San Antonio Rampage, Florida's AHL affiliate; loaned to Chicago Wolves (AHL) for last part of '04-'05

BOYES, BRAD
b. Mississauga, Ontario, April 17, 1982

2003-04 SJ	1	0	0	0	2
NHL Totals	1	0	0	0	2

–played 2004-05 with Providence Bruins, Boston's AHL affiliate, after being traded to Boston in March 2004

BOYLE, DAN
b. Ottawa, Ontario, July 12, 1976

2003-04 TB	78	9	30	39	60
NHL Totals	325	37	114	151	181

–began 2004-05 playing for Toronto in Original Stars Hockey League
–signed November 14, 2004 by Djurgarden (Swedish Elite League)
–played for Canada at 2005 World Championship (silver medal)

BOYNTON, NICK
b. Nobleton, Ontario, January 14, 1979

2003-04 BOS	81	6	24	30	98
NHL Totals	245	17	55	72	304

–signed January 26, 2005 by Nottingham Panthers (Elite Ice Hockey League, UK)

BRADLEY, MATT
b. Stittsville, Ontario, June 13, 1978

2003-04 PIT	82	7	9	16	65
NHL Totals	203	19	26	45	164

–began 2004-05 playing for Detroit in Original Stars Hockey League
–signed November 14, 2004 by Dornbirn (Austrian league, Division 2); left team on December 20, 2004

BRANDNER, CHRISTOPH
b. Bruck an der Mur, Austria, July 5, 1975

2003-04 MIN	35	4	5	9	8
NHL Totals	35	4	5	9	8

–played 2004-05 with Houston Aeros, Minnesota's AHL affiliate

BRASHEAR, DONALD
b. Bedford, Indiana, January 7, 1972

2003-04 PHI	64	6	7	13	212
NHL Totals	693	71	99	170	1,999

–played 2004-05 with Quebec Radio X (NAHL, Quebec)

BRATHWAITE, FRED
b. Ottawa, Ontario, November 24, 1972

2003-04 CBJ	21	4-11-1	1,050	59	0	3.37
NHL Totals	254	81-99-37	13,840	629	15	2.73

–signed June 19, 2004 by AK Bars Kazan (Super League, Russia)

BRENDL, PAVEL
b. Opocno, Czechoslovakia (Czech Republic), March 23, 1981

2003-04 CAR	18	5	3	8	8
NHL Totals	76	11	11	22	16

–signed September 17, 2004 by Ocelari Trinec (Extraleague, Czech Republic)
–signed October 14, 2004 by Olomouc (Czech league, Division 2)
–signed November 7, 2004 by Malmo (Swedish Elite League); released November 11, 2004
–signed November 15, 2004 by Jokipojat (Finnish league, Division 2)
–signed December 21, 2004 by Thurgau (Swiss league, Division 2); left Thurgau on January 11, 2005
–signed January 13, 2005 by Jokipojat (Finnish league, Division 2)

BRENNAN, KIP
b. Kingston, Ontario, August 27, 1980

2003-04 LA/ATL	23	1	0	1	96
NHL Totals	46	1	0	1	175

–played 2004-05 with Chicago Wolves, Atlanta's AHL affiliate

BREWER, ERIC
b. Vernon, British Columbia, April 17, 1979

2003-04 EDM	77	7	18	25	67
NHL Totals	404	34	79	113	262

–remained at home in B.C. for most of the season; did not play professionally in 2004-05

BRIERE, DANIEL
b. Gatineau, Quebec, October 6, 1977

2003-04 BUF	82	28	37	65	70
NHL Totals	354	105	118	223	228

–signed September 28, 2004 by SC Bern (Swiss league)
–played for IMG WorldStars in Europe in December 2004

BRIGLEY, TRAVIS
b. Coronation, Alberta, June 16, 1977

2003-04 COL	36	3	4	7	10
NHL Totals	55	3	6	9	16

–signed October 21, 2004 by Valerenga (Norwegian league)

BRIMANIS, ARIS
b. Cleveland, Ohio, March 14, 1972

2003-04 STL	13	0	0	0	4
NHL Totals	113	2	12	14	57

–played 2004-05 with Worcester IceCats, St. Louis's AHL affiliate

BRIND'AMOUR, ROD
b. Ottawa, Ontario, August 9, 1970

2003-04 CAR	78	12	26	38	28
NHL Totals	1,109	351	560	911	876

–signed February 16, 2005 by Kloten (Swiss league) as an emergency replacement for Jeff Halpern

BRISEBOIS, PATRICE
b. Montreal, Quebec, January 27, 1971

2003-04 MON	71	4	27	31	22
NHL Totals	791	79	263	342	501

–signed October 13, 2004 by Kloten (Swiss league); left team on November 22, 2004 because of recurring back pain and groin injury

BROCHU, MARTIN
b. Anjou, Quebec, March 10, 1973

2003-04 PIT	1	0-0-0	33	1	0	1.82
NHL Totals	9	0-5-0	369	22	0	3.58

–played part of 2004-05 with Verdun Dragons (NAHL, Quebec)

BRODEUR, MARTIN
b. Montreal, Quebec, May 6, 1972

2003-04 NJ	75	38-26-11	4,555	154	11	2.03
NHL Totals	740	403-217-105	43,511	1,573	75	2.17

–played with IMG WorldStars that toured Europe in December 2004
–played for Canada at 2005 World Championship (silver medal)

BROOKBANK, WADE
b. Lanigan, Saskatchewan, September 29, 1977

2003-04 NAS/VAN	29	2	0	2	133
NHL Totals	29	2	0	2	133

–played 2004-05 with Manitoba Moose, Vancouver's AHL affiliate

BROWN, BRAD
b. Baie Verte, Newfoundland, December 27, 1975

2003-04 MIN/BUF	43	0	3	3	66
NHL Totals	330	2	27	29	747

–did not play professionally in 2004-05

BROWN, CURTIS
b. Unity, Saskatchewan, February 12, 1976

2003-04 BUF/SJ	80	11	14	25	36
NHL Totals	554	111	145	256	294

–played 2004-05 with San Diego Gulls (ECHL)

BROWN, DUSTIN
b. Ithaca, New York, November 4, 1984

2003-04 LA	31	1	4	5	16
NHL Totals	31	1	4	5	16

–played 2004-05 with Manchester Monarchs, Los Angeles's AHL affiliate

BROWN, SEAN
b. Oshawa, Ontario, November 5, 1976

2003-04 NJ	39	0	3	3	44
NHL Totals	389	13	32	45	872

–did not play professionally in 2004-05

Daniel Briere spent 2004-05 with SC Bern in the Swiss league.

Anson Carter gets checked along the boards during the WorldStars 5-1 victory over HV 71 Jonkoping on December 17, 2004.

BRUNETTE, ANDREW
b. Sudbury, Ontario, August 24, 1973

2003-04 MIN	82	15	34	49	12
NHL Totals	542	121	223	344	166

–skated with University of Minnesota team; did not play professionally in 2004-05

BRYLIN, SERGEI
b. Moscow, Soviet Union (Russia), January 13, 1974

2003-04 NJ	82	14	19	33	20
NHL Totals	519	92	123	215	172

–signed November 4, 2004 by Khimik Voskresensk (Super League, Russia)

BRYZGALOV, ILYA
b. Togliatti, Soviet Union (Russia), June 22, 1980

2003-04 ANA	1	1-0-0	60	2	0	2.00
NHL Totals	2	1-0-0	92	3	0	1.96

–played 2004-05 with Cincinnati Might Ducks, Anaheim's AHL affiliate

BUCHBERGER, KELLY
b. Langenburg, Saskatchewan, December 2, 1966

2003-04 PIT	71	1	3	4	109
NHL Totals	1,182	105	204	309	2,297

–retired soon after the lockout was announced and became an assistant coach for the Edmonton Road Runners (AHL)

BULIS, JAN
b. Pardubice, Czechoslovakia (Czech Republic), March 18, 1978

2003-04 MON	72	13	17	30	30
NHL Totals	400	64	118	182	148

–signed September 17, 2004 by Pardubice (Extraleague, Czech Republic)

BURE, VALERI
b. Moscow, Soviet Union (Russia), June 13, 1974

2003-04 FLO/DAL	68	22	30	52	26
NHL Totals	621	174	226	400	221

–did not play professionally in 2004-05

BURKE, SEAN
b. Windsor, Ontario, January 29, 1967

2003-04 PHO/PHI	47	16-20-7	2,620	119	2	2.73
NHL Totals	762	304-321-101	43,419	2,142	35	2.96

–recovered from off-season hip injury and skated with other Flyers in South Jersey; did not play professionally in 2004-05

BURNETT, GARRETT
b. Coquitlam, British Columbia, September 23, 1975

2003-04 ANA	39	1	2	3	184
NHL Totals	39	1	2	3	184

–played 2004-05 with Danbury Trashers (UHL) and Flint Generals (UHL)

BURNS, BRENT
b. Ajax, Ontario, March 9, 1985

2003-04 MIN	36	1	5	6	12
NHL Totals	36	1	5	6	12

–played 2004-05 with Houston Aeros, Minnesota's AHL affiliate

BUTENSCHON, SVEN
b. Itzehoe, West Germany (Germany), March 22, 1976

2003-04 NYI	41	1	6	7	30
NHL Totals	132	2	12	14	76

–signed August 2, 2004 by Adler Mannheim (Deutsche Eishockey Liga, Germany)

BYLSMA, DAN
b. Grand Haven, Michigan, September 19, 1970

2003-04 ANA	11	0	0	0	0
NHL Totals	429	19	43	62	184

–retired at the end of 2003-04 season

CAIRNS, ERIC
b. Oakville, Ontario, June 27, 1974

2003-04 NYI	72	2	6	8	189
NHL Totals	406	9	31	40	1,053

–signed November 1, 2004 by London Racers (Elite Ice Hockey League, UK)

CAJANEK, PETR
b. Gottwaldov, Czechoslovakia (Czech Republic), August 18, 1975

2003-04 STL	70	12	14	26	16
NHL Totals	121	21	43	64	36

–signed September 5, 2004 by Zlin (Extraleague, Czech Republic)
–played for Czech Republic at 2005 World Championship (gold medal)

CALDER, KYLE
b. Mannville, Alberta, January 5, 1979

2003-04 CHI	66	21	18	39	29
NHL Totals	280	59	92	151	132

–signed January 20, 2005 by Sodertalje (Swedish Elite League)

CAMMALLERI, MIKE
b. Richmond Hill, Ontario, June 8, 1982

2003-04 LA	31	9	6	15	20
NHL Totals	59	14	9	23	42

–played 2004-05 with Manchester Monarchs, Los Angeles's AHL affiliate

CAMPBELL, BRIAN
b. Strathroy, Ontario, May 23, 1979

2003-04 BUF	53	3	8	11	12
NHL Totals	167	9	32	41	50

–signed October 19, 2004 by Jokerit Helsinki (SM-Liiga, Finland)

CAMPBELL, GREGORY
b. London, Ontario, December 17, 1983

2003-04 FLO	2	0	0	0	5
NHL Totals	2	0	0	0	5

–played 2004-05 with San Antonio Rampage, Florida's AHL affiliate

CARNEY, KEITH
b. Providence, Rhode Island, February 3, 1970

2003-04 ANA	69	2	5	7	42
NHL Totals	798	38	142	180	742

–remained at home to raise his four children; did not play professionally in 2004-05

CARON, SEBASTIAN
b. Amqui, Quebec, June 25, 1980

2003-04 PIT	40	9-24-5	2,213	138	1	3.74
NHL Totals	64	16-38-7	3,621	200	3	3.31

–played 2004-05 with Saguenay Fjord (NAHL, Quebec)

CARTER, ANSON
b. Toronto, Ontario, June 6, 1974

2003-04 NYR/WAS/LA	76	15	13	28	20
NHL Totals	529	158	180	338	170

–played for IMG WorldStars team that toured Europe in December 2004

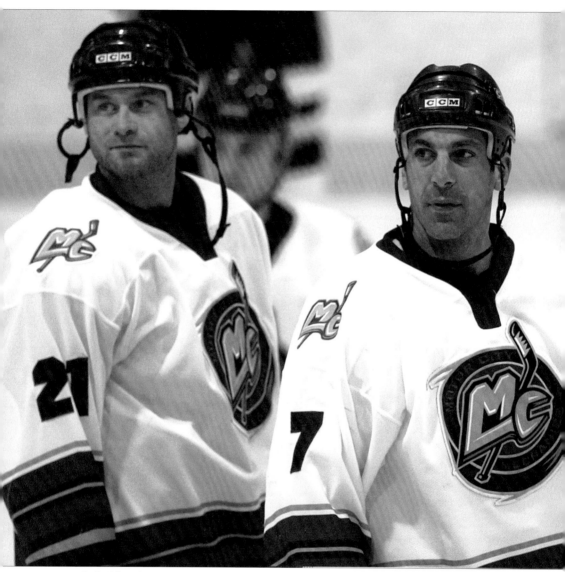

Bryan Smolinski (left) and Chris Chelios take a break during the pre-game warmup while playing for the Motor City Mechanics of the UHL.

CASSELS, ANDREW
b. Bramalea, Ontario, July 23, 1969

2003-04 CBJ	58	6	20	26	26
NHL Totals	984	200	520	720	396

–remained at home in Columbus and did not play professionally in 2004-05

CECHMANEK, ROMAN
b. Gottwaldov, Czechoslovakia (Czech Republic), March 2, 1971

2003-04 LA	49	18-21-6	2,701	113	5	2.51
NHL Totals	212	110-64-28	12,085	419	25	2.08

–signed September 17, 2004 by Vsetin (Extraleague, Czech Republic)

CHARA, ZDENO
b. Trencin, Czechoslovakia (Slovakia), March 18, 1977

2003-04 OTT	79	16	25	41	147
NHL Totals	459	41	91	132	766

–signed September 24, 2004 by Farjestad (Swedish Elite League)
–played for Slovakia at 2005 World Championship

CHARPENTIER, SEBASTIEN
b. Drummondville, Quebec, April 18, 1977

2003-04 WAS	7	0-6-0	369	21	0	3.41
NHL Totals	26	6-14-1	1,350	66	0	2.93

–played 2004-05 with St. Hyacinthe (NAHL, Quebec)

CHARTRAND, BRAD
b. Winnipeg, Manitoba, December 14, 1974

2003-04 LA	53	3	4	7	30
NHL Totals	215	25	25	50	122

–did not play professionally in 2004-05

CHEECHOO, JONATHAN
b. Moose Factory, Ontario, July 15, 1980

2003-04 SJ	81	28	19	47	33
NHL Totals	147	37	26	63	72

–signed December 21, 2004 with HV 71 Jonkoping (Swedish Elite League)

CHELIOS, CHRIS
b. Chicago, Illinois, January 25, 1962

2003-04 DET	69	2	19	21	61
NHL Totals	1,395	178	736	914	2,695

–trained with U.S. Olympic bobsled team in October-November 2004 to prepare for possible competition with the Greek National Team at the 2006 Turin Olympics
–signed February 1, 2005 with Motor City Mechanics (UHL)

CHIMERA, JASON
b. Edmonton, Alberta, May 2, 1979

2003-04 EDM	60	4	8	12	57
NHL Totals	130	19	17	36	93

–began 2004-05 playing for Detroit and New York in Original Stars Hockey League
–signed December 15, 2004 by Mastini-Varese (Serie A, Italy)

CHIODO, ANDY
b. Toronto, Ontario, April 25, 1983

2003-04 PIT	8	3-4-1	486	28	0	3.46
NHL Totals	8	3-4-1	486	28	0	3.46

–split 2004-05 season between Wilkes-Barre/Scranton Penguins, Pittsburgh's AHL affiliate, and Wheeling Nailers, Pittsburgh's ECHL affiliate

CHISTOV, STANISLAV
b. Chelyabinsk, Soviet Union (Russia), April 17, 1983

2003-04 ANA	56	2	16	18	26
NHL Totals	135	14	34	48	80

–played 2004-05 with Cincinnati Might Ducks, Anaheim's AHL affiliate

CHOUINARD, ERIC
b. Atlanta, Georgia, July 8, 1980

2003-04 PHI/MIN	48	6	4	10	6
NHL Totals	89	11	11	22	14

–signed October 14, 2004 by Salzburg (Austrian league); released December 29, 2004

CHOUINARD, MARC
b. Charlesbourg, Quebec, May 6, 1977

2003-04 MIN	45	11	10	21	17
NHL Totals	204	21	23	44	79

–signed January 1, 2005 by Frisk Tigers (Norwegian league)

CHOUINARD, MATHIEU
b. Laval, Quebec, April 11, 1980

2003-04 LA	1	0-0-0	3	0	0	0.00
NHL Totals	1	0-0-0	3	0	0	0.00

–split 2004-05 season between Cincinnati Might Ducks, Anaheim's AHL affiliate, and San Diego Gulls, Anaheim's ECHL affiliate

CHUBAROV, ARTEM
b. Gorky, Soviet Union (Russia), December 12, 1979

2003-04 VAN	65	12	7	19	14
NHL Totals	228	25	33	58	40

–signed June 19, 2004 by Moscow Dynamo (Super League, Russia)

CIBAK, MARTIN
b. Liptovsky Mikulas, Czechoslovakia (Slovakia), May 17, 1980

2003-04 TB	63	2	7	9	30
NHL Totals	89	3	12	15	38

–signed September 17, 2004 by Kosice (Extraleague, Slovakia)
–signed October 8, 2004 by Plzen (Extraleague, Czech Republic)
–played for Slovakia at Deutshcland Cup in November 2004
–signed January 31, 2005 by Kosice (Extraleague, Slovakia)

CIERNIK, IVAN
b. Levice, Czechoslovakia (Slovakia), October 30, 1977

2003-04 WAS	7	1	1	2	0
NHL Totals	89	12	14	26	32

–signed May 4, 2004 by Wolfsburg (Deutsche Eishockey Liga, Germany)

CLARK, BRETT
b. Wapella, Saskatchewan, December 23, 1976

2003-04 COL	12	1	1	2	6
NHL Totals	158	5	6	11	60

–played 2004-05 with Hershey Bears, Colorado's AHL affiliate

CLARK, CHRIS
b. South Windsor, Connecticut, March 8, 1976

2003-04 CAL	82	10	15	25	106
NHL Totals	278	35	36	71	363

–signed October 3, 2004 by SC Bern (Swiss league) but released a short time later because of poor play
–signed December 29, 2004 by Storhamar Dragons (Norwegian league)

CLARKE, NOAH
b. LaVerne, California, June 11, 1979

2003-04 LA	2	0	1	1	0
NHL Totals	2	0	1	1	0

–played 2004-05 with Manchester Monarchs, Los Angeles's AHL affiliate

CLEARY, DANIEL
b. Carbonear, Newfoundland, December 18, 1978

2003-04 PHO	68	6	11	17	42
NHL Totals	329	41	71	112	193

–signed September 6, 2004 by Mora (Swedish Elite League)

CLEMMENSEN, SCOTT
b. Des Moines, Iowa, July 23, 1977

2003-04 NJ	4	3-1-0	238	4	2	1.01
NHL Totals	6	3-1-0	258	5	2	1.16

–played 2004-05 with Albany River Rats, New Jersey's AHL affiliate

CLOUTIER, DAN
b. Mont Laurier, Quebec, April 22, 1976

2003-04 VAN	60	33-21-6	3,539	134	5	2.27
NHL Totals	305	123-121-33	16,476	725	15	2.64

–began 2004-05 playing for Toronto in Original Stars Hockey League
–signed January 20, 2005 by Klagenfurt AC (Austrian league)

CLYMER, BEN
b. Bloomington, Minnesota, April 11, 1978

2003-04 TB	66	2	8	10	50
NHL Totals	295	29	47	76	251

–signed December 2, 2004 by EHC Biel (Swiss league, Division 2)

COLAIACOVO, CARLO
b. Toronto, Ontario, January 27, 1983

2003-04 TML	2	0	1	1	2
NHL Totals	4	0	2	2	2

–played 2004-05 with St. John's Maple Leafs, Toronto's AHL affiliate

COLE, ERIK
b. Oswego, New York, November 6, 1978

2003-04 CAR	80	18	24	42	93
NHL Totals	214	48	61	109	200

–signed October 24, 2004 by Eisbaren Berlin (Deutsche Eishockey Liga, Germany)
–played for USA at 2005 World Championship

COMMODORE, MIKE
b. Fort Saskatchewan, Alberta, November 7, 1979

2003-04 CAL	12	0	0	0	25
NHL Totals	75	1	6	7	88

–played 2004-05 with Lowell Lock Monsters, Calgary's AHL affiliate

COMRIE, MIKE
b. Edmonton, Alberta, September 11, 1980

2003-04 PHI/PHO	49	12	12	24	28
NHL Totals	241	73	84	157	177

–began 2004-05 playing for Detroit in Original Stars Hockey League
–signed October 30, 2004 by Farjestad (Swedish Elite League); released December 9, 2004 by Farjestad after 10-game tryout

CONKLIN, TY
b. Anchorage, Alaska, March 30, 1976

2003-04 EDM	38	17-14-4	2,086	84	1	2.42
NHL Totals	42	19-14-4	2,234	88	1	2.36

–won gold medal with USA at Deutschland Cup in November 2004
–signed January 25, 2005 by Wolfsburg (Deutsche Eishockey Liga, Germany)
–played for USA at 2005 World Championship

CONROY, CRAIG
b. Potsdam, New York, September 4, 1971

2003-04 CAL	63	8	39	47	44
NHL Totals	609	118	222	340	337

–signed as a free agent by Los Angeles in the summer of 2004 and remained at home in upstate New York; did not play professionally in 2004-05

COOKE, MATT
b. Belleville, Ontario, September 7, 1978

2003-04 VAN	53	11	12	23	73
NHL Totals	379	58	81	139	426

–did not play professionally in 2004-05

CORAZZINI, CARL
b. Framingham, Massachusetts, April 21, 1979

2003-04 BOS	12	2	0	2	0
NHL Totals	12	2	0	2	0

–started 2004-05 with Providence Bruins, Boston's AHL affiliate, but traded during season to Hershey Bears, AHL affiliate of Colorado

CORSO, DANIEL
b. Montreal, Quebec, April 3, 1978

2003-04 ATL	7	0	1	1	0
NHL Totals	77	14	11	25	20

–played 2004-05 with Kassel (Deutsche Eishockey Liga, Germany)

CORSON, SHAYNE
b. Barrie, Ontario, August 13, 1966

2003-04 DAL	17	5	5	10	29
NHL Totals	1,156	273	420	693	2,357

–did not play professionally in 2004-05

CORVO, JOE
b. Oak Park, Illinois, June 20, 1977

2003-04 LA	72	8	17	25	36
NHL Totals	122	13	24	37	50

–played 2004-05 with Chicago Wolves (AHL)

COWAN, JEFF
b. Scarborough (Toronto), Ontario, September 27, 1976

2003-04 ATL/LA	71	11	16	27	92
NHL Totals	258	32	27	59	387

–began 2004-05 playing for Detroit in Original Stars Hockey League; stayed home and kept in shape the rest of the season

CROSS, CORY
b. Lloydminster, Alberta, January 3, 1971

2003-04 EDM	68	7	14	21	56
NHL Totals	603	31	92	123	625

–worked on an oil patch in Alberta all year that was so successful he considered retiring from hockey altogether to work on his business

CULLEN, MATT
b. Virginia, Minnesota, November 2, 1976

2003-04 FLO	56	6	13	19	24
NHL Totals	513	77	154	231	214

–signed September 18, 2004 by Cortina (Serie A, Italy)

CULLIMORE, JASSEN
b. Simcoe, Ontario, December 4, 1972

2003-04 TB	79	2	5	7	58
NHL Totals	524	19	47	66	504

–began 2004-05 playing for Detroit in Original Stars Hockey League

CUMMINS, JIM
b. Dearborn, Michigan, May 14, 1970

2003-04 COL	55	1	2	3	147
NHL Totals	511	24	36	60	1,538

–did not play professionally in 2004-05

CUTTA, JAKUB
b. Jablonec nad Nisou, Czechoslovakia (Czech Republic) December 29, 1981

2003-04 WAS	3	0	0	0	0
NHL Totals	8	0	0	0	0

–played 2004-05 with Portland Pirates, Washington's AHL affiliate

Pavel Datsyuk (#13) played most of 2004-05 with Moscow Dynamo and ended his year winning a bronze medal with Russia at the 2005 World Championship.

Mike Comrie played a handful of games with Farjestad in the Swedish Elite League in November 2004 before being released.

CZERKAWSKI, MARIUSZ
b. Radomsko, Poland, April 13, 1972

2003-04 NYI	81	25	24	49	16
NHL Totals	710	207	218	425	264

–signed September 9, 2004 by Djurgarden (Swedish Elite League)
–played for Poland at the final Olympic qualifying tournament in February 2005

DACKELL, ANDREAS
b. Gavle, Sweden, December 29, 1972

2003-04 MON	60	4	8	12	10
NHL Totals	613	91	159	250	162

–signed May 14, 2004 by Brynas (Swedish Elite League)

DAFOE, BYRON
b. Sussex, England, February 25, 1971

2003-04 ATL	18		4-11-1	973	51	0	3.14
NHL Totals	415		171-170-56	23,478	1,051	26	2.69

–did not play professionally in 2004-05

DAGENAIS, PIERRE
b. Blainville, Quebec, March 4, 1978

2003-04 MON	56	17	10	27	24
NHL Totals	110	30	16	46	42

–signed January 10, 2005 by Ajoie (Swiss league, B Division)

DAIGLE, ALEXANDRE
b. Montreal, Quebec, February 7, 1975

2003-04 MIN	78	20	31	51	14
NHL Totals	570	124	175	299	174

–played for IMG WorldStars team that toured Europe in December 2004
–signed February 5, 2005 by Forward Morges (Swiss league, Division 2)

DALEY, TREVOR
b. Toronto, Ontario, October 9, 1983

2003-04 DAL	27	1	5	6	14
NHL Totals	27	1	5	6	14

–played 2004-05 with Hamilton Bulldogs (AHL)

DAMPHOUSSE, VINCENT
b. Montreal, Quebec, December 17, 1967

2003-04 SJ	82	12	29	41	66
NHL Totals	1,378	432	773	1,205	1,190

–a member of the NHLPA's executive, he did not play anywhere this year, focusing instead on CBA negotiations between the league and players

DANDENAULT, MATHIEU
b. Sherbrooke, Quebec, February 3, 1976

2003-04 DET	65	3	9	12	40
NHL Totals	616	48	101	149	342

–signed December 27, 2004 by Asiago (Serie A, Italy)

DANTON, MIKE
b. Brampton, Ontario, October 21, 1980

2003-04 STL	68	7	5	12	141
NHL Totals	87	9	5	14	182

–jailed on November 8, 2004 for seven and a half years for attempting to have his agent, David Frost, killed

DARBY, CRAIG
b. Oneida, New York, September 26, 1972

2003-04 NJ	2	0	0	0	0
NHL Totals	196	21	35	56	32

–played 2004-05 with Springfield Indians, Tampa Bay's AHL affiliate, after signing with the Lightning as a free agent in the summer of 2004

DARCHE, MATHIEU
b. St. Laurent, Quebec, November 26, 1976

2003-04 NAS	2	0	0	0	0
NHL Totals	26	1	1	2	6

–played 2004-05 with Hershey Bears, Colorado's farm team, after signing with the Avalanche as a free agent in the summer of 2004

DATSYUK, PAVEL
b. Sverdlovsk, Soviet Union (Russia), July 20, 1978

2003-04 DET	75	30	38	68	35
NHL Totals	209	53	101	154	55

–signed June 19, 2004 by Moscow Dynamo (Super League, Russia)
–played for Russia at 2005 World Championship (bronze medal)

DAVISON, ROB
b. St. Catharines, Ontario, May 1, 1980

2003-04 SJ	55	0	3	3	92
NHL Totals	70	1	5	6	114

–signed October 5, 2004 by Cardiff Devils (Elite Ice Hockey League, UK)

DAZE, ERIC
b. Montreal, Quebec, July 2, 1975

2003-04 CHI	19	4	7	11	0
NHL Totals	600	226	172	398	174

–remained in Chicago for the balance of the season; did not play professionally in 2004-05

DELMORE, ANDY
b. LaSalle, Ontario, December 26, 1976

2003-04 BUF/SJ	37	2	5	7	29
NHL Totals	276	43	58	101	103

–signed July 21, 2004 by Adler Mannheim (Deutsche Eishockey Liga, Germany)
–played for Canada at Deutschland Cup in November 2004

DEMITRA, PAVOL
b. Dubnica, Czechoslovakia (Slovakia), November 29, 1974

2003-04 STL	68	23	35	58	18
NHL Totals	553	216	303	519	170

–signed September 17, 2004 by Dukla Trencin (Extraleague, Slovakia)
–played for Slovakia at 2005 World Championship

DEMPSEY, NATHAN
b. Spruce Grove, Alberta, July 14, 1974

2003-04 CHI/LA	75	12	20	32	32
NHL Totals	190	19	55	74	66

–signed February 9, 2005 by Eisbaren Berlin (Deutsche Eishockey Liga, Germany)

DENIS, MARC
b. Montreal, Quebec, August 1, 1977

2003-04 CBJ	66		21-36-7	3,796	162	5	2.56
NHL Totals	245		73-131-28	13,952	677	14	2.91

–did not play professionally in 2004-05

DESJARDINS, ERIC
b. Rouyn, Quebec, June 14, 1969

2003-04 PHI	48	1	11	12	28
NHL Totals	1,098	132	419	551	701

–remained at home in Quebec to train; did not play professionally in 2004-05

DEVEREAUX, BOYD
b. Seaforth, Ontario, April 16, 1978

2003-04 DET	61	6	9	15	20
NHL Totals	431	38	71	109	123

–did not play professionally in 2004-05

Peter Forsberg committed the full season to his old Swedish club team MoDo long before the NHL season was officially cancelled.

DE VRIES, GREG
b. Sundridge, Ontario, January 4, 1973

2003-04 NYR/OTT	66	3	13	16	43
NHL Totals	566	33	82	115	502

–did not play professionally in 2004-05

DIMAIO, ROB
b. Calgary, Alberta, February 19, 1968

2003-04 DAL	69	9	15	24	52
NHL Totals	833	102	158	260	810

–signed November 20, 2004 by Langnau (Swiss league)
–also played part of 2004-05 with Milano Vipers (Serie A, Italy)

DIMITRAKOS, NIKO
b. Boston, Massachusetts, May 21, 1979

2003-04 SJ	68	9	15	24	49
NHL Totals	89	15	22	37	57

–signed February 2, 2005 by SCL Tigers (Swiss league)

DINGMAN, CHRIS
b. Edmonton, Alberta, July 6, 1976

2003-04 TB	74	1	5	6	140
NHL Totals	351	15	18	33	747

–remained at home for the balance of the season; did not play
  professionally in 2004-05

DIPIETRO, RICK
b. Winthrop, Massachusetts, September 19, 1981

2003-04 NYI	50	23-18-5	2,844	112	5	2.36
NHL Totals	80	28-38-8	4,512	204	5	2.71

–spent most of 2004-05 playing rec. hockey on Long Island
–won gold medal with USA at Deutschland Cup in November
  2004
–played for USA at 2005 World Championship

DIVIS, REINHARD
b. Vienna, Austria, July 4, 1975

2003-04 STL	13	4-4-2	629	29	0	2.77
NHL Totals	16	6-4-2	737	30	0	2.44

–signed October 24, 2004 by Villach (Austrian league)

DOAN, SHANE
b. Halkirk, Alberta, October 10, 1976

2003-04 PHO	79	27	41	68	47
NHL Totals	648	142	209	351	588

–player representative for Phoenix did not play professionally in
  2004-05; remained at home with his family in Alberta for the
  balance of the season
–played for Canada at 2005 World Championship (silver medal)

DOIG, JASON
b. Montreal, Quebec, January 29, 1977

2003-04 WAS	65	2	9	11	105
NHL Totals	158	6	18	24	285

–remained at home in Montreal; did not play professionally in
  2004-05

DOMI, TIE
b. Windsor, Ontario, November 1, 1969

2003-04 TML	80	7	13	20	208
NHL Totals	943	99	130	229	3,406

–played with IMG All-Stars that toured Europe in December 2004

DONATO, TED
b. Boston, Massachusetts, April 28, 1969

2003-04 BOS	63	6	5	11	18
NHL Totals	796	150	197	347	396

–named head coach of Harvard Crimson on July 2, 2004

DONOVAN, SHEAN
b. Timmins, Ontario, January 22, 1975

2003-04 CAL	82	18	24	42	72
NHL Totals	618	85	92	177	420

–signed November 13, 2004 by Geneve-Servette (Swiss league); left
  Geneve-Servette on December 30, 2004

DOULL, DOUG
b. Green Bay, Nova Scotia, May 31, 1974

2003-04 BOS	35	0	1	1	132
NHL Totals	35	0	1	1	132

–played 2004-05 with Utah Grizzlies (AHL), Phoenix's AHL
  affiliate, after signing with the Coyotes as a free agent in the
  summer of 2004

DOWD, JIM
b. Brick, New Jersey, December 25, 1968

2003-04 MIN/MON	69	7	22	29	44
NHL Totals	511	57	146	203	289

–signed October 1, 2004 by Hamburg (Deutsche Eishockey Liga,
  Germany)

DOWNEY, AARON
b. Shelburne, Ontario, August 27, 1974

2003-04 DAL	37	1	1	2	77
NHL Totals	120	3	2	5	228

–began 2004-05 playing for Detroit in Original Stars Hockey
  League

DRAKE, DALLAS
b. Trail, British Columbia, February 4, 1969

2003-04 STL	79	13	22	35	65
NHL Totals	822	166	267	433	747

–lived in Michigan working out and staying in shape; did not play
  professionally in 2004-05

DRAPER, KRIS
b. Toronto, Ontario, May 24, 1971

2003-04 DET	67	24	16	40	31
NHL Totals	724	108	128	236	526

–signed October 31, 2004 by Geneve-Servette (Swiss league)
–played for IMG WorldStars team that toured Europe in December
  2004
–signed February 1, 2005 by Motor City Mechanics (UHL)
–played for Canada at 2005 World Championship (silver medal)

DRUKEN, HAROLD
b. St. John's, Newfoundland, January 26, 1979

2003-04 TML	9	0	4	4	2
NHL Totals	146	27	36	63	36

–played 2004-05 with St. John's Maple Leafs, Toronto's AHL affiliate

DRURY, CHRIS
b. Trumbull, Connecticut, August 20, 1976

2003-04 BUF	76	18	35	53	68
NHL Totals	470	126	202	328	290

–did not play professionally in 2004-05

DUBIELEWICZ, WADE
b. Invermere, British Columbia, January 30, 1978

2003-04 NYI	2	1-0-1	105	3	0	1.71
NHL Totals	2	1-0-1	105	3	0	1.71

–played 2004-05 with Bridgeport Sound Tigers, New York
  Islanders's AHL affiliate

DUMONT, J-P
b. Montreal, Quebec, April 1, 1978

2003-04 BUF	77	22	31	53	40
NHL Totals	380	101	115	216	208

–signed February 9, 2005 by SC Bern (Swiss league)

DUNHAM, MIKE
b. Johnson City, New York, June 1, 1972

2003-04 NYR	57	16-30-6	3,148	159	2	3.03
NHL Totals	358	129-163-39	19,895	892	18	2.69

–signed January 31, 2005 by Skelleftea (Swedish league, Division 2)
–played part of 2004-05 with Liptovsky Mikulas (Extraleague, Slovakia)

DUPUIS, PASCAL
b. Laval, Quebec, April 7, 1979

2003-04 MIN	59	11	15	26	20
NHL Totals	219	47	55	102	84

–signed January 14, 2005 by Ajoie (Swiss league, Division 2)

DUSABLON, BENOIT
b. Ste. Anne de la Perad, Quebec, August 1, 1979

2003-04 NYR	3	0	0	0	2
NHL Totals	3	0	0	0	2

–started 2004-05 with Hamilton Bulldogs (AHL)
–retired January 13, 2005

DVORAK, RADEK
b. Tabor, Czechoslovakia (Czech Republic), March 9, 1977

2003-04 EDM	78	15	35	50	26
NHL Totals	682	153	231	384	218

–signed September 15, 2004 by Ceske Budejovice (Czech league, Division 2)
–played for Czech Republic at 2005 World Championship (gold medal)

DWYER, GORDIE
b. Dalhousie, New Brunswick, January 25, 1978

2003-04 MON	2	0	0	0	7
NHL Totals	108	0	5	5	394

–played 2004-05 with Lowell Lock Monsters, Carolina's AHL affiliate, after signing with the Hurricanes as a free agent in the summer of 2004

DYKHUIS, KARL
b. Sept Iles, Quebec, July 8, 1972

2003-04 MON	9	0	0	0	2
NHL Totals	644	42	91	133	495

–signed January 3, 2005 with Amsterdam Bulldogs (Dutch league)

EASTWOOD, MIKE
b. Ottawa, Ontario, July 1, 1967

2003-04 PIT	82	4	15	19	40
NHL Totals	783	87	149	236	354

–did not play professionally in 2004-05

EATON, MARK
b. Wilmington, Delaware, May 6, 1977

2003-04 NAS	75	4	9	13	26
NHL Totals	244	13	30	43	94

–played 2004-05 with Grand Rapids Griffins (AHL)
–won gold medal with USA at Deutschland Cup in December 2004

EHRHOFF, CHRISTIAN
b. Moers, West Germany (Germany), July 6, 1982

2003-04 SJ	41	1	11	12	14
NHL Totals	41	1	11	12	14

–played 2004-05 with Cleveland Barons, San Jose's AHL affiliate
–played for Germany at 2005 World Championship

EKMAN, NILS
b. Stockholm, Sweden, March 11, 1976

2003-04 SJ	82	22	33	55	34
NHL Totals	153	33	46	79	110

–signed September 16, 2004 by Djurgarden (Swedish Elite League)

ELIAS, PATRIK
b. Trebic, Czechoslovakia (Czech Republic), April 13, 1976

2003-04 NJ	82	38	43	81	44
NHL Totals	558	207	252	459	275

–signed September 6, 2004 by Znojemsti Orli (Extraleague, Czech Republic)
–signed December 9, 2004 by Metallurg Magnitogorsk (Super League, Russia)

ELLIS, DAN
b. Saskatoon, Saskatchewan, June 19, 1980

2003-04 DAL	1	1-0-0	60	3	0	3.00
NHL Totals	1	1-0-0	60	3	0	3.00

–played 2004-05 with Hamilton Bulldogs (AHL)

ELLISON, MATT
b. Duncan, British Columbia, December 8, 1983

2003-04 CHI	10	0	1	1	0
NHL Totals	10	0	1	1	0

–played 2004-05 with Norfolk Admirals, Chicago's AHL affiliate

EMERY, RAY
b. Cayuga, Ontario, September 28, 1982

2003-04 OTT	3	2-0-0	126	5	0	2.38
NHL Totals	6	3-0-0	211	7	0	1.99

–played 2004-05 with Binghamton Senators, Ottawa's AHL affiliate

EMINGER, STEVE
b. Woodbridge, Ontario, October 31, 1983

2003-04 WAS	41	0	4	4	45
NHL Totals	58	0	6	6	69

–played 2004-05 with Portland Pirates, Washington's AHL affiliate

ERAT, MARTIN
b. Trebic, Czechoslovakia (Czech Republic), August 28, 1981

2003-04 NAS	76	16	33	49	38
NHL Totals	183	26	64	90	84

–signed September 5, 2004 by Zlin (Extraleague, Czech Republic)

ERIKSSON, ANDERS
b. Bollnas, Sweden, January 9, 1975

2003-04 CBJ	66	7	20	27	18
NHL Totals	412	21	109	130	158

–began 2004-05 playing for Toronto in Original Stars Hockey League
–signed October 29, 2004 by HV 71 Jonkoping (Swedish Elite League)

ERSKINE, JOHN
b. Kingston, Ontario, June 26, 1980

2003-04 DAL	32	0	1	1	84
NHL Totals	81	2	2	4	175

–played 2004-05 with Houston Aeros, Dallas's AHL affiliate

ESCHE, ROBERT
b. Whitesboro, New York, January 22, 1978

2003-04 PHI	40	21-11-7	2,322	79	3	2.04
NHL Totals	128	51-44-16	6,993	289	8	2.48

–Flyers' team representative at NHLPA meetings
–organized a charity game in Whitesboro, New York early in the season

EVANS, BRENNAN
b. North Battleford, Saskatchewan, January 6, 1982

2003-04 CAL	0	0	0	0	
NHL Totals	0	0	0	0	

–appeared only in playoffs in 2003-04
–played 2004-05 with Lowell Lock Monsters, Calgary's AHL affiliate

EXELBY, GARNET
b. Craik, Saskatchewan, August 16, 1981

2003-04 ATL	71	1	9	10	134
NHL Totals	86	1	11	12	175

–did not play professionally in 2004-05

FAHEY, JIM
b. Boston, Massachusetts, May 11, 1979

2003-04 SJ	15	0	2	2	18
NHL Totals	58	1	21	22	51

–played 2004-05 with Cleveland Barons, San Jose's AHL affiliate

FARRELL, MIKE
b. Edina, Minnesota, October 20, 1978

2003-04 NAS	1	0	0	0	0
NHL Totals	13	0	0	0	2

–did not play professionally in 2004-05

FAST, BRAD
b. Fort St. John, Saskatchewan, February 21, 1980

2003-04 CAR	1	1	0	1	0
NHL Totals	1	1	0	1	0

–split 2004-05 between Lowell Lock Monsters (AHL) and Florida Everblades (ECHL)

FATA, RICO
b. Sault Ste. Marie, Ontario, February 12, 1980

2003-04 PIT	73	16	18	34	54
NHL Totals	173	23	31	54	80

–signed August 15, 2004 by Asiago (Serie A, Italy)

FEDOROV, FEDOR
b. Moscow, Soviet Union (Russia), June 11, 1981

2003-04 VAN	8	0	1	1	4
NHL Totals	15	0	2	2	8

–signed November 15, 2004 by Spartak Moscow (Super League, Russia)
–signed February 16, 2005 by Metallurg Magnitogorsk (Super League, Russia)
–played for Russia at 2005 World Championship (bronze medal)

FEDOROV, SERGEI
b. Pskov, Soviet Union (Russia), December 13, 1969

2003-04 ANA	80	31	34	65	42
NHL Totals	988	431	588	1,019	629

–played for IMG WorldStars team that toured Europe in December 2004
–played with Spartak Moscow (Super Legaue, Russia)

FEDORUK, TODD
b. Redwater, Alberta, February 13, 1979

2003-04 PHI	49	1	4	5	136
NHL Totals	220	10	18	28	491

–played 2004-05 with Philadelphia Phantoms, Philadelphia Flyers' AHL affiliate

FEDOTENKO, RUSLAN
b. Kiev, Soviet Union (Ukraine), January 18, 1979

2003-04 TB	77	17	22	39	30
NHL Totals	305	69	64	133	189

–did not play professionally in 2004-05

FERENCE, ANDREW
b. Edmonton, Alberta, March 17, 1979

2003-04 CAL	72	4	12	16	53
NHL Totals	251	15	41	56	216

–began season skating with the Canmore Eagles of Alberta Junior Hockey League and acting as coach for team's defencemen
–signed December 1, 2004 by Ceske Budejovice (Czech Republic, Division 2)

FERENCE, BRAD
b. Calgary, Alberta, April 2, 1979

2003-04 PHO	63	0	5	5	103
NHL Totals	245	4	30	34	563

–signed October 28, 2004 by Morzine-Avoriaz (French league)

FERGUSON, SCOTT
b. Camrose, Alberta, January 6, 1973

2003-04 EDM	52	1	5	6	80
NHL Totals	203	7	14	21	288

–skated with Kelowna Rockets (WHL) to stay in shape at the start of the season
–played with Skovde IK (Swedish League, Division 2)

FERNANDEZ, MANNY
b. Etobicoke (Toronto), Ontario, August 26, 1974

2003-04 MIN	37	11-14-9	2,166	90	2	2.49
NHL Totals	191	73-79-24	10,859	455	10	2.51

–signed December 18, 2004 by Lulea (Swedish Elite League)

FIDDLER, VERN
b. Edmonton, Alberta, May 9, 1980

2003-04 NAS	17	0	0	0	23
NHL Totals	36	4	2	6	37

–played 2004-05 with Milwaukee Admirals, Nashville's AHL affiliate

FINLEY, JEFF
b. Edmonton, Alberta, April 14, 1967

2003-04 STL	53	0	1	1	34
NHL Totals	708	13	70	83	457

–did not play professionally in 2004-05

FISCHER, JIRI
b. Horovice, Czechoslovakia (Czech Republic), July 31, 1980

2003-04 DET	81	4	15	19	75
NHL Totals	283	8	44	52	262

–signed September 4, 2004 by Liberec (Extraleague, Czech Republic)
–played for Czech Republic at 2005 World Championship (gold medal)

FISHER, MIKE
b. Peterborough, Ontario, June 5, 1980

2003-04 OTT	24	4	6	10	39
NHL Totals	248	48	52	100	209

–signed November 1, 2004 by Zug (Swiss league); signed one-year contract extension on February 24, 2005, the first NHLer to commit to Europe for the 2005-06 season
–played for Canada at 2005 World Championship (silver medal)

FITZGERALD, TOM
b. Billerica, Massachusetts, August 28, 1968

2003-04 TML	69	7	10	17	52
NHL Totals	1,026	135	184	319	736

–signed as a free agent with Boston in the summer of 2004 but did not play anywhere in 2004-05

FITZPATRICK, RORY
b. Rochester, New York, January 11, 1975

2003-04 BUF	60	4	7	11	44
NHL Totals	154	5	13	18	94

–began 2004-05 playing for Toronto in Original Stars Hockey League
–played part of 2004-05 with Rochester Americans, Buffalo's AHL affiliate

FLEURY, MARC-ANDRE
b. Sorel, Quebec, November 28, 1984

2003-04 PIT	21	4-14-2	1,154	70	1	3.64
NHL Totals	21	4-14-2	1,154	70	1	3.64

–played 2004-05 with Wilkes-Barre/Scranton Penguins, Pittsburgh's AHL affiliate

FOCHT, DAN
b. Regina, Saskatchewan, December 31, 1977

2003-04 PIT	52	2	3	5	105
NHL Totals	82	2	6	8	145

–played 2004-05 with Hamilton Bulldogs (AHL)

FOOTE, ADAM
b. Toronto, Ontario, July 10, 1971

2003-04 COL	73	8	22	30	87
NHL Totals	799	55	179	234	1,140

–spent first part of 2004-05 recovering from a shoulder injury suffered during World Cup of Hockey 2004 and lived in Denver the balance of the year

FORBES, COLIN
b. New Westminster, British Columbia, February 16, 1976

2003-04 WAS	2	0	0	0	0
NHL Totals	302	33	28	61	211

–played 2004-05 with Lowell Lock Monsters (AHL) after signing with Carolina as a free agent in June 2004

FORSBERG, PETER
b. Ornskoldsvik, Sweden, July 20, 1973

2003-04 COL	39	18	37	55	30
NHL Totals	580	216	525	741	544

–signed September 18, 2004 by MoDo (Swedish Elite League); broke his wrist on January 20, 2005 and missed remainder of season

FORTIN, JEAN-FRANCOIS
b. Laval, Quebec, March 15, 1979

2003-04 WAS	2	0	0	0	0
NHL Totals	71	1	4	5	42

–played 2004-05 with Portland Pirates, Washington's AHL affiliate

FOSTER, KURTIS
b. Carp, Ontario, November 24, 1981

2003-04 ATL	3	0	1	1	0
NHL Totals	5	0	1	1	0

–played 2004-05 with Cincinnati Might Ducks, Anaheim's AHL affiliate, after signing with the Mighty Ducks of Anaheim as a free agent in the summer of 2004

FRANCIS, RON
b. Sault Ste. Marie, Ontario, March 1, 1963

2003-04 CAR/TML	80	13	27	40	14
NHL Totals	1,731	549	1,249	1,798	979

–did not play professionally in 2004-05

FRIESEN, JEFF
b. Meadow Lake, Saskatchewan, August 5, 1976

2003-04 NJ	81	17	20	37	26
NHL Totals	770	208	285	493	422

–did not play professionally in 2004-05

FRITSCHE, DAN
b. Cleveland, Ohio, July 13, 1985

2003-04 CBJ	19	1	0	1	12
NHL Totals	19	1	0	1	12

–returned to junior and played 2004-05 with Sarnia Sting and London Knights (OHL)

FROLOV, ALEXANDER
b. Moscow, Soviet Union (Russia), June 19, 1982

2003-04 LA	77	24	24	48	24
NHL Totals	156	38	41	79	58

–signed July 14, 2004 by CSKA Moscow (Super League, Russia)
–signed February 17, 2005 by Moscow Dynamo (Super League, Russia)

FUSSEY, OWEN
b. Winnipeg, Manitoba, April 2, 1983

2003-04 WAS	4	0	1	1	0
NHL Totals	4	0	1	1	0

–played 2004-05 with Portland Pirates, Washington's AHL affiliate

GABORIK, MARIAN
b. Trencin, Czechoslovakia (Slovakia), February 14, 1982

2003-04 MIN	65	18	22	40	20
NHL Totals	295	96	112	208	132

–signed July 5, 2004 by Dukla Trencin (Extraleague, Slovakia)
–signed December 21, 2004 by Farjestad (Swedish Elite League); left team on January 30, 2005
–re-signed January 31, 2005 by Dukla Trencin
–played for Slovakia at 2005 World Championship

GAGNE, SIMON
b. Ste. Foy, Quebec, February 29, 1980

2003-04 PHI	80	24	21	45	29
NHL Totals	354	113	132	245	117

–played for Canada at 2005 World Championship (silver medal)

GAINEY, STEVE
b. Montreal, Quebec, January 26, 1979

2003-04 DAL/PHI	7	0	0	0	7
NHL Totals	13	0	1	1	14

–played 2004-05 with Epinal (French league), the same team for which his father, Bob, played at the end of his career

GAMACHE, SIMON
b. Thetford Mines, Quebec, January 3, 1981

2003-04 ATL/NAS	9	1	1	2	0
NHL Totals	11	1	1	2	2

–played 2004-05 with Milwaukee Admirals, Nashville's AHL affiliate

GARON, MATHIEU
b. Chandler, Quebec, January 9, 1978

2003-04 MON	19	8-6-2	1,003	38	0	2.27
NHL Totals	43	16-20-3	2,335	97	4	2.49

–played 2004-04 with Manchester Monarchs (AHL)

GAUTHIER, DENIS
b. Montreal, Quebec, October 1, 1976

2003-04 CAL	80	1	15	16	113
NHL Totals	384	13	45	58	515

–did not play professionally in 2004-05

GELINAS, MARTIN
b. Shawinigan, Quebec, June 5, 1970

2003-04 CAL	76	17	18	35	70
NHL Totals	1,052	269	286	555	684

–signed September 23, 2004 by Forward Morges (Swiss league, Division 2)
–signed February 17, 2005 by Lugano (Swiss league)

Derian Hatcher (right) was one of several NHLers to sign in the UHL and upset players who, making a paltry salary, were bumped off the team to accommodate the big-ticket stars.

GERBER, MARTIN
b. Burgdorf, Switzerland, September 3, 1974

2003-04 ANA	32	11-12-4	1,698	64	2	2.26
NHL Totals	54	17-23-7	2,901	103	3	2.13

–signed September 17, 2004 by Langnau (Swiss league)
–signed November 7, 2004 by Farjestad (Swedish Elite League)
–played for Switzerland at final Olympic qualifying tournament in February 2005
–played for Switzerland at 2005 World Championship

GERNANDER, KEN
b. Coleraine, Minnesota, June 30, 1969

2003-04 NYR	2	0	0	0	2
NHL Totals	12	2	3	5	6

–played 2004-05 with Hartford Wolf Pack, New York Rangers' AHL affiliate

GIGUERE, JEAN-SEBASTIEN
b. Montreal, Quebec, May 16, 1977

2003-04 ANA	55	17-31-6	3,210	140	3	2.62
NHL Totals	237	90-109-25	13,727	568	19	2.48

–signed January 31, 2005 by Hamburg (Deutsche Eishockey Liga, Germany)

GILL, HAL
b. Concord, Massachusetts, April 6, 1975

2003-04 BOS	82	2	7	9	99
NHL Totals	546	19	68	87	464

–signed November 25, 2004 by Lukko Rauma (SM-Liiga, Finland)
–played for USA at 2005 World Championship

GIONTA, BRIAN
b. Rochester, New York, January 18, 1979

2003-04 NJ	75	21	8	29	36
NHL Totals	166	37	28	65	67

–began 2004-05 playing for Toronto in Original Stars Hockey League
–won gold medal with USA at Deutschland Cup in November 2004
–played for Albany River Rats, New Jersey's AHL affiliate
–played for USA at 2005 World Championship

GIROUX, RAY
b. North Bay, Ontario, July 20, 1976

2003-04 NJ	11	0	3	3	4
NHL Totals	38	0	13	13	22

–played 2004-05 with Houston Aeros, Minnesota's AHL affiliate, after signing with the Wild as a free agent in the summer of 2004

GLEASON, TIM
b. Southfield, Michigan, January 29, 1983

2003-04 LA	47	0	7	7	21
NHL Totals	47	0	7	7	21

–played 2004-05 with Manchester Monarchs, Los Angeles's AHL affiliate

GOC, MARCEL
b. Calw, West Germany (Germany), August 24, 1983

2003-04 SJ	0	0	0	0
NHL Totals	0	0	0	0

–appeared only in playoffs in 2003-04
–played 2004-05 with Cleveland Barons, San Jose's AHL affiliate
–played for Germany at 2005 World Championship

GODARD, ERIC
b. Vernon, British Columbia, March 7, 1980

2003-04 NYI	31	0	1	1	97
NHL Totals	50	0	1	1	145

–played 2004-05 with Bridgeport Sound Tigers, New York Islanders' AHL affiliate

GOMEZ, SCOTT
b. Anchorage, Alaska, December 23, 1979

2003-04 NJ	80	14	56	70	70
NHL Totals	394	70	236	306	278

–played 2004-05 with Alaska Aces (ECHL); suffered broken pelvis on April 16, 2005 and missed rest of season

GONCHAR, SERGEI
b. Chelyabinsk, Soviet Union (Russia), April 13, 1974

2003-04 WAS/BOS	71	11	47	58	56
NHL Totals	669	148	277	425	529

–signed September 21, 2004 by Metallurg Magnitogorsk (Super League, Russia); played for Magnitogorsk at 2005 Spengler Cup (December 26-31, 2004)
–played for IMG WorldStars team that toured Europe in December 2004

GORDON, BOYD
b. Unity, Saskatchewan, October 19, 1983

2003-04 WAS	41	1	5	6	8
NHL Totals	41	1	5	6	8

–played 2004-05 with Portland Pirates, Washington's AHL affiliate

GOREN, LEE
b. Winnipeg, Manitoba, December 26, 1977

2003-04 FLO	2	0	1	1	0
NHL Totals	37	4	2	6	14

–played 2004-05 with Manitoba Moose, Vancouver's AHL affiliate, after signing with the Canucks as a free agent in the summer of 2004

GRAHAME, JOHN
b. Denver, Colorado, August 31, 1975

2003-04 TB	29	18-9-1	1,688	58	1	2.06
NHL Totals	122	53-44-14	6,848	288	7	2.52

–did not play professionally in 2004-05

GRAND-PIERRE, JEAN-LUC
b. Montreal, Quebec, February 2, 1977

2003-04 CBJ/ATL/WAS	56	3	2	5	52
NHL Totals	269	7	13	20	311

–signed December 10, 2004 by Troja-Ljungby (Swedish league, Division 2)

GRATTON, BENOIT
b. Montreal, Quebec, December 28, 1976

2003-04 MON	4	0	1	1	4
NHL Totals	58	6	10	16	58

–signed June 9, 2004 by Lugano (Swiss league); loaned February 8, 2005 to EHC Chur (Swiss league)

GRATTON, CHRIS
b. Brantford, Ontario, July 5, 1975

2003-04 PHO/COL	81	13	19	32	111
NHL Totals	851	174	296	470	1,351

–did not play professionally in 2004-05

GREBESHKOV, DENIS
b. Yaroslavl, Soviet Union (Russia), October 11, 1983

2003-04 LA	4	0	1	1	0
NHL Totals	4	0	1	1	0

–played 2004-05 with Manchester Monarchs, Los Angeles's AHL affiliate

GREEN, JOSH
b. Camrose, Alberta, November 16, 1977

2003-04 CAL/NYR	50	5	6	11	32
NHL Totals	239	29	32	61	154

–played 2004-05 with Manitoba Moose (AHL)

Olli Jokinen was busy in 2004-05, playing in Switzerland, Sweden, and Finland before representing his country (Finland) at the 2005 World Championship.

Dany Heatley started the year in Switzerland with Bern before an eye injury and his court case brought him home.

GREEN, MIKE
b. Victoria, British Columbia, August 23, 1979

2003-04 FLO/NYR	24	1	3	4	4
NHL Totals	24	1	3	4	4

–signed August 2, 2004 by Nurnberg (Deutsche Eishockey Liga, Germany)

GREEN, TRAVIS
b. Castlegar, British Columbia, December 20, 1970

2003-04 BOS	64	11	5	16	67
NHL Totals	857	182	249	431	658

–did not play professionally in 2004-05

GRENIER, MARTIN
b. Laval, Quebec, November 2, 1980

2003-04 VAN/NYR	7	1	0	1	9
NHL Totals	15	1	0	1	14

–played 2004-05 with Hartford Wolf Pack, New York Rangers' AHL affiliate

GRIER, MIKE
b. Detroit, Michigan, January 5, 1975

2003-04 WAS/BUF	82	9	20	29	36
NHL Totals	612	105	139	244	364

–did not play professionally in 2004-05

GROSEK, MICHAL
b. Vyskov, Czechoslovakia (Czech Republic), June 1, 1975

2003-04 BOS	33	3	2	5	33
NHL Totals	526	84	137	221	509

–played 2004-05 with Geneve-Servette (Swiss league)

GRUDEN, JOHN
b. Virginia, Minnesota, June 4, 1970

2003-04 WAS	11	1	0	1	6
NHL Totals	92	1	8	9	46

–missed most of 2003-04 because of a concussion and did not play professionally in 2004-05

GUERIN, BILL
b. Worcester, Massachusetts, November 9, 1970

2003-04 DAL	82	34	35	69	109
NHL Totals	879	315	308	623	1,258

–as a member of the NHLPA's executive committee, he focused on negotiations and did not play professionally in 2004-05

HACKETT, JEFF
b. London, Ontario, June 1, 1968

2003-04 PHI	27	10-10-6	1,630	65	3	2.39
NHL Totals	500	166-244-56	28,125	1,361	26	2.90

–retired February 9, 2004 after suffering serious case of vertigo

HAGMAN, NIKLAS
b. Espoo, Finland, December 5, 1979

2003-04 FLO	75	10	13	23	22
NHL Totals	233	28	46	74	50

–played 2004-05 with Davos (Swiss league); won gold medal with Davos at 2005 Spengler Cup (December 26-31, 2004) and later league championship
–played for Finland at 2005 World Championship

HAHL, RIKU
b. Hameenlinna, Finland, November 1, 1980

2003-04 COL	28	0	1	1	12
NHL Totals	92	5	8	13	38

–signed September 15, 2004 by HPK Hameenlinna (SM-Liiga, Finland)
–played for Finland at 2005 World Championship

HAINSEY, RON
b. Bolton, Connecticut, March 24, 1981

2003-04 MON	11	1	1	2	4
NHL Totals	32	1	1	2	6

–played 2004-05 with Hamilton Bulldogs, Montreal's AHL affiliate

HAJT, CHRIS
b. Saskatoon, Saskatchewan, July 5, 1978

2003-04 WAS	5	0	0	0	2
NHL Totals	6	0	0	0	2

–split 2004-05 between Augusta Lynx (ECHL) and Portland Pirates, Washington's AHL affiliate

HALE, DAVID
b. Colorado Springs, Colorado, June 18, 1981

2003-04 NJ	65	0	4	4	72
NHL Totals	65	0	4	4	72

–played 2004-05 with Albany River Rats, New Jersey's AHL affiliate, though missed much of the season with a kidney ailment

HALL, ADAM
b. Kalamazoo, Michigan, August 14, 1980

2003-04 NAS	79	13	14	27	37
NHL Totals	159	29	27	56	68

–signed October 11, 2004 by KalPa (Finnish league, Division 2)
–played for USA at 2005 World Championship

HALPERN, JEFF
b. Potomac, Maryland, May 3, 1976

2003-04 WAS	79	19	27	46	56
NHL Totals	368	76	94	170	272

–signed October 8, 2004 by Ajoie (Swiss league, B Division); left Ajoie on November 23, 2004 because of homesickness
–won gold medal with USA at Deutschland Cup in November 2004
–signed December 30, 2004 by Kloten (Swiss league)
–played for USA at 2005 World Championship

HAMEL, DENIS
b. Lachute, Quebec, May 10, 1977

2003-04 OTT	5	0	0	0	0
NHL Totals	135	13	9	22	67

–played 2004-05 with Binghamton Senators, Ottawa's AHL affiliate

HAMHUIS, DAN
b. Smithers, British Columbia, December 13, 1982

2003-04 NAS	80	7	19	26	57
NHL Totals	80	7	19	26	57

–played 2004-05 with Milwaukee Admirals, Nashville's AHL affiliate

HAMILTON, JEFF
b. Englewood, Ohio, September 4, 1977

2003-04 NYI	1	0	0	0	0
NHL Totals	1	0	0	0	0

–played 2004-05 with Hartford Wolf Pack (AHL)

HAMRLIK, ROMAN
b. Zlin, Czechoslovakia (Czech Republic), April 12, 1974

2003-04 NYI	81	7	22	29	68
NHL Totals	873	117	324	441	985

–signed August 4, 2004 by Zlin (Extraleague, Czech Republic)

HANDZUS, MICHAL
b. Banska Bystrica, Czechoslovakia (Slovakia), March 11, 1977

2003-04 PHI	82	20	38	58	82
NHL Totals	436	101	147	248	269

–signed October 27, 2004 by Zvolen (Extraleague, Slovakia)
–played for Slovakia at 2005 World Championship

Jaromir Jagr had the most successful year of any NHLer. He led Avangard Omsk to both the European Champions' Cup and the league championship and then won gold with the Czech Republic at the World Championship.

HANKINSON, CASEY
b. Edina, Minnesota, May 8, 1976

2003-04 ANA	4	0	0	0	4
NHL Totals	18	0	1	1	13

–signed October 7, 2004 by La Chaux-de-fonds (Swiss league)
–won gold medal with USA at Deutschland Cup in November 2004
–signed December 3, 2004 by Cincinnati Mighty Ducks, Anaheim's AHL affiliate, and played the rest of the year there

HANNAN, SCOTT
b. Richmond, British Columbia, January 23, 1979

2003-04 SJ	82	6	15	21	48
NHL Totals	348	15	64	79	233

–played for Canada at 2005 World Championship (silver medal)

HARTIGAN, MARK
b. Fort St. John, British Columbia, October 15, 1977

2003-04 CBJ	9	1	3	4	6
NHL Totals	34	6	5	11	14

–played 2004-05 with Syracuse Crunch, Columbus's AHL affiliate

HARTNELL, SCOTT
b. Regina, Saskatchewan, April 18, 1982

2003-04 NAS	59	18	15	33	87
NHL Totals	291	46	78	124	347

–signed October 21, 2004 by Valerenga (Norwegian league)

HARVEY, TODD
b. Hamilton, Ontario, February 17, 1975

2003-04 SJ	47	4	5	9	38
NHL Totals	608	86	130	216	918

–played 2004-05 with Cambridge Hornets (OHA Senior A)

HASEK, DOMINIK
b. Pardubice, Czechoslovakia (Czech Republic), January 29, 1965

2003-04 DET	14	8-3-2	817	30	2	2.20	
NHL Totals	595	296-192-82	34,562	1,284	63	2.23	

–attended training camp of Binghamton Senators, Ottawa's AHL affiliate, to rehab injured groin, but only other games this year were with IMG WorldStars tour to Europe in December 2004

HATCHER, DERIAN
b. Sterling Heights, Michigan, June 4, 1972

2003-04 DET	15	0	4	4	8
NHL Totals	842	71	227	298	1,388

–signed February 1, 2005 by Motor City Mechanics (UHL)

HAVELID, NICLAS
b. Stockholm, Sweden, April 12, 1973

2003-04 ANA	79	6	20	26	28
NHL Totals	310	24	61	85	152

–signed August 9, 2004 by Sodertalje (Swedish Elite League)

HAVLAT, MARTIN
b. Mlada Boleslav, Czechoslovakia (Czech Republic), April 19, 1981

2003-04 OTT	68	31	37	68	46
NHL Totals	280	96	123	219	162

–signed September 24, 2004 by Znojemsti Orli (Extraleague, Czech Republic)
–signed November 10, 2004 by Moscow Dynamo (Super League, Russia); left Moscow Dynamo on January 5, 2005
–re-signed January 18, 2005 by Znojemsti Orli
–signed January 31, 2005 by Sparta Praha (Extraleague, Czech Republic)

HEALEY, PAUL
b. Edmonton, Alberta, March 20, 1975

2003-04 NYR	4	0	0	0	0
NHL Totals	75	6	14	20	30

–played 2004-05 with San Antonio Rampage, Florida's AHL affiliate, after being traded to the Panthers in March 2004
–played part of 2004-05 with Edmonton Road Runners (AHL)

HEATLEY, DANY
b. Freiburg, West Germany (Germany), January 21, 1981

2003-04 ATL	31	13	12	25	18
NHL Totals	190	80	101	181	132

–signed October 13, 2004 by SC Bern (Swiss league) and played with the team until suffering an eye injury on November 6, 2004 which required surgery to the orbital bone (returned home to Calgary to recover)
–appeared in an Atlanta court on February 4, 2005 and pleaded guilty to second-degree vehicular homicide, driving too fast for conditions, failure to maintain a lane, and speeding in connection with the death of teammate Dan Snyder from a car accident on September 29, 2003. He received three years' probation and was ordered to make 150 speeches (50 per year for three years) on the dangers of speeding.
–signed February 9, 2005 by AK Bars Kazan (Super League, Russia)
–played for Canada at 2005 World Championship (silver medal)

HECHT, JOCHEN
b. Mannheim, West Germany (Germany), June 21, 1977

2003-04 BUF	64	15	37	52	49
NHL Totals	333	73	123	196	215

–signed August 2, 2004 by Adler Mannheim (Deutsche Eishockey Liga, Germany)
–played for Germany at 2005 World Championship

HEDBERG, JOHAN
b. Leksand, Sweden, May 3, 1973

2003-04 VAN	21	8-6-2	1,098	46	3	2.51
NHL Totals	137	54-63-14	7,930	374	10	2.83

–signed August 1, 2004 by Leksand (Swedish league, Division 2)

HEDICAN, BRET
b. St. Paul, Minnesota, August 10, 1970

2003-04 CAR	81	7	17	24	64
NHL Totals	798	47	187	234	693

–did not play professionally in 2004-05

HEDIN, PIERRE
b. Ornskoldsvik, Sweden, February 19, 1978

2003-04 TML	3	0	1	1	0
NHL Totals	3	0	1	1	0

–signed September 18, 2004 by MoDo (Swedish Elite League)

HEEREMA, JEFF
b. Thunder Bay, Ontario, January 17, 1980

2003-04 STL	22	1	2	3	4
NHL Totals	32	4	2	6	6

–played 2004-05 with Manitoba Moose, Vancouver's AHL affiliate, after signing with the Canucks as a free agent in the summer of 2004

HEINS, SHAWN
b. Eganville, Ontario, December 24, 1973

2003-04 ATL	17	0	4	4	16
NHL Totals	125	4	12	16	154

–signed July 15, 2004 by Berlin (Deutsche Eishockey Liga, Germany)
–played for Canada at Deutschland Cup in November 2004

HEJDUK, MILAN
b. Usti-nad-Labem, Czechoslovakia (Czech Republic), February 14, 1976

2003-04 COL	82	35	40	75	20
NHL Totals	470	197	219	416	154

–signed September 18, 2004 by Pardubice (Extraleague, Czech Republic)

HELMER, BRYAN
b. Sault Ste. Marie, Ontario, July 15, 1972

2003-04 PHO	17	0	1	1	10
NHL Totals	134	8	15	23	133

–played 2004-05 with Grand Rapids Griffins, Detroit's AHL affiliate, after signing with the Red Wings as a free agent in the summer of 2004

HEMSKY, ALES
b. Pardubice, Czechoslovakia (Czech Republic), August 13, 1983

2003-04 EDM	71	12	22	34	14
NHL Totals	130	18	46	64	28

–signed September 18, 2004 by Pardubice (Extraleague, Czech Republic)
–played for Czech Republic at 2005 World Championship (gold medal)

HENDRICKSON, DARBY
b. Richfield, Minnesota, August 28, 1972

2003-04 MIN/COL	34	2	3	5	12
NHL Totals	518	65	64	129	370

–signed October 2, 2004 by Riga 2000 (Latvian league) to play with his good friend, Sergei Zholtok, but after Zholtok died during a game after suffering a heart attack, Hendrickson returned home to the U.S. and did not play professionally the rest of the season.

HENRY, ALEX
b. Elliot Lake, Ontario, October 18, 1979

2003-04 MIN	71	2	4	6	106
NHL Totals	112	2	4	6	186

–signed January 15, 2005 by Kaufbeuren (Germany, Division 2)

HENRY, BURKE
b. Ste. Rose, Manitoba, January 21, 1979

2003-04 CHI	23	2	4	6	24
NHL Totals	39	2	6	8	33

–split 2004-05 between San Antonio Rampage, Florida's AHL affiliate, after signing with the Panthers as a free agent in the summer of 2004, and Milwaukee Admirals (AHL, on loan)

HIGGINS, CHRIS
b. Smithtown, New York, June 2, 1983

2003-04 MON	2	0	0	0	0
NHL Totals	2	0	0	0	0

–played 2004-05 with Hamilton Bulldogs, Montreal's AHL affiliate

HILBERT, ANDY
b. Lansing, Michigan, February 6, 1981

2003-04 BOS	18	2	0	2	9
NHL Totals	38	3	3	6	18

–played 2004-05 with Providence Bruins, Boston's AHL affiliate

HILL, SEAN
b. Duluth, Minnesota, February 14, 1970

2003-04 CAR	80	13	26	39	84
NHL Totals	682	57	187	244	786

–signed as a free agent by Florida during the summer of 2004 but did not play professionally during 2004-05

HINOTE, DAN
b. Leesburg, Florida, January 30, 1977

2003-04 COL	59	4	7	11	57
NHL Totals	280	22	30	52	206

–signed December 22, 2004 by MoDo (Swedish Elite League)

HLAVAC, JAN
b. Prague, Czechoslovakia (Czech Republic), September 20, 1976

2003-04 NYR	72	5	21	26	16
NHL Totals	356	78	111	189	98

–signed August 9, 2004 by Sparta Praha (Extraleague, Czech Republic); played for Sparta Praha at 2005 Spengler Cup (December 26-31, 2004)
–played for Czech Republic at 2005 World Championship (gold medal)

HNIDY, SHANE
b. Neepawa, Manitoba, November 8, 1975

2003-04 OTT/NAS	46	0	7	7	82
NHL Totals	198	4	18	22	353

–played part of 2004-05 with Florida Everblades (ECHL)

HNILICKA, MILAN
b. Pardubice, Czechoslovakia (Czech Republic), June 25, 1973

2003-04 LA	2	0-1-0		80	5	0	3.75
NHL Totals	121	29-67-13	6,509	359	5		3.31

–signed May 18, 2004 by Liberec (Extraleague, Czech Republic)
–played for Czech Republic at 2005 World Championship (gold medal)

HOLDEN, JOSH
b. Calgary, Alberta, January 18, 1978

2003-04 TML	1	0	0	0	0
NHL Totals	60	5	9	14	16

–signed July 24, 2004 by Forward Morges (Swiss league, B Division)
–signed September 19, 2004 by Hameenlinna (SM-Liiga, Finland)

HOLIK, BOBBY
b. Jihlava, Czechoslovakia (Czech Republic), January 1, 1971

2003-04 NYR	82	25	31	56	96
NHL Totals	1,024	281	361	642	1,102

–spent most of the season on his ranch in Florida; did not play professionally in 2004-05

HOLLAND, JASON
b. Morinville, Alberta, April 30, 1976

2003-04 LA	52	3	3	6	24
NHL Totals	81	4	5	9	36

–signed October 24, 2004 by Alleghe (Serie A, Italy); left Alleghe on December 12, 2004 and played the rest of the season with Manchester Monarchs, Los Angeles's AHL affiliate

HOLMQVIST, MIKAEL
b. Stockholm, Sweden, June 8, 1979

2003-04 ANA	21	2	0	2	25
NHL Totals	21	2	0	2	25

–played 2004-05 with Cincinnati Mighty Ducks, Anaheim's AHL affiliate

HOLMSTROM, TOMAS
b. Pitea, Sweden, January 23, 1973

2003-04 DET	67	15	15	30	38
NHL Totals	541	96	140	236	387

–signed September 16, 2004 by Lulea (Swedish Elite League)

HOLZINGER, BRIAN
b. Parma, Ohio, October 10, 1972

2003-04 PIT/CBJ	74	7	15	22	40
NHL Totals	547	93	145	238	339

–did not play professionally in 2004-05

Darius Kasparaitis was one of several big NHL names to play for AK Bars Kazan in 2004-05.

HORCOFF, SHAWN
b. Trail, British Columbia, September 17, 1978

2003-04 EDM	80	15	25	40	73
NHL Totals	268	44	67	111	156

–signed September 6, 2004 by Mora (Swedish Elite League)

HORDICHUK, DARCY
b. Kamsack, Saskatchewan, August 10, 1980

2003-04 FLO	57	3	1	4	158
NHL Totals	130	4	2	6	434

–began 2004-05 playing with Detroit in Original Stars Hockey
  League

HORTON, NATHAN
b. Welland, Ontario, May 29, 1985

2003-04 FLO	55	14	8	22	57
NHL Totals	55	14	8	22	57

–played 2004-05 with San Antonio Rampage, Florida's AHL
  affiliate

HOSSA, MARCEL
b. Ilava, Czechoslovakia (Slovakia), October 12, 1981

2003-04 MON	15	1	1	2	8
NHL Totals	59	10	9	19	24

–signed September 25, 2004 by Mora (Swedish Elite League)
–played for Slovakia at Deutschland Cup in November 2004
–played for Slovakia at 2005 World Championship

HOSSA, MARIAN
b. Stara Lubovna, Czechoslovakia (Slovakia), January 12, 1979

2003-04 OTT	81	36	46	82	46
NHL Totals	467	188	202	390	243

–signed September 16, 2004 by Dukla Trencin (Extraleague,
  Slovakia)
–signed November 11, 2004 by Mora IK (Swedish Elite League);
  left Mora IK on January 30, 2005
–re-signed January 31, 2005 by Dukla Trencin
–played for Slovakia at 2005 World Championship

HRDINA, JAN
b. Hradec Kralove, Czechoslovakia (Czech Republic), February 5, 1976

2003-04 PHO/NJ	68	12	21	33	40
NHL Totals	438	91	173	264	263

–signed October 4, 2004 by Kladno (Extraleague, Czech Republic)

HUDLER, JIRI
b. Olomouc, Czechoslovakia (Czech Republic), January 4, 1984

2003-04 DET	12	1	2	3	10
NHL Totals	12	1	2	3	10

–began 2004-05 with Grand Rapids Griffins, Detroit's AHL
  affiliate
–signed December 2, 2004 by Vsetin (Extraleague, Czech Republic)

HUET, CRISTOBAL
b. St. Martin d'Heres, France, September 3, 1975

2003-04 LA	41	10-16-10	2,199	89	3	2.43
NHL Totals	53	14-20-11	2,740	110	4	2.41

–signed September 14, 2004 by Adler Mannheim (Deutsche
  Eishockey Liga, Germany)
–played for France at final Olympic qualifying tournament in
  February 2005

HULL, BRETT
b. Belleville, Ontario, August 9, 1964

2003-04 DET	81	25	43	68	12
NHL Totals	1,264	741	649	1,390	458

–did not play professionally in 2004-05

HULL, JODY
b. Petrolia, Ontario, February 2, 1969

2003-04 OTT	1	0	0	0	0
NHL Totals	831	124	137	261	156

–did not play professionally in 2004-05

HULSE, CALE
b. Edmonton, Alberta, November 10, 1973

2003-04 PHO	82	3	17	20	123
NHL Totals	580	16	75	91	937

–married the actress/model Gena Lee Nolan (*Baywatch*) during the
  season; did not play professionally in 2004-05

HUML, IVAN
b. Kladno, Czechoslovakia (Czech Republic), September 6, 1981

2003-04 BOS	7	0	0	0	6
NHL Totals	49	6	12	18	36

–signed September 5, 2004 by Kladno (Extraleague, Czech
  Republic)

HUNTER, TRENT
b. Red Deer, Alberta, July 5, 1980

2003-04 NYI	77	25	26	51	16
NHL Totals	85	25	30	55	20

–signed November 8, 2004 by Nykoping (Swedish league, Division 2)

HUSELIUS, KRISTIAN
b. Osterhaninge, Sweden, November 10, 1978

2003-04 FLO	76	10	21	31	24
NHL Totals	233	53	66	119	58

–signed July 29, 2004 by Linkoping (Swedish Elite League);
  suspended by Linkoping in early February after he and teammate Henrik Tallinder and Mora's
  Andreas Lilja were charged with (and acquitted of) rape
–signed February 23, 2004 by Rapperswill-Jona (Swiss league), the
  same day Swedish police re-opened the case (which was later
  dropped)

HUSSEY, MATT
b. New Haven, Connecticut, May 28, 1979

2003-04 PIT	3	2	1	3	0
NHL Totals	3	2	1	3	0

–played 2004-05 with Wilkes-Barre/Scranton Penguins, Pittsburgh's
  AHL affiliate

HUTCHINSON, ANDREW
b. Evanston, Illinois, March 24, 1980

2003-04 NAS	18	4	4	8	4
NHL Totals	18	4	4	8	4

–played 2004-05 with Milwaukee Admirals, Nashville's AHL
  affiliate

IGINLA, JAROME
b. Edmonton, Alberta, July 1, 1977

2003-04 CAL	81	41	32	73	84
NHL Totals	626	250	253	503	422

–did not play professionally during 2004-05

IRBE, ARTURS
b. Riga, Soviet Union (Latvia), February 2, 1967

2003-04 CAR	10		5-2-1	564	23	0	2.45
NHL Totals	568	218-236-79	32,066	1,513	33	2.83

–one of the NHLPA's vice presidents, Irbe worked on an agreement
  with the league and did not play professionally in 2004-05
–played for Latvia at 2005 World Championship

Goalie Nikolai Khabibulin spent most of the 2004-05 season in net for AK Bars Kazan in Russia.

Finnish star Saku Koivu rejoined TPS Turku during the lockout, the team he began his pro career with prior to joining Montreal in 1994.

ISBISTER, BRAD
b. Edmonton, Alberta, May 7, 1977

2003-04 EDM	51	10	8	18	54
NHL Totals	409	93	90	183	517

–signed February 2, 2005 by Slovan Bratislava (Extraleague, Slovakia); left team on February 8, 2005
–signed February 12, 2005 by HC Innsbruck (Austrian league)

JACKMAN, BARRET
b. Trail, British Columbia, March 5, 1981

2003-04 STL	15	1	2	3	41
NHL Totals	98	4	18	22	231

–started 2004-05 playing rec. hockey in Brentwood Hockey League in St. Louis
–signed February 3, 2005 by Missouri River Otters (UHL)

JACKMAN, RIC
b. Toronto, Ontario, June 28, 1978

2003-04 TML/PIT	54	9	21	30	27
NHL Totals	136	10	25	35	94

–signed September 17, 2004 by Bjorkloven (Swedish league, Division 2)

JACKMAN, TIM
b. Minot, North Dakota, November 14, 1981

2003-04 CBJ	19	1	2	3	16
NHL Totals	19	1	2	3	16

–played 2004-05 with Syracuse Crunch, Columbus's AHL affiliate

JAGR, JAROMIR
b. Kladno, Czechoslovakia (Czech Republic), February 15, 1972

2003-04 WAS/NYR	77	31	43	74	38
NHL Totals	1,027	537	772	1,309	699

–signed September 17, 2004 by Kladno (Extraleague, Czech Republic)
–signed November 7, 2004 by Avangard Omsk (Super League, Russia); scored winning goal in European Champions Cup final at 14:38 of overtime of final game
–played for Czech Republic at 2005 World Championship (gold medal)

JANIK, DOUG
b. Agawam, Massachusetts, March 26, 1980

2003-04 BUF	4	0	0	0	19
NHL Totals	10	0	0	0	21

–played 2004-05 with Rochester Americans, Buffalo's AHL affiliate

JASPERS, JASON
b. Thunder Bay, Ontario, April 8, 1981

2003-04 PHO	3	0	0	0	2
NHL Totals	9	0	1	1	6

–split 2004-05 between Utah Grizzlies, Phoenix's AHL affiliate, and Springfield Falcons (AHL, on loan)

JILLSON, JEFF
b. North Smithfield, Rhode Island, July 24, 1980

2003-04 BOS/BUF	64	4	13	17	54
NHL Totals	138	9	32	41	92

–played 2004-05 with Rochester Americans, Buffalo's AHL affiliate

JOHANSSON, ANDREAS
b. Hofors, Sweden, May 19, 1973

2003-04 NAS	47	12	15	27	26
NHL Totals	377	81	88	169	190

–played 2004-05 with Geneve-Servette (Swiss league)

JOHANSSON, CALLE
b. Goteborg, Sweden, February 14, 1967

2003-04 TML	8	0	6	6	0
NHL Totals	1,109	119	416	535	519

–had come out of retirement late in 2003-04 to play for Toronto as the playoffs approached, but retired after the season

JOHNSON, AARON
b. Port Hawkesbury, Nova Scotia, April 30, 1983

2003-04 CBJ	29	2	6	8	32
NHL Totals	29	2	6	8	32

–played 2004-05 with Syracuse Crunch, Columbus's AHL affiliate

JOHNSON, BRENT
b. Farmington, Michigan, March 12, 1977

2003-04 STL/PHO	18	5-9-2	979	41	1	2.52
NHL Totals	151	77-53-13	8,542	325	12	2.28

–did not play professionally in 2004-05

JOHNSON, CRAIG
b. St. Paul, Minnesota, March 18, 1972

2003-04 ANA/TML/WAS	64	2	9	11	28
NHL Totals	557	75	98	173	260

–played 2004-05 with Hamburg (Deutsche Eishockey Liga, Germany)

JOHNSON, GREG
b. Thunder Bay, Ontario, March 16, 1971

2003-04 NAS	82	14	18	32	33
NHL Totals	717	134	216	350	335

–did not play professionally in 2004-05

JOHNSON, MATT
b. Welland, Ontario, November 23, 1975

2003-04 MIN	57	7	1	8	177
NHL Totals	473	23	20	43	1,523

–stayed at his home near Detroit; did not play professionally in 2004-05

JOHNSON, MIKE
b. Scarborough (Toronto), Ontario, October 3, 1974

2003-04 PHO	11	1	9	10	10
NHL Totals	480	100	185	285	217

–began 2004-05 playing for Detroit in Original Stars Hockey League
–signed January 31, 2005 by Farjestad (Swedish Elite League)

JOHNSON, RYAN
b. Thunder Bay, Ontario, June 14, 1976

2003-04 STL	69	4	7	11	8
NHL Totals	344	19	45	64	116

–signed February 3, 2005 by Missouri River Otters (UHL)

JOHNSSON, KIM
b. Malmo, Sweden, March 16, 1976

2003-04 PHI	80	13	29	42	26
NHL Totals	395	45	124	169	192

–signed September 18, 2004 by Ambri-Piotta (Swiss league); left Ambri-Piotta on November 29, 2004
–signed December 21, 2004 by Rogle BK (Swedish Elite League)

JOKINEN, OLLI
b. Kuopio, Finland, December 5, 1978

2003-04 FLO	82	26	32	58	81
NHL Totals	477	97	113	210	494

–signed September 15, 2004 by Kloten (Swiss league)
–played part of 2004-05 with Sodertalje (Swedish Elite League)
–signed January 30, 2005 by HIFK Helsinki (SM-Liiga, Finland)
–played for Finland at 2005 World Championship

JONES, RANDY
b. Quispamsis, New Brunswick, July 23, 1981

2003-04 PHI	5	0	0	0	0
NHL Totals	5	0	0	0	0

–played 2004-05 with Philadelphia Phantoms, Philadelphia Flyers' AHL affiliate

JONES, TY
b. Richland, Washington, February 22, 1979

2003-04 FLO	6	0	0	0	7
NHL Totals	14	0	0	0	19

–played 2004-05 with San Antonio Rampage, Florida's AHL affiliate

JONSSON, KENNY
b. Angelholm, Sweden, October 6, 1974

2003-04 NYI	79	5	24	29	22
NHL Totals	686	63	204	267	298

–signed December 20, 2004 by Rogle (Swedish league, Division 2)
–played for Sweden at 2005 World Championship

JOSEPH, CURTIS
b. Keswick, Ontario, April 29, 1967

2003-04 DET	31	16-10-3	1,708	68	2	2.39
NHL Totals	798	396-289-90	46,396	2,124	43	2.75

–did not play professionally during 2004-05

JOVANOVSKI, ED
b. Windsor, Ontario, June 26, 1976

2003-04 VAN	56	7	16	23	64
NHL Totals	643	78	206	284	1,027

–spent first part of the season recovering from a knee injury and did not play professionally in 2004-05
–played for Canada at 2005 World Championship (silver medal)

JUNEAU, JOE
b. Pont Rouge, Quebec, January 5, 1968

2003-04 MON	70	5	10	15	20
NHL Totals	828	156	416	572	272

–announced his retirement after the 2003-04 season

KABERLE, FRANTISEK
b. Kladno, Czechoslovakia (Czech Republic), November 8, 1973

2003-04 ATL	67	3	26	29	30
NHL Totals	309	20	91	111	114

–signed September 17, 2004 by Kladno (Extraleague, Czech Republic)
–signed January 31, 2005 by MoDo (Swedish Elite League)
–played for Czech Republic at 2005 World Championship (gold medal)

KABERLE, TOMAS
b. Rakovnik, Czechoslovakia (Czech Republic), March 2, 1978

2003-04 TML	71	3	28	31	18
NHL Totals	443	41	183	224	110

–signed September 17, 2004 by Kladno (Extraleague, Czech Republic)
–played for Czech Republic at 2005 World Championship (gold medal)

KALININ, DMITRI
b. Chelyabinsk, Soviet Union (Russia), July 22, 1980

2003-04 BUF	77	10	24	34	42
NHL Totals	283	24	66	90	167

–signed September 25, 2004 by Metallurg Magnitogorsk (Super League, Russia); played for Magnitogorsk at 2005 Spengler Cup (December 26-31, 2004)
–played for Russia at 2005 World Championship (bronze medal)

KANE, BOYD
b. Swift Current, Saskatchewan, April 18, 1978

2003-04 PHI	7	0	0	0	7
NHL Totals	7	0	0	0	7

–played 2004-05 with Philadelphia Phantoms, Philadelphia Flyers' AHL affiliate

KAPANEN, NIKO
b. Hattula, Finland, April 29, 1978

2003-04 DAL	67	1	5	6	16
NHL Totals	158	6	35	41	62

–signed June 9, 2004 by Zug (Swiss league)
–played for Finland at 2005 World Championship

KAPANEN, SAMI
b. Vantaa, Finland, June 14, 1973

2003-04 PHI	74	12	18	30	14
NHL Totals	622	161	230	391	125

–signed November 17, 2004 by KalPa (Finnish league, Division 2)

KARIYA, PAUL
b. Vancouver, British Columbia, October 16, 1974

2003-04 COL	51	11	25	36	22
NHL Totals	657	311	394	705	235

–did not play professionally in 2004-05

KARPOVTSEV, ALEXANDER
b. Moscow, Soviet Union (Russia), April 7, 1970

2003-04 CHI/NYI	27	0	8	8	18
NHL Totals	590	34	154	188	426

–signed August 21, 2004 by Lokomotiv Yaroslavl (Super League, Russia)
–played for Russia at 2005 World Championship (bronze medal)

KASPARAITIS, DARIUS
b. Elektrenai, Soviet Union (Lithuania), October 16, 1972

2003-04 NYR	44	1	9	10	48
NHL Totals	772	25	128	153	1,252

–signed October 22, 2004 by AK Bars Kazan (Super League, Russia)

KAVANAGH, PAT
b. Ottawa, Ontario, March 14, 1979

2003-04 VAN	3	1	0	1	2
NHL Totals	6	2	0	2	2

–played 2004-05 with Binghamton Senators, Ottawa's AHL affiliate, after signing with the Senators as a free agent in the summer of 2004

KEANE, MIKE
b. Winnipeg, Manitoba, May 29, 1967

2003-04 VAN	64	8	9	17	20
NHL Totals	1,161	168	302	470	881

–did not play professionally in 2004-05

KEITH, MATT
b. Edmonton, Alberta, April 11, 1983

2003-04 CHI	20	2	3	5	10
NHL Totals	20	2	3	5	10

–played 2004-05 with Norfolk Admirals, Chicago's AHL affiliate

KELLY, CHRIS
b. Toronto, Ontario, November 11, 1980

2003-04 OTT	4	0	0	0	0
NHL Totals	4	0	0	0	0

–played 2004-05 with Binghamton Senators, Ottawa's AHL affiliate

KELLY, STEVE
b. Vancouver, British Columbia, October 26, 1976

2003-04 LA	3	0	0	0	0
NHL Totals	147	9	12	21	83

–signed May 4, 2004 by Adler Mannheim (Deutsche Eishockey Liga, Germany)
–played for Canada at Deutschland Cup in November 2004

KESLER, RYAN
b. Detroit, Michigan, August 31, 1984

2003-04 VAN	28	2	3	5	16
NHL Totals	28	2	3	5	16

–played 2004-05 with Manitoba Moose, Vancouver's AHL affiliate

KHABIBULIN, NIKOLAI
b. Sverdlovsk, Soviet Union (Russia), January 13, 1973

2003-04 TB	55	28-19-7	3,274	127	3	2.33
NHL Totals	476	209-187-58	27,107	1,177	35	2.61

–signed November 8, 2004 by AK Bars Kazan (Super League, Russia)

KHAVANOV, ALEXANDER
b. Moscow, Soviet Union (Russia), January 30, 1972

2003-04 STL	48	3	7	10	18
NHL Totals	284	21	69	90	173

–signed September 25, 2004 by SKA St. Petersburg (Super League, Russia); left St. Petersburg on October 4, 2004

KIDD, TREVOR
b. Dugald, Manitoba, March 26, 1972

2003-04 TML	15	6-5-2	883	48	1	3.26
NHL Totals	387	140-162-52	21,426	1,014	19	2.84

–signed January 31, 2005 by Orebro (Swedish league, Division 3)

KILGER, CHAD
b. Cornwall, Ontario, November 27, 1976

2003-04 MON/TML	41	3	3	6	16
NHL Totals	500	66	79	145	224

–remained at home with his family in Cornwall, skating with the local Provincial Junior team; did not play professionally in 2004-05

KING, JASON
b. Corner Brook, Newfoundland, September 14, 1981

2003-04 VAN	47	12	9	21	8
NHL Totals	55	12	11	23	8

–played 2004-05 with Manitoba Moose, Vancouver's AHL affiliate

KIPRUSOFF, MIIKKA
b. Turku, Finland, October 26, 1976

2003-04 CAL	38	24-10-4	2,301	65	4	1.69
NHL Totals	85	38-31-7	4,691	178	7	2.27

–signed September 20, 2004 by Timra (Swedish Elite League)

KLATT, TRENT
b. Robbinsdale, Minnesota, January 30, 1971

2003-04 LA	82	17	26	43	46
NHL Totals	782	143	200	343	307

–member of NHLPA executive remained at home to work on negotiations with NHL; did not play professionally in 2004-05

KLEE, KEN
b. Indianapolis, Indiana, April 24, 1971

2003-04 TML	66	4	25	29	36
NHL Totals	636	47	93	140	644

–remained at home in Denver with his family

KLEMM, JON
b. Cranbrook, British Columbia, January 8, 1970

2003-04 CHI/DAL	77	2	5	7	44
NHL Totals	637	37	91	128	342

–did not play professionally in 2004-05

KLESLA, ROSTISLAV
b. Novy Jicin, Czechoslovakia (Czech Republic), March 21, 1982

2003-04 CBJ	47	2	11	13	27
NHL Totals	202	14	33	47	178

–signed September 17, 2004 by Vsetin (Extraleague, Czech Republic)
–signed January 29, 2005 by HPK Hameenlinna (SM-Liiga, Finland)

KLOUCEK, TOMAS
b. Prague, Czechoslovakia (Czech Republic), March 7, 1980

2003-04 NAS/ATL	42	0	1	1	35
NHL Totals	140	2	8	10	248

–signed September 17, 2004 by Slava Praha (Extraleague, Czech Republic)
–loaned January 31, 2005 to Liberec (Extraleague, Czech Republic)

KNUBLE, MIKE
b. Toronto, Ontario, July 4, 1972

2003-04 BOS	82	21	25	46	32
NHL Totals	510	101	107	208	224

–signed August 2, 2004 by Linkoping (Swedish Elite League)
–played for USA at 2005 World Championship

KNUTSEN, ESPEN
b. Oslo, Norway, January 12, 1972

2003-04 CBJ	14	0	4	4	2
NHL Totals	207	30	81	111	105

–played 2004-05 with Djurgarden (Swedish Elite League)

KOBASEW, CHUCK
b. Osoyoos, British Columbia, April 17, 1982

2003-04 CAL	70	6	11	17	51
NHL Totals	93	10	13	23	59

–played 2004-05 with Lowell Lock Monsters, Calgary's AHL affiliate

KOIVU, SAKU
b. Turku, Finland, November 23, 1974

2003-04 MON	68	14	41	55	52
NHL Totals	497	120	278	398	342

–signed October 21, 2004 by TPS Turku (SM-Liiga, Finland)

KOLANOS, KRYS
b. Calgary, Alberta, July 27, 1981

2003-04 PHO	41	4	6	10	24
NHL Totals	100	15	17	32	72

–signed October 25, 2004 by Espoo (SM-Liiga, Finland); left Espoo on December 28, 2004
–signed February 16, 2005 by Krefeld (Deutsche Eishockey Liga, Germany)

KOLNIK, JURAJ
b. Nitra, Czechoslovakia (Slovakia), November 13, 1980

2003-04 FLO	53	14	11	25	14
NHL Totals	99	20	15	35	26

–played 2004-05 with San Antonio Rampage, Florida's AHL affiliate

KOLTSOV, KONSTANTIN
b. Minsk, Soviet Union (Belarus), April 17, 1981

2003-04 PIT	82	9	20	29	30
NHL Totals	84	9	20	29	30

–signed September 15, 2004 by Dynamo Minsk (Belarus league)
–also played part of 2004-05 with Spartak Moscow (Super League, Russia)
–played for Belarus at 2005 World Championship

Alexei Kovalev, playing for AK Bars Kazan, is dumped in front of the goal.

KOLZIG, OLAF
b. Johannesburg, South Africa, April 9, 1970

2003-04 WAS	63	19-35-9	3,738	180	2	2.89
NHL Totals	544	234-220-63	31,417	1,342	33	2.56

–spent the first part of the season as a goalie consultant with the Tri-City Americans (WHL)
–signed February 2, 2005 by Eisbaren Berlin (Deutsche Eishockey Liga, Germany)

KOMARNISKI, ZENITH
b. Edmonton, Alberta, August 13, 1978

2003-04 CBJ	2	0	0	0	0
NHL Totals	21	1	1	2	10

–played 2004-05 with Syracuse Crunch, Columbus's AHL affiliate

KOMISAREK, MIKE
b. Islip Terrace, New York, January 19, 1982

2003-04 MON	46	0	4	4	34
NHL Totals	67	0	5	5	62

–played 2004-05 with Hamilton Bulldogs, Montreal's AHL affiliate, though missed most of the season with a hip injury

KONDRATIEV, MAXIM
b. Togliatti, Soviet Union (Russia), January 20, 1983

2003-04 TML/NYR	7	0	0	0	2
NHL Totals	7	0	0	0	2

–signed November 11, 2004 by Lada Togliatti (Super League, Russia)
–played part of 2004-05 with Hartford Wolf Pack, New York Rangers' AHL affiliate

KONOWALCHUK, STEVE
b. Salt Lake City, Utah, November 11, 1972

2003-04 WAS/COL	82	19	21	40	70
NHL Totals	769	165	216	381	689

–remained in Denver with his family; did not play professionally in 2004-05

KOROLEV, IGOR
b. Moscow, Soviet Union (Russia), September 6, 1970

2003-04 CHI	62	3	10	13	22
NHL Totals	795	119	227	346	330

–signed July 13, 2004 by Lokomotiv Yaroslavl (Super League, Russia)

KOROLYUK, ALEXANDER
b. Moscow, Soviet Union (Russia), January 14, 1976

2003-04 SJ	63	19	18	37	18
NHL Totals	296	62	80	142	140

–signed September 25, 2004 by Vityaz Chekhov (Russian league, Division 2)
–signed February 14, 2005 by Khimik Voskresensk (Super League, Russia)

KOSTOPOULOS, TOM
b. Mississauga, Ontario, January 24, 1979

2003-04 PIT	60	9	13	22	67
NHL Totals	79	10	16	26	76

–played 2004-05 with Manchester Monarchs (AHL)

KOTALIK, ALES
b. Jindrichuv Hradec, Czechoslovakia (Czech Republic), December 23, 1978

2003-04 BUF	62	15	11	26	41
NHL Totals	143	37	28	65	73

–signed September 6, 2004 by Liberec (Extraleague, Czech Republic)

KOVALCHUK, ILYA
b. Tver, Soviet Union (Russia), April 15, 1983

2003-04 ATL	81	41	46	87	63
NHL Totals	227	108	97	205	148

–signed August 22, 2004 by AK Bars Kazan (Super League, Russia)
–played for Russia at 2005 World Championship (bronze medal)

KOVALEV, ALEXEI
b. Togliatti, Soviet Union (Russia), February 24, 1973

2003-04 NYR/MON	78	14	31	45	66
NHL Totals	849	292	388	680	902

–signed November 3, 2004 by AK Bars Kazan (Super League, Russia)
–captained Russian team at Sweden Hockey Games
–played for Russia at 2005 World Championship (bronze medal)

KOZLOV, VIKTOR
b. Togliatti, Soviet Union (Russia), February 14, 1975

2003-04 FLO/NJ	59	13	20	33	18
NHL Totals	599	132	234	366	170

–signed July 11, 2004 by Lada Togliatti (Super League, Russia)
–played for Russia at 2005 World Championship (bronze medal)

KOZLOV, VYACHESLAV
b. Voskresensk, Soviet Union (Russia), May 3, 1972

2003-04 ATL	76	20	32	52	74
NHL Totals	800	252	307	559	532

–signed September 15, 2004 by Khimik Voskresensk (Super League, Russia)
–signed February 17, 2005 by AK Bars Kazan (Super League, Russia)

KRAFT, MILAN
b. Plzen, Czechoslovakia (Czech Republic), January 17, 1980

2003-04 PIT	66	19	21	40	18
NHL Totals	207	41	41	82	52

–signed September 17, 2004 by Karlovy Vary (Extraleague, Czech Republic)

KRAJICEK, LUKAS
b. Prostejov, Czechoslovakia (Czech Republic), March 11, 1983

2003-04 FLO	18	1	6	7	12
NHL Totals	23	1	6	7	12

–played 2004-05 with San Antonio Rampage, Florida's AHL affiliate

KRESTANOVICH, JORDAN
b. Langley, British Columbia, June 14, 1981

2003-04 COL	14	0	0	0	6
NHL Totals	22	0	2	2	6

–played 2004-05 with Pensacola Ice Pilots (ECHL)

KROG, JASON
b. Fernie, British Columbia, October 9, 1975

2003-04 ANA	80	6	12	18	16
NHL Totals	175	18	34	52	34

–signed August 24, 2004 by Villach (Austrian league)

KRONWALL, NIKLAS
b. Stockholm, Sweden, January 12, 1981

2003-04 DET	20	1	4	5	16
NHL Totals	20	1	4	5	16

–played 2004-05 with Grand Rapids Griffins, Detroit's AHL affiliate
–played for Sweden at 2005 World Championship

KUBA, FILIP
b. Ostrava, Czechoslovakia (Czech Republic), December 29, 1976

2003-04 MIN	77	5	19	24	28
NHL Totals	310	28	86	114	119

–skated with teammates at the University of Minnesota to keep in shape; did not play professionally in 2004-05

KUBINA, PAVEL
b. Celadna, Czechoslovakia (Czech Republic), April 15, 1977

2003-04 TB	81	17	18	35	85
NHL Totals	455	60	111	171	567

–signed September 17, 2004 by Vitkovice (Extraleague, Czech Republic); suspended late in season for 15 games after suggesting that a referee was bribed during game seven of the Vitkovice-Zlin semi-final
–played for IMG WorldStars team that toured Europe in December 2004
–played for Czech Republic at 2005 World Championship (gold medal)

KUDROC, KRISTIAN
b. Michalovce, Czechoslovakia (Slovakia), May 21, 1981

2003-04 FLO	2	0	0	0	2
NHL Totals	26	2	2	4	38

–signed December 20, 2004 by Hammarby (Swedish league, Division 2)

KUKKONEN, LASSE
b. Oulu, Finland, September 18, 1981

2003-04 CHI	10	0	1	1	4
NHL Totals	10	0	1	1	4

–signed September 11, 2004 by Karpat Oulu (SM-Liiga, Finland)
–played for Finland at 2005 World Championship

KULESHOV, MIKHAIL
b. Perm, Soviet Union (Russia), January 7, 1981

2003-04 COL	3	0	0	0	0
NHL Totals	3	0	0	0	0

–signed November 15, 2004 by Molot-Prikamie (Super League, Russia)

KUNITZ, CHRIS
b. Regina, Saskatchewan, September 26, 1979

2003-04 ANA	21	0	6	6	12
NHL Totals	21	0	6	6	12

–played 2004-05 with Cincinnati Might Ducks, Anaheim's AHL affiliate

KURKA, TOMAS
b. Most, Czechoslovakia (Czech Republic), December 14, 1981

2003-04 CAR	3	0	0	0	0
NHL Totals	17	3	2	5	2

–signed September 25, 2004 by Litvinov (Extraleague, Czech Republic)
–signed December 16, 2004 by Providence Bruins (AHL)

KUTLAK, ZDENEK
b. Budejovice, Czechoslovakia (Czech Republic), February 13, 1980

2003-04 BOS	2	0	0	0	0
NHL Totals	16	1	2	3	4

–signed May 16, 2004 by Karlovy Vary (Extraleague, Czech Republic)

KUZNETSOV, MAXIM
b. Pavlodar, Soviet Union (Kazakhstan), March 24, 1977

2003-04 LA	16	0	1	1	20
NHL Totals	136	2	8	10	137

–signed June 7, 2004 by SKA St. Petersburg (Super League, Russia)

KVASHA, OLEG
b. Moscow, Soviet Union (Russia), July 26, 1978

2003-04 NYI	81	15	36	51	48
NHL Totals	429	68	117	185	297

–signed September 25, 2004 by Severstal Cherepovits (Super League, Russia)
–loaned December 20, 2004 to CSKA Moscow (Super League, Russia)

KWIATKOWSKI, JOEL
b. Kindersley, Saskatchewan, March 22, 1977

2003-04 WAS	80	6	6	12	89
NHL Totals	149	7	11	18	119

–played 2004-05 with San Antonio Rampage, Florida's AHL affiliate, after signing with the Panthers as a free agent in the summer of 2004
–played part of 2004-05 with St. John's Maple Leafs (AHL)

LAAKSONEN, ANTTI
b. Tammela, Finland, October 3, 1973

2003-04 MIN	77	12	14	26	20
NHL Totals	361	62	68	130	96

–did not play professionally in 2004-05

LABARBERA, JASON
b. Burnaby, British Columbia, January 18, 1980

2003-04 NYR	4	1-2-0	198	16	0	4.85
NHL Totals	5	1-2-0	208	16	0	4.62

–played 2004-05 with Hartford Wolf Pack, New York Rangers' AHL affiliate

LACHANCE, SCOTT
b. Charlottesville, Virginia, October 22, 1972

2003-04 CBJ	77	0	4	4	44
NHL Totals	819	31	112	143	567

–did not play professionally in 2004-05

LACOUTURE, DAN
b. Hyannis, Massachusetts, April 18, 1977

2003-04 NYR	59	5	2	7	82
NHL Totals	265	16	23	39	278

–played 2004-05 with Providence Bruins (AHL)

LAFLAMME, CHRISTIAN
b. St. Charles, Quebec, November 24, 1976

2003-04 STL	16	0	1	1	20
NHL Totals	324	2	45	47	282

–signed May 16, 2004 by Kassel (Deutsche Eishockey Liga, Germany)

LAICH, BROOKS
b. Medicine Hat, Alberta, June 23, 1983

2003-04 OTT/WAS	5	0	1	1	2
NHL Totals	5	0	1	1	2

–played 2004-05 with Portland Pirates, Washington's AHL affiliate

LAING, QUINTIN
b. Rosetown, Saskatchewan, June 8, 1979

2003-04 CHI	3	0	1	1	0
NHL Totals	3	0	1	1	0

–played 2004-05 with Norfolk Admirals, Chicago's AHL affiliate

LALIME, PATRICK
b. St. Bonaventure, Quebec, July 7, 1974

2003-04 OTT	57	25-23-7	3,324	127	5	2.29
NHL Totals	322	167-112-32	18,553	738	33	2.39

–signed by the St. Louis Blues as a free agent in the summer of 2004 but did not play professionally during 2004-05

LAMOTHE, MARC
b. New Liskeard, Ontario, February 27, 1974

2003-04 DET	2	1-0-1	125	3	0	1.44
NHL Totals	4	2-1-1	241	13	0	3.24

–signed June 14, 2004 by Lokomotiv Yaroslavl (Super League, Russia)

LAMPMAN, BRYCE
b. Rochester, Minnesota, August 31, 1982

2003-04 NYR	8	0	0	0	0
NHL Totals	8	0	0	0	0

–played 2004-05 with Hartford Wolf Pack, New York Rangers' AHL affiliate

LANG, ROBERT
b. Teplice, Czechoslovakia (Czech Republic), December 19, 1970

2003-04 WAS/DET	69	30	49	79	24
NHL Totals	646	174	293	467	170

–played for IMG WorldStars team that toured Europe in December 2004

LANGDON, DARREN
b. Deer Lake, Newfoundland, January 8, 1971

2003-04 MON	64	0	3	3	135
NHL Totals	507	16	22	38	1,229

–signed as a free agent by the New Jersey Devils in the summer of 2004
–signed with Deer Lake Red Wings of the West Coast Senior Hockey League after season officially cancelled and ran his local bar, *Langers*

LANGENBRUNNER, JAMIE
b. Duluth, Minnesota, July 24, 1975

2003-04 NJ	53	10	16	26	43
NHL Totals	577	125	197	322	492

– signed January 24, 2005 by Ingolstadt (Deutsche Eishockey Liga, Germany)

LANGFELD, JOSH
b. Fridley, Minnesota, July 17, 1977

2003-04 OTT	38	7	10	17	16
NHL Totals	51	7	11	18	22

–played 2004-05 with Binghamton Senators, Ottawa's AHL affiliate

LANGKOW, DAYMOND
b. Edmonton, Alberta, September 27, 1976

2003-04 PHO	81	21	31	52	40
NHL Totals	625	136	218	354	374

–did not play professionally in 2004-05

LAPERRIERE, IAN
b. Montreal, Quebec, January 19, 1974

2003-04 LA	62	10	12	22	58
NHL Totals	694	78	126	204	1,242

–signed by Colorado Avalanche as a free agent in the summer of 2004 but did not play professionally in 2004-05

LAPOINTE, CLAUDE
b. Lachine, Quebec, October 11, 1968

2003-04 PHI	42	5	3	8	32
NHL Totals	879	127	178	305	721

–did not play professionally in 2004-05

LAPOINTE, MARTIN
b. Ville St. Pierre, Quebec, September 12, 1973

2003-04 BOS	78	15	10	25	67
NHL Totals	757	148	165	313	1,143

–did not play professionally in 2004-05

LARAQUE, GEORGES
b. Montreal, Quebec, December 7, 1976

2003-04 EDM	66	6	11	17	99
NHL Totals	418	41	58	99	753

–signed January 31, 2005 by AIK Stockholm (Swedish league, Division 3)

LARIONOV, IGOR
b. Voskresensk, Soviet Union (Russia), December 3, 1960

2003-04 NJ	49	1	10	11	20
NHL Totals	921	169	475	644	474

–retired after 2003-04 season, though played in a farewell game in his honour in Moscow on December 13, 2004

LAROSE, CORY
b. Campbellton, New Brunswick, May 14, 1975

2003-04 NYR	7	0	1	1	4
NHL Totals	7	0	1	1	4

–played 2004-05 with Chicago Wolves, Atlanta's AHL affiliate, after signing with the Thrashers as a free agent in the summer of 2004

LARSEN, BRAD
b. Nakusp, British Columbia, June 28, 1977

2003-04 COL/ATL	32	2	2	4	13
NHL Totals	98	4	12	16	62

–played 2004-05 with Chicago Wolves, Atlanta's AHL affiliate

LAW, KIRBY
b. McCreary, Manitoba, March 11, 1977

2003-04 PHI	6	0	1	1	2
NHL Totals	9	0	1	1	4

–played 2004-05 with Houston Aeros, Minnesota's AHL affiliate, after signing with the Wild as a free agent in the summer of 2004

LEAHY, PAT
b. Brighton, Massachusetts, June 9, 1979

2003-04 BOS	6	0	0	0	0
NHL Totals	6	0	0	0	0

–played part of 2004-05 with Providence Bruins (AHL)

LECAVALIER, VINCENT
b. Ile Bizard, Quebec, April 21, 1980

2003-04 TB	81	32	34	66	52
NHL Totals	467	146	181	327	284

–signed November 4, 2004 by AK Bars Kazan (Super League, Russia)

LECLAIR, JOHN
b. St. Albans, Vermont, July 5, 1969

2003-04 PHI	75	23	32	55	51
NHL Totals	873	382	379	761	428

–curtailed workouts with other Flyers in the South Jersey area because of back pain

LECLAIRE, PASCAL
b. Repentigny, Quebec, November 7, 1982

2003-04 CBJ	2	0-2-0	119	7	0	3.53
NHL Totals	2	0-2-0	119	7	0	3.53

–played 2004-05 with Syracuse Crunch, Columbus's AHL affiliate

LECLERC, MIKE
b. Winnipeg, Manitoba, November 10, 1976

2003-04 ANA	10	1	3	4	4
NHL Totals	291	54	78	132	251

–did not play professionally in 2004-05

103

LEEB, BRAD
b. Red Deer, Alberta, August 27, 1979

2003-04 TML	1	0	0	0	0
NHL Totals	5	0	0	0	2

–played 2004-05 with St. John's Maple Leafs, Toronto's AHL affiliate

LEETCH, BRIAN
b. Corpus Christi, Texas, March 3, 1968

2003-04 NYR/TML	72	15	36	51	34
NHL Totals	1,144	242	754	996	535

–did not play professionally in 2004-05
–spent part of the season fishing in the Bahamas with Mark Messier and the rest of the year with his family in Cape Cod; did not play professionally in 2004-05

LEGACE, MANNY
b. Toronto, Ontario, February 4, 1973

2003-04 DET	41	23-10-5	2,325	82	3	2.12
NHL Totals	146	77-35-18	8,123	301	6	2.22

–signed December 20, 2004 by Khimik Voskresensk (Super League, Russia); returned in early 2005 to Toronto and stayed with his parents

LEGWAND, DAVID
b. Detroit, Michigan, August 17, 1980

2003-04 NAS	82	18	29	47	46
NHL Totals	362	72	122	194	202

–won gold medal with USA at Deutschland Cup in November 2004
–signed January 27, 2005 by Basel (Swiss league, Division 2)
–played for USA at 2005 World Championship

LEHTINEN, JERE
b. Espoo, Finland, June 24, 1973

2003-04 DAL	58	13	13	26	20
NHL Totals	568	157	184	341	134

–remained at home in Dallas with his family; did not play professionally in 2004-05

LEHTONEN, KARI
b. Helsinki, Finland, November 16, 1983

2003-04 ATL	4	4-0-0	239	5	1	1.25
NHL Totals	4	4-0-0	239	5	1	1.25

–played 2004-05 with Chicago Wolves, Atlanta's AHL affiliate

LEIGHTON, MICHAEL
b. Petrolia, Ontario, May 19, 1981

2003-04 CHI	34	6-18-8	1,988	99	2	2.99
NHL Totals	42	8-21-10	2,435	120	3	2.96

–played 2004-05 with Norfolk Admirals, Chicago's AHL affiliate

LEMIEUX, MARIO
b. Montreal, Quebec, October 5, 1965

2003-04 PIT	10	1	8	9	6
NHL Totals	889	683	1,018	1,701	818

–Pittsburgh Penguins owner did not play professionally in 2004-05

LEOPOLD, JORDAN
b. Golden Valley, Minnesota, August 3, 1980

2003-04 CAL	82	9	24	33	24
NHL Totals	140	13	34	47	36

–continued his recovery from a concussion he suffered prior to the World Cup of Hockey 2004 and skated with his local university team in Minnesota
–played for USA at 2005 World Championship

LESCHYSHYN, CURTIS
b. Thompson, Manitoba, September 21, 1969

2003-04 OTT	56	1	4	5	16
NHL Totals	1,033	47	165	212	669

–remained in Denver and skated with NHLers in the area; did not play professionally in 2004-05

LESSARD, FRANCIS
b. Montreal, Quebec, May 30, 1979

2003-04 ATL	62	1	1	2	181
NHL Totals	85	1	3	4	268

–did not play professionally in 2004-05

LETOWSKI, TREVOR
b. Thunder Bay, Ontario, April 5, 1977

2003-04 CBJ	73	15	17	32	16
NHL Totals	399	63	84	147	125

–signed January 7, 2005 by Fribourg-Gotteron (Swiss league)

LIDSTROM, NICKLAS
b. Vasteras, Sweden, April 28, 1970

2003-04 DET	81	10	18	38	18
NHL Totals	1,016	173	553	726	276

– did not play professionally in 2004-05

LILES, JOHN-MICHAEL
b. Zionsville, Indiana, November 25, 1980

2003-04 COL	79	10	24	34	28
NHL Totals	79	10	24	34	28

–signed August 22, 2004 by Kassel (Deutsche Eishockey Liga, Germany)
–played for IMG WorldStars team that toured Europe in December 2004
–signed December 29, 2004 by Iserlohn (Deutsche Eishockey Liga, Germany)
–played for USA at 2005 World Championship

LILJA, ANDREAS
b. Landskrona, Sweden, July 13, 1975

2003-04 FLO	79	3	4	7	90
NHL Totals	180	8	19	27	186

–signed September 15, 2004 by Mora (Swedish Elite League); suspended by Mora in early February for the rest of the season after he and fellow Swedes Kristian Huselius and Henrik Tallinder were accused of (and later acquitted of) rape
–signed February 25, 2005 by Ambri-Piotta (Swiss league), two days after Swedish police re-opened the case (which was later dropped)

LINDEN, TREVOR
b. Medicine Hat, Alberta, April 11, 1970

2003-04 VAN	82	14	22	36	26
NHL Totals	1,161	349	465	814	831

–president of NHLPA did not play professionally in 2004-05

LINDROS, ERIC
b. London, Ontario, February 28, 1973

2003-04 NYR	39	10	22	32	60
NHL Totals	678	356	461	817	1,285

–did not play professionally in 2004-05
–studied Business at University of Toronto

LINDSAY, BILL
b. Fernie, British Columbia, May 17, 1971

2003-04 ATL	24	0	0	0	25
NHL Totals	777	83	141	224	922

–began 2004-05 playing with Toronto in Original Stars Hockey League
–played 2004-05 for Long Beach Ice Dogs (ECHL)

LING, DAVID
b. Halifax, Nova Scotia, January 9, 1975

2003-04 CBJ	50	1	2	3	98
NHL Totals	93	4	4	8	191

–played 2004-05 with St. John's Maple Leafs (AHL)

LITTLE, NEIL
b. Medicine Hat, Alberta, December 18, 1971

2003-04 PHI	1	0-1-0	33	2	0	3.64
NHL Totals	2	0-2-0	93	6	0	3.87

–played 2004-05 with Philadelphia Phantoms, Philadelphia Flyers'
  AHL affiliate

LOMBARDI, MATT
b. Montreal, Quebec, March 18, 1982

2003-04 CAL	79	16	13	29	32
NHL Totals	79	16	13	29	32

–played the last part of 2004-05 with Lowell Lock Monsters,
  Calgary's AHL affiliate, after missing most of the year with post-
  concussion symptoms resulting from an eblow received during
  2004 playoffs

LOW, REED
b. Moose Jaw, Saskatchewan, June 21, 1976

2003-04 STL	57	0	2	2	141
NHL Totals	250	3	16	19	694

–remained in St. Louis where he owned and operated a salon called
  Uppercuts

LOWRY, DAVE
b. Sudbury, Ontario, February 14, 1965

2003-04 CAL	18	1	1	2	11
NHL Totals	1,084	164	187	351	1,191

–did not play professionally in 2004-05

LOYNS, LYNN
b. Naicam, Saskatchewan, February 21, 1981

2003-04 SJ/CAL	14	0	2	2	2
NHL Totals	33	3	2	5	21

–played 2004-05 with Lowell Lock Monsters, Calgary's
  AHL affiliate

LUKOWICH, BRAD
b. Cranbrook, British Columbia, August 12, 1976

2003-04 TB	79	5	14	19	24
NHL Totals	373	15	48	63	257

–played 2004-05 with Fort Worth Brahmas (CHL)

LUNDMARK, JAMIE
b. Edmonton, Alberta, January 16, 1981

2003-04 NYR	56	2	8	10	33
NHL Totals	111	10	19	29	49

–signed September 21, 2004 by Bolzano (Serie A, Italy)
–played most of 2004-05 with Hartford Wolf Pack, New York
  Rangers' AHL affiliate

LUOMA, MIKKO
b. Jyvaskyla, Finland, June 22, 1976

2003-04 EDM	3	0	1	1	0
NHL Totals	3	0	1	1	0

–signed June 9, 2004 by Malmo (Swedish Elite League)

LUONGO, ROBERTO
b. Montreal, Quebec, April 4, 1979

2003-04 FLO	72	25-33-14	4,252	172	7	2.43
NHL Totals	266	80-138-33	14,829	653	23	2.64

–married on June 18, 2005 in Florida
–played for Canada at 2005 World Championship (silver medal)

LUPUL, JOFFREY
b. Edmonton, Alberta, September 23, 1983

2003-04 ANA	75	13	21	34	28
NHL Totals	75	13	21	34	28

–played 2004-05 with Cincinnati Mighty Ducks, Anaheim's
  AHL affiliate

LYDMAN, TONI
b. Lahti, Finland, September 25, 1977

2003-04 CAL	67	4	16	20	30
NHL Totals	289	19	74	93	140

–spent first part of 2004-05 recovering from a concussion suffered
  late in the '03-'04 season
–signed January 31, 2005 by HIFK Helsinki (SM-Liiga, Finland)

LYNCH, DOUG
b. North Vancouver, British Columbia, April 4, 1983

2003-04 EDM	2	0	0	0	0
NHL Totals	2	0	0	0	0

–played 2004-05 with Edmonton Road Runners, Edmonton Oilers'
  AHL affiliate

LYSAK, BRETT
b. Edmonton, Alberta, December 30, 1980

2003-04 CAR	2	0	0	0	2
NHL Totals	2	0	0	0	2

–played 2004-05 with Iserlohn (Deutsche Eishockey Liga,
  Germany)

MACDONALD, CRAIG
b. Antigonish, Nova Scotia, April 7, 1977

2003-04 FLO/BOS	52	0	6	6	33
NHL Totals	110	2	10	12	53

–played 2004-05 with Lowell Lock Monsters (AHL)

MACDONALD, JASON
b. Charlottetown, Prince Edward Island, April 1, 1974

2003-04 NYR	4	0	0	0	19
NHL Totals	4	0	0	0	19

–split 2004-05 between Regina Pats (WHL) and St. John's Maple
  Leafs (AHL)

MACINNIS, AL
b. Inverness, Nova Scotia, July 11, 1963

2003-04 STL	3	0	2	2	6
NHL Totals	1,416	340	934	1,274	1,511

–missed most of 2003-04 with serious eye injury and did not play
  professionally in 2004-05
–spent most of 2004-05 coaching his son's pee wee team in St.
  Louis where 12-year-old Carson played

MACKENZIE, DEREK
b. Sudbury, Ontario, June 11, 1981

2003-04 ATL	12	0	1	1	10
NHL Totals	13	0	1	1	12

–played 2004-05 with Chicago Wolves, Atlanta's AHL affiliate

MACLEAN, DON
b. Sydney, Nova Scotia, January 14, 1977

2003-04 CBJ	4	1	0	1	0
NHL Totals	29	6	3	9	6

–signed July 2, 2004 by Espoo (SM-Liiga, Finland)

MACMILLAN, JEFF
b. Durham, Ontario, March 30, 1979

2003-04 DAL	4	0	0	0	0
NHL Totals	4	0	0	0	0

–played 2004-05 with Hartford Wolf Pack, New York Rangers'
  AHL affiliate, after signing with the Rangers as a free agent in the
  summer of 2004

MADDEN, JOHN
b. Barrie, Ontario, May 4, 1973

2003-04 NJ	80	12	23	35	22
NHL Totals	400	85	78	163	91

–signed November 29, 2004 by HIFK Helsinki (SM-Liiga, Finland); left team on December 12, 2004

MAIR, ADAM
b. Hamilton, Ontario, February 15, 1979

2003-04 BUF	81	6	14	20	146
NHL Totals	212	14	28	42	375

–did not play professionally in 2004-05

MAJESKY, IVAN
b. Banska Bystrica, Czechoslovakia (Slovakia), September 2, 1976

2003-04 ATL	63	3	7	10	76
NHL Totals	145	7	15	22	168

–signed November 12, 2004 by Sparta Praha (Extraleague, Czech Republic); played for Sparta Praha at 2005 Spengler Cup (December 26-31, 2004)
–played for Slovakia at 2005 World Championship

MALAKHOV, VLADIMIR
b. Sverdlovsk, Soviet Union (Russia), August 30, 1968

2003-04 NYR/PHI	62	3	16	19	55
NHL Totals	683	82	255	337	671

–did not play professionally in 2004-05

MALEC, TOMAS
b. Skalica, Czechoslovakia (Slovakia), May 13, 1982

2003-04 CAR	2	0	0	0	2
NHL Totals	43	0	2	2	45

–played 2004-05 with Cincinnati Mighty Ducks, Anaheim's AHL affiliate, after being traded to Anaheim in the summer of 2004

MALHOTRA, MANNY
b. Mississauga, Ontario, May 18, 1980

2003-04 DAL/CBJ	65	12	13	25	28
NHL Totals	346	35	42	77	165

–signed October 8, 2004 by ZM Olimpija (Slovenian league)
–signed December 20, 2004 by HV 71 Jonkoping (Swedish Elite League)

MALIK, MAREK
b. Ostrava, Czechoslovakia (Czech Republic), June 24, 1975

2003-04 VAN	78	3	16	19	45
NHL Totals	464	27	87	114	388

–signed September 17, 2004 by Vitkovice (Extraleague, Czech Republic)

MALONE, RYAN
b. Pittsburgh, Pennsylvania, December 1, 1979

2003-04 PIT	81	22	21	43	64
NHL Totals	81	22	21	43	64

–signed September 29, 2004 by Espoo (SM-Liiga, Finland); released by Espoo on October 28, 2004 after a poor start
–won gold medal with USA at Deutschland Cup in November 2004
–signed January 3, 2005 by SV Ritten Renon (Serie A, Italy)
–signed February 25, 2005 by Ambri-Piotta (Swiss league)

MALTBY, KIRK
b. Guelph, Ontario, December 22, 1972

2003-04 DET	79	14	19	33	80
NHL Totals	717	102	109	221	645

–played for Canada at 2005 World Championship (silver medal)

MANLOW, ERIC
b. Belleville, Ontario, April 7, 1975

2003-04 NYI	18	0	2	2	2
NHL Totals	37	2	4	6	8

–played 2004-05 with Grand Rapids Griffins, Detroit's AHL affiliate, after signing with the Red Wings as a free agent in the summer of 2004

MAPLETOFT, JUSTIN
b. Lloydminster, Saskatchewan, January 11, 1981

2003-04 NYI	27	1	4	5	6
NHL Totals	38	3	6	9	8

–played 2004-05 with Bridgeport Sound Tigers, New York Islanders' AHL affiliate

MARA, PAUL
b. Ridgewood, New Jersey, September 7, 1979

2003-04 PHO	81	6	36	42	48
NHL Totals	346	37	94	131	311

–signed October 29, 2004 by Hannover (Deutsche Eishockey Liga, Germany)
–won gold medal with USA at Deutschland Cup in November 2004

MARCHANT, TODD
b. Buffalo, New York, August 12, 1973

2003-04 CBJ	77	9	25	34	34
NHL Totals	756	145	232	377	524

–did not play professionally in 2004-05

MARCHMENT, BRYAN
b. Scarborough (Toronto), Ontario, May 1, 1969

2003-04 TML	75	1	3	4	106
NHL Totals	889	39	140	179	2,232

–remained at home in Toronto working at his own business re-fitting trucks

MARKKANEN, JUSSI
b. Imatra, Finland, May 8, 1975

2003-04 NYR/EDM	33	10-14-3	1,638	65	2	2.38
NHL Totals	69	23-26-8	3,602	140	7	2.33

–signed September 25, 2004 by Lada Togliatti (Super League, Russia)

MARKOV, ANDREI
b. Voskresensk, Soviet Union (Russia), December 20, 1978

2003-04 MON	69	6	22	28	20
NHL Totals	267	30	82	112	96

–signed June 19, 2004 by Moscow Dynamo (Super League, Russia)
–played for Russia at 2005 World Championship (bronze medal)

MARKOV, DANNY
b. Moscow, Soviet Union (Russia), July 30, 1976

2003-04 CAR/PHI	78	6	13	19	95
NHL Totals	414	25	95	120	335

–signed November 15, 2004 by Vityaz Chekhov (Russian league, Division 2)

MARLEAU, PATRICK
b. Aneroid, Saskatchewan, September 15, 1979

2003-04 SJ	80	28	29	57	24
NHL Totals	558	153	174	327	193

–remained on the family farm in Aneroid for most of the year
–played for Canada at 2005 World Championship (silver medal)

Bryan McCabe had a not very successful run with HV 71 Jonkoping in Sweden, playing only a few games before being released.

MARSHALL, GRANT
b. Mississauga, Ontario, June 9, 1973

2003-04 NJ	65	8	7	15	67
NHL Totals	624	84	130	214	723

–remained at home with his family in P.E.I.; did not play professionally in 2004-05

MARSHALL, JASON
b. Cranbrook, British Columbia, February 22, 1971

2003-04 MIN/SJ	24	1	6	7	26
NHL Totals	503	16	47	63	970

–signed January 22, 2005 by Plzen (Extraleague, Czech Republic)

MARTENSSON, TONY
b. Upplands Vasby, Sweden, June 23, 1980

2003-04 ANA	6	1	1	2	0
NHL Totals	6	1	1	2	0

–signed May 17, 2004 by Linkoping (Swedish Elite League)

MARTIN, PAUL
b. Minneapolis, Minnesota, March 5, 1981

2003-04 NJ	70	6	18	24	4
NHL Totals	70	6	18	24	4

–signed November 4, 2004 by Fribourg-Gotteron (Swiss league)
–won gold medal with USA at Deutschland Cup in November 2004
–played for USA at 2005 World Championship

MARTINEK, RADEK
b. Havlickuv Brod, Czechoslovakia (Czech Republic), August 31, 1976

2003-04 NYI	47	4	3	7	43
NHL Totals	136	7	18	25	85

–signed September 17, 2004 by Ceske Budejovice (Czech Republic league, Division 2)

MARTINS, STEVE
b. Gatineau, Quebec, April 13, 1972

2003-04 STL	25	1	0	1	22
NHL Totals	263	20	24	44	142

–signed September 7, 2004 by JYP Jyvaskyla (SM-Liiga, Finland)

MASON, CHRIS
b. Red Deer, Alberta, April 20, 1976

2003-04 NAS	17	4-4-1	744	27	1	2.18
NHL Totals	21	4-5-1	872	35	1	2.41

–signed November 30, 2004 by Valerenga (Norwegian league)

MATVICHUK, RICHARD
b. Edmonton, Alberta, February 5, 1973

2003-04 DAL	75	1	20	21	36
NHL Totals	733	38	129	167	584

–signed February 2, 2005 by Slovan Bratislava (Extraleague, Slovakia); left Slovan Bratislava on February 8, 2005

MAULDIN, GREG
b. Boston, Massachusetts, June 10, 1982

2003-04 CBJ	6	0	0	0	4
NHL Totals	6	0	0	0	4

–played 2004-05 with Syracuse Crunch, Columbus's AHL affiliate

MAY, BRAD
b. Toronto, Ontario, November 29, 1971

2003-04 VAN	70	5	6	11	137
NHL Totals	804	120	146	266	1,937

–organized a charity game on December 12, 2004 at the Pacific Coliseum, Vancouver

MAYERS, JAMAL
b. Toronto, Ontario, October 24, 1974

2003-04 STL	80	6	5	11	91
NHL Totals	368	36	47	83	447

–began 2004-05 playing with Toronto in Original Stars Hockey League
–signed November 16, 2004 by Hammarby (Swedish league, Division 2)
–finished 2004-05 with Missouri River Otters (UHL)

MCALLISTER, CHRIS
b. Saskatoon, Saskatchewan, June 16, 1975

2003-04 COL/NYR	46	0	1	1	74
NHL Totals	301	4	17	21	634

–signed January 7, 2005 by Newcastle Vipers (British Ice Hockey League, UK)

MCAMMOND, DEAN
b. Grand Cache, Alberta, June 15, 1973

2003-04 CAL	64	17	13	30	18
NHL Totals	645	135	192	327	354

–played 2004-05 with Albany River Rats (AHL)

MCCABE, BRYAN
b. St. Catharines, Ontario, June 8, 1975

2003-04 TML	75	16	37	53	86
NHL Totals	708	76	194	270	1,262

–signed October 29, 2004 by HV 71 Jonkoping (Swedish Elite League); left HV 71 on December 12, 2004 and returned to his family on Long Island
–spent most of season advising teammates of NHL-NHLPA negotiations as player rep for Toronto

MCCARTHY, SANDY
b. Toronto, Ontario, June 15, 1972

2003-04 BOS/NYR	50	4	1	5	30
NHL Totals	736	72	76	148	1,534

–did not play professionally in 2004-05

MCCARTHY, STEVE
b. Trail, British Columbia, February 3, 1981

2003-04 CHI	25	1	3	4	8
NHL Totals	134	3	13	16	45

–did not play professionally in 2004-05

MCCARTY, DARREN
b. Burnaby, British Columbia, April 1, 1972

2003-04 DET	43	6	5	11	50
NHL Totals	643	119	154	273	1,275

–spent part of the season touring with his band, Grinder

MCCAULEY, ALYN
b. Brockville, Ontario, May 29, 1977

2003-04 SJ	82	20	27	47	28
NHL Totals	402	56	83	139	84

–returned home to Gananoque, Ontario, and took courses through Athabasca University

MCCORMICK, CODY
b. London, Ontario, April 18, 1983

2003-04 COL	44	2	3	5	73
NHL Totals	44	2	3	5	73

–played 2004-05 with Hershey Bears, Colorado's AHL affiliate

MCDONALD, ANDY
b. Strathroy, Ontario, August 25, 1977

2003-04 ANA	79	9	21	30	24
NHL Totals	194	27	53	80	54

–signed September 17, 2004 by Ingolstadt (Deutsche Eishockey Liga, Germany)

MCDONELL, KENT
b. Williamstown, Ontario, March 1, 1979

2003-04 CBJ	29	1	2	3	36
NHL Totals	32	1	2	3	36

–started 2004-05 with Dundas Real McCoys (OHA Senior A)
–signed December 30, 2004 by Duisburg (German league, Division 2)
–also played 2004-05 with Bergen Flyers (Norwegian league)

MCEACHERN, SHAWN
b. Waltham, Massachusetts, February 28, 1969

2003-04 ATL	82	17	38	55	76
NHL Totals	883	254	317	571	484

–signed January 24, 2005 by Malmo (Swedish Elite League)

MCGILLIS, DAN
b. Hawkesbury, Ontario, July 1, 1972

2003-04 BOS	80	5	23	28	65
NHL Totals	607	56	176	232	534

–did not play professionally in 2004-05

MCKEE, JAY
b. Kingston, Ontario, September 8, 1977

2003-04 BUF	43	2	3	5	41
NHL Totals	507	12	70	82	413

–remained in the Buffalo area and skated with other Sabres players

MCKENNA, STEVE
b. Toronto, Ontario, August 21, 1973

2003-04 PIT	49	1	2	3	85
NHL Totals	373	18	14	32	824

–signed October 26, 2004 by Nottingham Panthers (Elite Ice Hockey League, UK)

MCKENZIE, JIM
b. Gull Lake, Saskatchewan, November 3, 1969

2003-04 NAS	61	1	3	4	88
NHL Totals	880	48	52	100	1,739

–remained in Nashville for the balance of the season

MCLAREN, KYLE
b. Humboldt, Saskatchewan, June 18, 1977

2003-04 SJ	64	2	22	24	60
NHL Totals	514	36	120	156	460

–did not play professionally in 2004-05

MCLAREN, STEVE
b. Owen Sound, Ontario, February 3, 1975

2003-04 STL	6	0	0	0	25
NHL Totals	6	0	0	0	25

–played 2004-05 with Springfield Falcons, Tampa Bay's AHL affiliate, after signing with the Lightning as a free agent in the summer of 2004

MCLEAN, BRETT
b. Comox, British Columbia, August 14, 1978

2003-04 CHI	76	11	20	31	54
NHL Totals	78	11	20	31	54

–signed September 24, 2004 by Malmo (Swedish Elite League)

MCLENNAN, JAMIE
b. Edmonton, Alberta, June 30, 1971

2003-04 CAL/NYR	30	13-12-3	1,690	65	4	2.31
NHL Totals	228	75-100-33	12,623	551	13	2.62

–signed February 17, 2005 by Guildford Flames (British Ice Hockey League, UK)

MCNEILL, GRANT
b. Vermillion, Alberta, June 8, 1983

2003-04 FLO	3	0	0	0	5
NHL Totals	3	0	0	0	5

–split 2004-05 with San Antonio Rampage, Florida's AHL affiliate, and Texas Wildcatters (ECHL)

MELICHAR, JOSEF
b. Ceske Budejovice, Czechoslovakia (Czech Republic), January 20, 1979

2003-04 PIT	82	3	5	8	62
NHL Totals	168	3	10	13	153

–signed September 17, 2004 by Sparta Praha (Extraleague, Czech Republic)

MELLANBY, SCOTT
b. Montreal, Quebec, June 11, 1966

2003-04 STL	68	14	17	31	76
NHL Totals	1,291	340	430	770	2,361

–signed with Atlanta as a free agent in the summer of 2004 but did not play professionally in 2004-05
–spent 2004-05 as an assistant coach for the Missouri River Otters (UHL)

MELOCHE, ERIC
b. Montreal, Quebec, May 1, 1976

2003-04 PIT	25	3	7	10	20
NHL Totals	61	8	9	17	32

–played 2004-05 with Philadelphia Phantoms, Philadelphia Flyers' AHL affiliate, after signing with the Flyers as a free agent in the summer of 2004

MESSIER, ERIC
B. Drummondville, Quebec, October 29, 1973

2003-04 FLO	21	0	3	3	16
NHL Totals	406	25	50	75	146

–did not play professionally in 2004-05

MESSIER, MARK
b. Edmonton, Alberta, January 18, 1961

2003-04 NYR	76	18	25	43	42
NHL Totals	1,756	694	1,193	1,887	1,910

–did not play professionally in 2004-05

MEYER, FREDDY
b. Sanbornville, New Hampshire, January 4, 1981

2003-04 PHI	1	0	0	0	0
NHL Totals	1	0	0	0	0

–played 2004-05 with Philadelphia Phantoms, Philadelphia Flyers' AHL affiliate

MEZEI, BRANISLAV
b. Nitra, Czechoslovakia (Slovakia), October 8, 1980

2003-04 FLO	45	0	7	7	80
NHL Totals	122	3	13	16	155

–signed September 25, 2004 by Trinec (Extraleague, Czech Republic)
–played for Slovakia at Deutschland Cup in November 2004
–signed January 30, 2005 by Dukla Trencin (Extraleague, Slovakia)

MICHALEK, MILAN
b. Jindrichuv Hradec, Czechoslovakia (Czech Republic), December 7, 1984

2003-04 SJ	2	1	0	1	4
NHL Totals	2	1	0	1	4

–played 2004-05 with Cleveland Barons, San Jose's AHL affiliate

MICHALEK, ZBYNEK
b. Jindrichuv Hradec, Czechoslovakia (Czech Republic),
December 23, 1982

2003-04 MIN	22	1	1	2	4
NHL Totals	22	1	1	2	4

–played 2004-05 with Houston Aeros, Minnesota's AHL affiliate

MIETTINEN, ANTTI
b. Hameenlinna, Finland, July 3, 1980

2003-04 DAL	16	1	0	1	0
NHL Totals	16	1	0	1	0

–started 2004-05 in Finland
–played most of 2004-05 with Hamilton Bulldogs (AHL)

MILLER, AARON
b. Buffalo, New York, August 11, 1971

2003-04 LA	35	1	2	3	32
NHL Totals	482	24	70	94	303

–played for USA at 2005 World Championship

MILLER, KEVIN
b. Lansing, Michigan, September 1, 1965

2003-04 DET	4	0	2	2	0
NHL Totals	620	150	185	335	429

–played part of 2004-05 with Flint Generals (UHL)

MILLER, KIP
b. Lansing, Michigan, June 11, 1969

2003-04 WAS	66	9	22	31	8
NHL Totals	449	74	165	239	105

–played 2004-05 with Grand Rapids Griffins (AHL)

MILLER, RYAN
b. East Lansing, Michigan, July 17, 1980

2003-04 BUF	3	0-3-0	178	15	0	5.06
NHL Totals	18	6-11-1	1,090	55	1	3.03

–played 2004-05 with Rochester Americans, Buffalo's AHL affiliate

MILLEY, NORM
b. Toronto, Ontario, February 14, 1980

2003-04 BUF	2	0	0	0	2
NHL Totals	15	0	3	3	8

–played 2004-05 with Rochester Americans, Buffalo's AHL affiliate

MINK, GRAHAM
b. Stowe, Vermont, May 21, 1979

2003-04 WAS	2	0	0	0	2
NHL Totals	2	0	0	0	2

–played 2004-05 with Portland Pirates, Washington's AHL affiliate

MIRONOV, BORIS
b. Moscow, Soviet Union (Russia), March 21, 1972

2003-04 NYR	75	3	13	16	86
NHL Totals	716	76	231	307	891

–did not play professionally in 2004-05

MITCHELL, WILLIE
b. Port McNeill, British Columbia, April 23, 1977

2003-04 MIN	70	1	13	14	83
NHL Totals	242	7	44	51	275

–did not play professionally in 2004-05

MODANO, MIKE
b. Livonia, Michigan, June 7, 1970

2003-04 DAL	76	14	30	44	46
NHL Totals	1,101	458	648	1,106	714

–played for USA at 2005 World Championship

MODIN, FREDRIK
b. Sundsvall, Sweden, October 8, 1974

2003-04 TB	82	29	28	57	32
NHL Totals	585	152	156	308	259

–signed October 5, 2004 by Timra (Swedish Elite League)

MODRY, JAROSLAV
b. Ceske Budejovice, Czechoslovakia (Czech Republic),
February 27, 1971

2003-04 LA	79	5	27	32	44
NHL Totals	490	40	145	185	330

–signed October 20, 2004 by Liberec (Extraleague, Czech
Republic)

MOEN, TRAVIS
b. Stewart Valley, Saskatchewan, April 6, 1982

2003-04 CHI	82	4	2	6	142
NHL Totals	82	4	2	6	142

–played 2004-05 with Norfolk Admirals, Chicago's AHL affiliate

MOGILNY, ALEXANDER
b. Khabarovsk, Soviet Union (Russia), February 18, 1969

2003-04 TML	37	8	22	30	12
NHL Totals	956	461	546	1,007	426

–underwent second hip surgery and spent the rest of the season on
the Injured Reserve List

MONTADOR, STEVE
b. Vancouver, British Columbia, December 21, 1979

2003-04 CAL	26	1	2	3	50
NHL Totals	87	3	5	8	190

–signed September 17, 2004 by Mulhouse (French league); left
Mulhouse on January 25, 2005

MOORE, DOMINIC
b. Thornhill, Ontario, August 3, 1980

2003-04 NYR	5	0	3	3	0
NHL Totals	5	0	3	3	0

–played 2004-05 with Hartford Wolf Pack, New York Rangers'
AHL affiliate

MOORE, STEVE
b. Windsor, Ontario, September 22, 1978

2003-04 COL	57	5	7	12	37
NHL Totals	69	5	7	12	41

–suffered career-threatening injuries on March 3, 2004 and has yet
to play again
–filed civil suit in Denver against Todd Bertuzzi in February 2005
alleging civil conspiracy, assault, battery, negligence, and outra-
geous behaviour

MORAN, BRAD
b. Abbotsford, British Columbia, March 20, 1979

2003-04 CBJ	2	1	1	2	2
NHL Totals	5	1	1	2	2

–played 2004-05 with Syracuse Crunch, Columbus's AHL affiliate

MORAN, IAN
b. Cleveland, Ohio, August 24, 1972

2003-04 BOS	35	1	4	5	28
NHL Totals	476	20	49	69	311

–began 2004-05 playing with Toronto in Original Stars Hockey
League
–signed November 3, 2004 by Bofors IK (Swedish league, Division
2); left Bofors IK on December 12, 2004 after struggling to adapt
–signed January 22, 2005 by Nottingham Panthers (Elite Ice
Hockey League, UK)

MOREAU, ETHAN
b. Huntsville, Ontario, September 22, 1975

2003-04 EDM	81	20	12	32	96
NHL Totals	604	105	91	196	733

–signed December 20, 2004 by Villach (Austrian league)

MORGAN, GAVIN
b. Scarborough (Toronto), Ontario, July 9, 1976

2003-04 DAL	6	0	0	0	21
NHL Totals	6	0	0	0	21

–played 2004-05 with Hamilton Bulldogs, Montreal's AHL affiliate, after signing with the Canadiens as a free agent in the summer of 2004

MORGAN, JASON
b. St. John's, Newfoundland, October 9, 1976

2003-04 CAL/NAS	19	0	4	4	4
NHL Totals	33	1	4	5	8

–played 2004-05 with Norfolk Admirals, Chicago's AHL affiliate, after signing with the Blackhawks as a free agent in the summer of 2004

MOROZOV, ALEKSEY
b. Moscow, Soviet Union (Russia), February 16, 1977

2003-04 PIT	75	16	34	50	25
NHL Totals	451	84	135	219	98

–signed September 25, 2004 by AK Bars Kazan (Super League, Russia)

MORRIS, DEREK
b. Edmonton, Alberta, August 24, 1978

2003-04 COL/PHO	83	6	26	32	49
NHL Totals	501	51	192	243	502

–did not play professionally in 2004-05

MORRISON, BRENDAN
b. Pitt Meadows, British Columbia, August 15, 1975

2003-04 VAN	82	22	38	60	50
NHL Totals	471	111	231	342	190

–played 2004-05 with Linkoping (Swedish Elite League)
–played for Canada at 2005 World Championship (silver medal)

MORRISONN, SHAONE
b. Vancouver, British Columbia, December 23, 1982

2003-04 BOS/WAS	33	1	7	8	10
NHL Totals	44	1	7	8	18

–played 2004-05 with Portland Pirates, Washington's AHL affiliate

MORROW, BRENDEN
b. Carlyle, Saskatchewan, January 16, 1979

2003-04 DAL	81	25	24	49	121
NHL Totals	370	97	107	204	573

–played 2004-05 with Oklahoma City Blazers (CHL)
–played for Canada at 2005 World Championship (silver medal)

MOTZKO, JOE
b. Bemidji, Minnesota, March 14, 1980

2003-04 CBJ	2	0	0	0	0
NHL Totals	2	0	0	0	0

–played 2004-05 with Syracuse Crunch, Columbus's AHL affiliate

MOWERS, MARK
b. Decature, Georgia, February 16, 1974

2003-04 DET	52	3	8	11	4
NHL Totals	137	8	21	29	20

–began 2004-05 playing with Toronto in Original Stars Hockey League
–signed December 21, 2004 by Malmo (Swedish Elite League); left Malmo on January 24, 2005
–signed February 4, 2005 by Fribourg-Gotteron (Swiss league)

MUIR, BRYAN
b. Winnipeg, Manitoba, June 8, 1973

2003-04 LA	2	0	1	1	2
NHL Totals	181	5	15	20	167

–signed October 18, 2004 by MoDo (Swedish Elite League)
–signed January 31, 2005 by Espoo (SM-Liiga, Finland)
–played part of 2004-05 with Krefeld (Deutsche Eishockey Liga, Germany)

MUNRO, ADAM
b. St. George, Ontario, November 12, 1982

2003-04 CHI	7	1-5-1	425	26	0	3.66
NHL Totals	7	1-5-1	425	26	0	3.66

–split 2004-05 between Norfolk Admirals, Chicago's AHL affiliate, and Atlantic City Boardwalk Bullies (ECHL)

MURLEY, MATT
b. Troy, New York, December 17, 1979

2003-04 PIT	18	1	1	2	14
NHL Totals	18	1	1	2	14

–played 2004-05 with Wilkes-Barre/Scranton Penguins, Pittsburgh's AHL affiliate

MURRAY, GARTH
b. Regina, Saskatchewan, September 17, 1982

2003-04 NYR	20	1	0	1	24
NHL Totals	20	1	0	1	24

–played 2004-05 with Hartford Wolf Pack, New York Rangers' AHL affiliate

MURRAY, GLEN
b. Halifax, Nova Scotia, November 1, 1972

2003-04 BOS	81	32	28	60	56
NHL Totals	823	268	255	523	533

–played for IMG WorldStars team that toured Europe in December 2004

MURRAY, MARTY
b. Lylton, Manitoba, February 16, 1975

2003-04 CAR	66	5	7	12	8
NHL Totals	242	31	40	71	37

–remained at home in Clear Lake, Manitoba; did not play professionally in 2004-05

MURRAY, REM
b. Stratford, Ontario, October 9, 1972

2003-04 NAS	39	8	9	17	12
NHL Totals	551	93	120	213	159

–did not play professionally in 2004-05

MYRVOLD, ANDERS
b. Lorenskog, Norway, August 12, 1975

2003-04 DET	8	0	1	1	2
NHL Totals	33	0	5	5	12

–signed September 15, 2004 by Valerenga (Norwegian league)
–played for Norway at final Olympic qualifying tournament in February 2005

NABOKOV, EVGENI
b. Ust-Kamenogorsk (Oskemen), Soviet Union (Kazakhstan), July 25, 1975

2003-04 SJ	59	31-19-8	3,456	127	9	2.20
NHL Totals	258	121-94-29	14,698	572	26	2.34

–signed December 2, 2004 by Metallurg Magnitogorsk (Super League, Russia); played for Magnitogorsk at 2005 Spengler Cup (December 26-31, 2004)

NAGY, LADISLAV
b. Saca, Czechoslovakia (Slovakia), June 1, 1979

2003-04 PHO	55	24	28	52	46
NHL Totals	266	79	95	174	212

–signed September 17, 2004 by Kosice (Extraleague, Slovakia)
–signed December 17, 2004 by Mora (Swedish Elite League)

NASH, RICK
b. Brampton, Ontario, June 16, 1984

2003-04 CBJ	80	41	16	57	87
NHL Totals	154	58	38	96	165

–signed August 3, 2004 by Davos (Swiss league); won gold medal
  with Davos at 2005 Spengler Cup (December 26-31, 2004) and
  named tournament MVP, and later won Swiss championship
  with Davos
–played for IMG WorldStars team that toured Europe in December
  2004
–played for Canada at 2005 World Championship (silver medal)

NASH, TYSON
b. Edmonton, Alberta, March 11, 1975

2003-04 PHO	69	3	5	8	110
NHL Totals	324	27	31	58	589

–did not play professionally in 2004-05

NASLUND, MARKUS
b. Ornskoldsvik, Sweden, July 30, 1973

2003-04 VAN	78	35	49	84	58
NHL Totals	790	290	339	629	513

–signed December 20, 2004 by MoDo (Swedish Elite League)

NAZAROV, ANDREI
b. Chelyabinsk, Soviet Union (Russia), May 22, 1974

2003-04 PHO	33	1	2	3	125
NHL Totals	569	53	71	124	1,403

–signed September 25, 2004 by Avangard Omsk (Super League,
  Russia); won European Champions Cup with Avangard Omsk
–played part of 2004-05 with Metallurg Magnitogorsk (Super
  League, Russia)

NECKAR, STANISLAV
b. Ceske Budejovice, Czechoslovakia (Czech Republic),
December 22, 1975

2003-04 NAS/TB	1	0	1	1	0
NHL Totals	510	12	41	53	316

–signed December 16, 2004 by Ceske Budejovice (Czech Republic,
  Division 2)

NEDOROST, ANDREJ
b. Trencin, Czechoslovakia (Slovakia), April 30, 1980

2003-04 CBJ	9	2	0	2	6
NHL Totals	28	2	3	5	12

–signed January 22, 2005 by Karlovy Vary (Extraleague, Czech
  Republic)

NEDOROST, VACLAV
b. Budejovice, Czechoslovakia (Czech Republic), March 16, 1982

2003-04 FLO	32	4	3	7	12
NHL Totals	99	10	10	20	34

–signed September 4, 2004 by Liberec (Extraleague, Czech
  Republic)

NEDVED, PETR
b. Liberec, Czechoslovakia (Czech Republic), December 9, 1971

2003-04 NYR/EDM	81	19	27	46	46
NHL Totals	889	301	379	680	610

–signed September 17, 2004 by Sparta Praha (Extraleague, Czech
  Republic)
–played for IMG WorldStars team that toured Europe in December
  2004

NEIL, CHRIS
b. Markdale, Ontario, June 18, 1979

2003-04 OTT	82	8	8	16	194
NHL Totals	222	24	19	43	572

–played the end of 2004-05 with Binghamton Senators, Ottawa's
  AHL affiliate

NICHOL, SCOTT
b. Edmonton, Alberta, December 31, 1974

2003-04 CHI	75	7	11	18	145
NHL Totals	208	20	25	45	415

–signed October 26, 2004 by London Racers (Elite Ice Hockey
  League, UK); left London on November 25, 2005
–re-signed January 26, 2005 by London (Elite Ice Hockey League,
  Britain)

NICKULAS, ERIC
b. Hyannis, Massachusetts, March 25, 1975

2003-04 STL/CHI	65	8	12	20	52
NHL Totals	102	13	19	32	74

–played 2004-05 with Norfolk Admirals (AHL), Chicago's AHL
  affiliate, after being claimed on waivers by the Blackhawks in
  February 2004

NIEDERMAYER, ROB
b. Cassiar, British Columbia, December 28, 1974

2003-04 ANA	55	12	16	28	34
NHL Totals	696	129	207	336	575

–signed January 17, 2005 by Ferencvaros (Hungarian league)

NIEDERMAYER, SCOTT
b. Edmonton, Alberta, August 31, 1973

2003-04 NJ	81	14	40	54	44
NHL Totals	892	112	364	476	478

– did not play professionally in 2004-05

NIEMINEN, VILLE
b. Tampere, Finland, April 6, 1977

2003-04 CHI/CAL	79	5	16	21	58
NHL Totals	271	39	52	91	227

–signed July 22, 2004 by Tappara (SM-Liiga, Finland)

NIEUWENDYK, JOE
b. Oshawa, Ontario, September 10, 1966

2003-04 TML	64	22	28	50	26
NHL Totals	1,177	533	529	1,062	627

–did not play professionally in 2004-05

NIINIMAA, JANNE
b. Raahe, Finland, May 22, 1975

2003-04 NYI	82	9	19	28	64
NHL Totals	637	51	249	300	611

–signed October 6, 2004 by Karpat Oulu (SM-Liiga, Finland)
–signed November 17, 2004 by Malmo (Swedish Elite League);
  released by Malmo on December 21, 2004
–re-signed January 3, 2005 by Karpat Oulu (SM-Liiga, Finland)

NIITTYMAKI, ANTERO
b. Turku, Finland, June 18, 1980

2003-04 PHI	3	3-0-0	180	3	0	1.00
NHL Totals	3	3-0-0	180	3	0	1.00

–played 2004-05 with Philadelphia Phantoms, Philadelphia Flyers'
  AHL affiliate

NIKOLISHIN, ANDREI
b. Vorkuta, Soviet Union (Russia), March 25, 1973

2003-04 COL	49	5	7	12	24
NHL Totals	628	93	187	280	270

–signed June 4, 2004 by CSKA Moscow (Super League, Russia)

NILSON, MARCUS
b. Balsta, Sweden, March 1, 1978

2003-04 FLO/CAL	83	11	13	24	40
NHL Totals	341	53	78	131	207

–signed September 16, 2004 by Djurgarden (Swedish Elite League)

NOLAN, OWEN
b. Belfast, Ireland, February 12, 1972

2003-04 TML	65	19	29	48	110
NHL Totals	915	349	386	735	1,600

–remained with family in San Jose running his two pubs; did not play professionally in 2004-05

NORONEN, MIKA
b. Tampere, Finland, June 17, 1979

2003-04 BUF	5	11-17-2	1,796	77	2	2.57
NHL Totals	63	21-29-6	3,313	141	3	2.55

–signed November 2, 2004 by HPK Hameenlinna (SM-Liiga, Finland)

NORSTROM, MATTIAS
b. Stockholm, Sweden, January 2, 1972

2003-04 LA	74	1	13	14	44
NHL Totals	684	10	104	114	515

–played for IMG WorldStars team that toured Europe in December 2004
–signed January 11, 2005 by AIK Stockholm (Swedish league, Division 3)
–played for Sweden at 2005 World Championship

NORTON, BRAD
b. Cambridge, Massachusetts, February 13, 1975

2003-04 LA/WAS	36	0	2	2	94
NHL Totals	111	3	7	10	236

–did not play professionally in 2004-05

NOVOSELTSEV, IVAN
b. Golitsino, Soviet Union (Russia), January 23, 1979

2003-04 FLO/PHO	34	3	4	7	14
NHL Totals	234	31	44	75	112

–signed July 28, 2004 by Lada Togliatti (Super League, Russia)
–signed December 20, 2004 by Spartak Moscow (Super League, Russia)

NUMMINEN, TEPPO
b. Tampere, Finland, July 3, 1968

2003-04 DAL	62	3	14	17	18
NHL Totals	1,160	111	440	551	423

–did not play professionally in 2004-05

NURMINEN, PASI
b. Lahti, Finland, December 17, 1975

2003-04 ATL	64	25-30-7	3,738	173	3	2.78
NHL Totals	125	48-54-12	7,059	338	5	2.87

–signed September 15, 2004 by Pelicans (SM-Liiga, Finland)
–signed November 2, 2004 by Salavat Yulaev (Super League, Russia)
–signed November 8, 2004 by Malmo (Swedish Elite League)

NYCHOLAT, LAWRENCE
b. Calgary, Alberta, May 7, 1979

2003-04 NYR	9	0	0	0	6
NHL Totals	9	0	0	0	6

–played 2004-05 with Hartford Wolf Pack, New York Rangers' AHL affiliate

NYLANDER, MICHAEL
b. Stockholm, Sweden, October 3, 1972

2003-04 WAS/BOS	18	1	13	14	22
NHL Totals	648	140	307	447	294

–missed most of 2003-04 with a broken leg
–signed September 25, 2004 by Karpat Oulu (SM-Liiga, Finland); left Karpat Oulu on December 12, 2004
–signed December 20, 2004 by SKA St. Petersburg (Super League, Russia)
–signed February 14, 2005 by AK Bars Kazan (Super League, Russia)

OATES, ADAM
b. Weston, Ontario, August 27, 1962

2003-04 EDM	60	2	16	18	8
NHL Totals	1,337	341	1,079	1,420	415

–announced retirement shortly after end of 2003-04 season

ODELEIN, LYLE
b. Quill Lake, Saskatchewan, July 21, 1968

2003-04 FLO	82	4	12	16	88
NHL Totals	1,029	50	201	251	2,266

–did not play professionally in 2004-05

O'DONNELL, SEAN
b. Ottawa, Ontario, October 13, 1971

2003-04 BOS	82	1	10	11	110
NHL Totals	693	21	119	140	1,235

–played for IMG WorldStars team that toured Europe in December 2004

OHLUND, MATTIAS
b. Pitea, Sweden, September 9, 1976

2003-04 VAN	82	14	20	34	73
NHL Totals	480	54	158	212	400

–signed December 21, 2004 by Lulea (Swedish Elite League); left Lulea on December 29, 2004

OLIVER, DAVID
b. Sechelt, British Columbia, April 17, 1971

2003-04 DAL	36	7	5	12	12
NHL Totals	230	49	49	98	84

–signed January 13, 2005 by Guildford Flames (British Ice Hockey League, UK)

OLIWA, KRZYSZTOF
b. Tychy, Poland, April 12, 1973

2003-04 CAL	65	3	2	5	247
NHL Totals	407	17	28	45	1,447

–signed October 1, 2004 by Podhale Nowy Targ (Polish league)
–played for Poland at final Olympic qualifying tournament in February 2005

OLSON, JOSH
b. Grand Forks, North Dakota, July 13, 1981

2003-04 FLO	5	1	0	1	0
NHL Totals	5	1	0	1	0

–split 2004-05 between San Antonio Rampage, Florida's AHL affiliate, and Hershey Bears (AHL)

O'NEILL, JEFF
b. Richmond Hill, Ontario, February 23, 1976

2003-04 CAR	67	14	20	34	60
NHL Totals	673	198	218	416	552

–did not play professionally in 2004-05

Brad Richards of the Stanley Cup-winning Tampa Bay Lightning started 2004-05 with AK Bars Kazan before an injury sent him home.

ORPIK, BROOKS
b. San Francisco, California, September 26, 1980

2003-04 PIT	79	1	9	10	127
NHL Totals	85	1	9	10	129

–remained at home in Boston coaching his younger brother's midget club

ORR, COLTON
b. Winnipeg, Manitoba, March 3, 1982

2003-04 BOS	1	0	0	0	0
NHL Totals	1	0	0	0	0

–played 2004-05 with Providence Bruins, Boston's AHL affiliate

ORSZAGH, VLADIMIR
b. Banska Bystrica, Czechoslovakia (Slovakia), May 24, 1977

2003-04 NAS	82	16	21	37	74
NHL Totals	273	50	60	110	180

–signed October 6, 2004 by Zvolen (Extraleague, Slovakia)
–played for Slovakia at 2005 World Championship

ORTMEYER, JED
b. Omaha, Nebraska, September 3, 1978

2003-04 NYR	58	2	4	6	16
NHL Totals	58	2	4	6	16

–played 2004-05 with Hartford Wolf Pack, New York Rangers' AHL affiliate

OSGOOD, CHRIS
b. Peace River, Alberta, November 26, 1972

2003-04 STL	67	31-25-8	3,861	144	3	2.24
NHL Totals	568	305-177-66	32,604	1,324	41	2.44

–did not play professionally in 2004-05

OTT, STEVE
b. Summerside, Prince Edward Island, August 19, 1982

2003-04 DAL	73	2	10	12	152
NHL Totals	99	5	14	19	183

–played 2004-05 with Hamilton Bulldogs (AHL)

OUELLET, MAXIME
b. Beauport, Quebec, June 17, 1981

2003-04 WAS	6	2-3-1	365	19	1	3.12
NHL Totals	8	2-4-1	441	22	1	2.99

–played 2004-05 with Portland Pirates, Washington's AHL affiliate

OZOLINSH, SANDIS
b. Riga, Soviet Union (Latvia), August 3, 1972

2003-04 ANA	36	5	11	16	24
NHL Totals	779	158	367	525	578

–played for Latvia at final Olympic qualifying tournament in February 2005
–spent most of the season at home in southern California

PAHLSSON, SAMUEL
b. Ornskoldsvik, Sweden, December 17, 1977

2003-04 ANA	82	8	14	22	52
NHL Totals	272	22	44	66	116

–played 2004-05 with Vastra Frolunda (Swedish Elite League)
–plated for Sweden at 2005 World Championship

PALFFY, ZIGGY
b. Skalica, Czechoslovakia (Slovakia), May 5, 1972

2003-04 LA	35	16	25	41	12
NHL Totals	642	318	353	671	310

–signed September 15, 2004 by Sparta Praha (Extraleague, Czech Republic)
–signed October 7, 2004 by HK 36 Skalica (Extraleague, Slovakia)
–re-signed November 16, 2004 by Slavia Praha
–played for Slovakia at 2005 World Championship

PANDOLFO, JAY
b. Winchester, Massachusetts, December 27, 1974

2003-04 NJ	82	13	13	26	14
NHL Totals	488	55	78	133	92

–signed December 27, 2004 by Salzburg (Austrian league)

PANDOLFO, MIKE
b. Winchester, Massachusetts, September 15, 1979

2003-04 CBJ	3	0	0	0	0
NHL Totals	3	0	0	0	0

–played 2004-05 with Syracuse Crunch, Columbus's AHL affiliate

PAPINEAU, JUSTIN
b. Ottawa, Ontario, January 15, 1980

2003-04 NYI	64	8	5	13	8
NHL Totals	81	11	8	19	12

–played 2004-05 with Bridgeport Sound Tigers, New York Islanders' AHL affiliate

PARK, RICHARD
b. Seoul, South Korea, May 27, 1976

2003-04 MIN	73	13	12	25	28
NHL Totals	308	42	47	89	110

–signed November 8, 2004 by Malmo (Swedish Elite League); released by Malmo on December 12, 2004 because of poor play
–won gold medal with USA at Deutschland Cup in November 2004
–signed January 4, 2005 by Langnau (Swiss league)
–played for USA at 2005 World Championship

PARKER, SCOTT
b. Hanford, California, January 29, 1978

2003-04 SJ	50	1	3	4	101
NHL Totals	252	5	13	18	563

–did not play professionally in 2004-05

PARRISH, MARK
b. Edina, Minnesota, February 2, 1977

2003-04 NYI	59	24	11	35	18
NHL Totals	442	144	110	254	170

–played for USA at 2005 World Championship

PASSMORE, STEVE
b. Thunder Bay, Ontario, January 29, 1973

2003-04 CHI	9	2-6-0	478	23	0	2.89
NHL Totals	93	23-44-12	5,045	235	2	2.79

–signed August 30, 2004 by Adler Mannheim (Deutsche Eishockey Liga, Germany)

PATRICK, JAMES
b. Winnipeg, Manitoba, June 14, 1963

2003-04 BUF	55	4	7	11	12
NHL Totals	1,280	149	490	639	759

–did not play professionally in 2004-05; remained at home in Buffalo and worked out regularly in the gym and doing yoga

PAYER, SERGE
b. Rockland, Ontario, May 7, 1979

2003-04 OTT	5	0	1	1	2
NHL Totals	48	5	2	7	23

–played 2004-05 with San Antonio Rampage, Florida's AHL affiliate, after signing with the Panthers as a free agent in the summer of 2004

PEAT, STEPHEN
b. Princeton, British Columbia, March 10, 1980

2003-04 WAS	64	5	0	5	90
NHL Totals	129	8	2	10	232

–played part of 2004-05 with Danbury Trashers (UHL)

PECA, MICHAEL
b. Toronto, Ontario, March 26, 1974

2003-04 NYI	76	11	29	40	71
NHL Totals	622	151	220	371	560

–did not play professionally in 2004-05

PELLERIN, SCOTT
b. Shediac, New Brunswick, January 9, 1970

2003-04 STL	2	0	0	0	2
NHL Totals	536	72	126	198	320

–did not play professionally in 2004-05

PELLETIER, JEAN-MARC
b. Atlanta, Georgia, March 4, 1978

2003-04 PHO	4	1-1-0	175	12	0	4.11
NHL Totals	7	1-4-0	354	23	0	3.90

–split 2004-05 between Utah Grizzlies, Phoenix's AHL affiliate, and
  Springfield Falcons (AHL)

PELUSO, MIKE
b. Bismarck, North Dakota, September 2, 1974

2003-04 PHI	1	0	0	0	0
NHL Totals	38	4	2	6	19

–did not play professionally in 2004-05

PERREAULT, YANIC
b. Sherbrooke, Quebec, April 4, 1971

2003-04 MON	69	16	15	31	40
NHL Totals	671	195	212	407	314

–did not play professionally in 2004-05

PERRIN, ERIC
b. Montreal, Quebec, November 1, 1975

2003-04 TB	4	0	0	0	0
NHL Totals	4	0	0	0	0

–played 2004-05 with Hershey Bears (AHL)

PERROTT, NATHAN
b. Owen Sound, Ontario, December 8, 1976

2003-04 TML	40	1	2	3	116
NHL Totals	63	2	4	6	195

–played 2004-05 with St. John's Maple Leafs, Toronto's AHL
  affiliate

PETERS, ANDREW
b. St. Catharines, Ontario, May 5, 1980

2003-04 BUF	42	2	0	2	151
NHL Totals	42	2	0	2	151

–signed August 20, 2004 by Bodens IK (Swedish league,
  Division 2); left Bodens IK on October 20, 2004
–re-signed by Bodens IK on January 14, 2005

PETROVICKY, RONALD
b. Zilina, Czechoslovakia (Slovakia), February 15, 1977

2003-04 ATL	78	16	15	31	123
NHL Totals	251	30	36	66	339

–signed September 17, 2004 by SKP Zilina (Extraleague, Slovakia);
  left SKP Zilina on January 11, 2005
–signed January 23, 2005 by Brynas (Swedish Elite League)

PETTINEN, TOMI
b. Ylojarvi, Finland, June 17, 1977

2003-04 NYI	4	0	0	0	2
NHL Totals	6	0	0	0	2

–signed June 7, 2004 by Lukko Rauma (SM-Liiga, Finland)

PETTINGER, MATT
b. Edmonton, Alberta, October 22, 1980

2003-04 WAS	71	7	5	12	37
NHL Totals	143	14	8	22	83

–signed October 8, 2004 by ZM Olimpija (Slovenian league); left
  ZM Olimpia on December 6, 2004

PHILLIPS, CHRIS
b. Calgary, Alberta, March 9, 1978

2003-04 OTT	82	7	16	23	46
NHL Totals	467	31	88	119	286

–signed November 2, 2004 by Brynas (Swedish Elite League)
–played for Canada at 2005 World Championship (silver medal)

PIHLMAN, THOMAS
b. Espoo, Finland, November 13, 1982

2003-04 NJ	2	0	0	0	2
NHL Totals	2	0	0	0	2

–played 2004-05 with Albany River Rats, New Jersey's AHL
  affiliate

PILAR, KAREL
b. Prague, Czechoslovakia (Czech Republic), December 23, 1977

2003-04 TML	50	2	17	19	22
NHL Totals	50	6	24	30	42

–signed August 9, 2004 by Sparta Praha (Extraleague, Czech
  Republic); played for Sparta Praha at 2005 Spengler Cup
  (December 26-31, 2004)

PIRJETA, LASSE
b. Oulu, Finland, April 4, 1974

2003-04 CBJ/PIT	70	8	14	22	20
NHL Totals	121	19	24	43	32

–played 2004-05 with HIFK Helsinki (SM-Liiga, Finland); played
  for Helsinki at 2005 Spengler Cup (December 26-31, 2004)

PIRNES, ESA
b. Oulu, Finland, April 1, 1977

2003-04 LA	57	3	8	11	12
NHL Totals	57	3	8	11	12

–signed July 30, 2004 by Lukko Rauma (SM-Liiga, Finland)

PIROS, KAMIL
b. Most, Czechoslovakia (Czech Republic), November 20, 1978

2003-04 ATL/FLO	17	1	1	2	4
NHL Totals	28	4	4	8	10

–signed November 15, 2004 by Khimik Voskresensk (Super
  League, Russia)

PISANI, FERNANDO
b. Edmonton, Alberta, December 27, 1976

2003-04 EDM	76	16	14	30	46
NHL Totals	111	24	19	43	56

–signed October 24, 2004 by Langnau (Swiss league); left Langnau
  on November 8, 2004
–signed December 23, 2004 by Asiago (Serie A, Italy)

PITKANEN, JONI
b. Oulu, Finland, September 19, 1983

2003-04 PHI	71	8	19	27	44
NHL Totals	71	8	19	27	44

–played 2004-05 with Philadelphia Phantoms, Philadelphia Flyers'
  AHL affiliate

PITTIS, DOMENIC
b. Calgary, Alberta, October 1, 1974

2003-04 BUF	4	0	0	0	4
NHL Totals	86	5	11	16	71

–signed April 4, 2004 by Kloten (Swiss league)
–played for Canada at Deutschland Cup in November 2004

PIVKO, LIBOR
b. Novy Vicin, Czechoslovakia (Czech Republic), March 29, 1980

2003-04 NAS	1	0	0	0	0
NHL Totals	1	0	0	0	0

–played 2004-05 with Milwaukee Admirals, Nashville's AHL affiliate

PLEKANEC, TOMAS
b. Kladno, Czechoslovakia (Czech Republic), October 31, 1982

2003-04 MON	2	0	0	0	0
NHL Totals	2	0	0	0	0

–played 2004-05 with Hamilton Bulldogs, Montreal's AHL affiliate

POAPST, STEVE
b. Cornwall, Ontario, January 3, 1969

2003-04 CHI	53	2	2	4	26
NHL Totals	245	8	23	31	126

–did not play professionally in 2004-05

POCK, THOMAS
b. Klagenfurt, Austria, December 2, 1981

2003-04 NYR	6	2	2	4	0
NHL Totals	6	2	2	4	0

–split 2004-05 between Charlotte Checkers (ECHL) and Hartford Wolf Pack, New York Rangers' AHL affiliate, after signing with the Rangers as a free agent in the summer of 2004
–loaned February 7-16, 2005 by Hartford when Pock played for Austrian national team during final round of 2006 Olympic qualifying tournaments (Austria failed to qualify)
–played for Austria at 2005 World Championship

PODKONICKY, ANDREI
b. Zvolen, Czechoslovakia (Slovakia), May 9, 1978

2003-04 WAS	2	0	0	0	0
NHL Totals	8	1	0	1	2

–signed May 2, 2004 by Liberec (Extraleague, Czech Republic)

POHL, JOHN
b. Rochester, Minnesota, June 29, 1979

2003-04 STL	1	0	0	0	0
NHL Totals	1	0	0	0	0

–played part of 2004-05 with Worcester IceCats, St. Louis's AHL affiliate

POLLOCK, JAME
b. Quebec City, Quebec, June 16, 1979

2003-04 STL	9	0	0	0	6
NHL Totals	9	0	0	0	6

–signed April 6, 2004 by Kloten (Swiss league)
–played for Canada at Deutschland Cup in November 2004
–signed February 22, 2005 by Lugano (Swiss league)

POMINVILLE, JASON
b. Repentigny, Quebec, November 30, 1982

2003-04 BUF	1	0	0	0	0
NHL Totals	1	0	0	0	0

–played 2004-05 with Rochester Americans, Buffalo's AHL affiliate

PONIKAROVSKY, ALEXEI
b. Kiev, Soviet Union (Ukraine), April 9, 1980

2003-04 TML	73	9	19	28	44
NHL Totals	116	12	25	37	69

–signed November 13, 2004 by Khimik Voskresensk (Super League, Russia)

POPOVIC, MARK
b. Stoney Creek, Ontario, October 11, 1982

2003-04 ANA	1	0	0	0	0
NHL Totals	1	0	0	0	0

–played 2004-05 with Cincinnati Mighty Ducks, Anaheim's AHL affiliate

POTHIER, BRIAN
b. New Bedford, Massachusetts, April 15, 1977

2003-04 OTT	55	2	6	8	24
NHL Totals	105	7	16	23	54

–played 2004-05 with Binghamton Senators, Ottawa's AHL affiliate

POTI, TOM
b. Worcester, Massachusetts, March 22, 1977

2003-04 NYR	67	10	14	24	47
NHL Totals	443	49	136	185	316

–remained at home in New England; did not play professionally in 2004-05

POTVIN, FELIX
b. Anjou, Quebec, June 23, 1971

2003-04 BOS	28		12-8-6	1,605	67	4 2.50
NHL Totals	635		266-260-85	36,765	1,694	32 2.76

–did not play professionally in 2004-05

PRATT, NOLAN
b. Fort McMurray, Alberta, August 14, 1975

2003-04 TB	58	1	3	4	42
NHL Totals	374	7	34	41	403

–began 2004-05 playing with Detroit in Original Stars Hockey League
–signed January 15, 2005 by Duisburg (German league, Division 2)

PREISSING, TOM
b. Rosemount, Minnesota, December 3, 1978

2003-04 SJ	69	2	17	19	12
NHL Totals	69	2	17	19	12

–signed November 15, 2004 by Krefeld (Deutsche Eishockey Liga, Germany)
–won gold medal with USA at Deutschland Cup in November 2004

PRIMEAU, KEITH
b. Toronto, Ontario, November 24, 1971

2003-04 PHI	54	7	15	22	80
NHL Totals	900	265	347	612	1,535

–skated with other Flyers in South Jersey; did not play professionally in 2004-05

PRIMEAU, WAYNE
b. Scarborough (Toronto), Ontario, June 4, 1976

2003-04 SJ	72	9	20	29	90
NHL Totals	499	42	86	128	546

–remained at home in Toronto working out; did not play professionally in 2004-05

PRONGER, CHRIS
b. Dryden, Ontario, October 10, 1974

2003-04 STL	80	14	40	54	88
NHL Totals	722	94	306	400	1,098

–attended Webster University in St. Louis during 2004-05 season, taking courses in business management theory and introduction to law

PRONGER, SEAN
b. Thunder Bay, Ontario, November 30, 1972

2003-04 VAN	3	0	1	1	4
NHL Totals	260	23	36	59	159

–signed June 2, 2004 by Frankfurt (Deutsche Eishockey Liga, Germany)

PROSPAL, VACLAV
b. Ceske Budejovice, Czechoslovakia (Czech Republic), February 17, 1975

2003-04 ANA	82	19	35	54	54
NHL Totals	549	107	241	348	290

–signed September 17, 2004 by Ceske Budejovice (Czech Republic, Division 2)
–played for Czech Republic at 2005 World Championship (gold medal)

PRUSEK, MARTIN
b. Ostrava, Czechoslovakia (Czech Republic), December 11, 1975

2003-04 OTT	29	16-6-3	1,528	54	3	2.12
NHL Totals	48	28-9-4	2,525	94	3	2.23

–signed August 20, 2004 by Znojemsti Orli (Extraleague, Czech Republic)

PURINTON, DALE
b. Fort Wayne, Indiana, October 11, 1976

2003-04 NYR	40	1	1	2	117
NHL Totals	181	4	16	20	578

–played 2004-05 with Victoria Salmon Kings (ECHL); suspended by coach Bryan Maxwell for the remainder of the season in March 2005

PUSHOR, JAMIE
b. Lethbridge, Alberta, February 11, 1973

2003-04 CBJ/NYR	14	0	0	0	2
NHL Totals	517	13	44	57	648

–played 2004-05 with Syracuse Crunch (AHL)

PYATT, TAYLOR
b. Thunder Bay, Ontario, August 19, 1981

2003-04 BUF	63	8	12	20	25
NHL Totals	267	36	50	86	137

–signed November 16, 2004 by Hammarby (Swedish league, Division 2)

QUINT, DERON
b. Durham, New Hampshire, March 12, 1976

2003-04 CHI	51	4	7	11	18
NHL Totals	458	46	97	143	166

–signed December 20, 2004 by Bolzano (Serie A, Italy)

QUINTAL, STEPHANE
b. Boucherville, Quebec, October 22, 1968

2003-04 MON	73	3	5	8	82
NHL Totals	1,037	63	180	243	1,320

–signed December 27, 2004 by Asiago (Serie A, Italy)

RACHUNEK, KAREL
b. Gottwaldow, Czechoslovakia (Czech Republic), August 27, 1979

2003-04 OTT/NYR	72	2	19	21	33
NHL Totals	258	12	89	101	149

–signed September 6, 2004 by Znojemsti Orli (Extraleague, Czech Republic)
–signed November 1, 2004 by Lokomotiv Yaroslavl (Super League, Russia)

RADIVOJEVIC, BRANKO
b. Piestany, Czechoslovakia (Slovakia), November 24, 1980

2003-04 PHO/PHI	77	10	22	32	72
NHL Totals	174	26	39	65	139

–signed September 17, 2004 by Vsetin (Extraleague, Czech Republic)
–signed January 27, 2005 by Lulea (Swedish Elite League)

RADULOV, IGOR
b. Nizhny Tagil, Soviet Union (Russia), August 23, 1982

2003-04 CHI	36	4	7	11	18
NHL Totals	43	9	7	16	22

–started 2004-05 with Norfolk Admirals, Chicago's AHL affiliate
–signed December 20, 2004 by Spartak Moscow (Super League, Russia)

RAFALSKI, BRIAN
b. Dearborn, Michigan, September 28, 1973

2003-04 NJ	69	6	30	36	24
NHL Totals	377	30	177	207	110

–New Jersey player representative at NHLPA meetings spent most of the season at home in Wisconsin

RAGNARSSON, MARCUS
b. Ostervala, Sweden, August 13, 1971

2003-04 PHI	70	7	9	16	58
NHL Totals	632	37	140	177	482

–signed January 30, 2005 by Almtuna (Swedish league, Division 2)

RASMUSSEN, ERIK
b. Minneapolis, Minnesota, March 28, 1977

2003-04 NJ	69	7	6	13	41
NHL Totals	407	44	64	108	248

–did not play professionally in 2004-05

RATHJE, MIKE
b. Mannville, Alberta, May 11, 1974

2003-04 SJ	80	2	17	19	46
NHL Totals	671	27	128	155	439

–spent most of the season rehabilitating a bulging disc injury in his lower back and raising twins born in November 2004

RAY, ROB
b. Stirling, Ontario, June 8, 1968

2003-04 OTT	6	1	0	1	14
NHL Totals	900	14	50	91	3,207

–status in limbo as he sought to receive monthly stipend issued by NHLPA

RAYCROFT, ANDREW
b. Belleville, Ontario, May 4, 1980

2003-04 BOS	57	29-18-9	3,420	117	3	2.05
NHL Totals	78	35-27-10	4,434	164	3	2.22

–began 2004-05 playing with Detroit in Original Stars Hockey League
–signed November 6, 2004 by Djurgarden (Swedish Elite League)
–signed January 17, 2005 by Tappara (SM-Liiga, Finland)

REASONER, MARTY
b. Honeoye Falls, New York, February 26, 1977

2003-04 EDM	17	2	6	8	10
NHL Totals	234	36	61	97	121

–signed January 30, 2005 by Salzburg (Austrian league)

RECCHI, MARK
b. Kamloops, British Columbia, February 1, 1968

2003-04 PHI	82	26	49	75	47
NHL Totals	1,173	456	745	1,201	780

–signed November 10, 2004 by TPS Turku (SM-Liiga, Finland) but never played for the team in 2004-05

Calgary Flames forward Oleg Saprykin (standing) spent 2004-05 with CSKA Moscow.

REDDEN, WADE
b. Lloydminster, Saskatchewan, June 12, 1977

2003-04 OTT	81	17	26	43	65
NHL Totals	629	78	208	286	403

–began 2004-05 recovering at home in Calgary from shoulder injury suffered while playing for Team Canada at the World Cup of Hockey 2004
–played for Canada at 2005 World Championship (silver medal)

REGEHR, ROBYN
b. Recife, Brazil, April 19, 1980

2003-04 CAL	82	4	14	18	74
NHL Totals	363	12	42	54	370

–played for IMG WorldStars team that toured Europe in December 2004
–played for Canada at 2005 World Championship (silver medal)

REICH, JEREMY
b. Craik, Saskatchewan, February 11, 1979

2003-04 CBJ	9	0	1	1	20
NHL Totals	9	0	1	1	20

–played 2004-05 with Syracuse Crunch, Columbus's AHL affiliate, as well as Houston Aeros (AHL)

REICHEL, ROBERT
b. Litvinov, Czechoslovakia (Czech Republic), June 25, 1971

2003-04 TML	69	11	19	30	30
NHL Totals	830	252	378	630	388

–signed August 20, 2004 by Chemopetrol Litvinov (Extraleague, Czech Republic)

REID, BRANDON
b. Kirkland, Quebec, March 9, 1981

2003-04 VAN	3	0	1	1	0
NHL Totals	10	2	4	6	0

–signed July 7, 2004 by Hamburg (Deutsche Eishockey Liga, Germany)

REINPRECHT, STEVE
b. Edmonton, Alberta, May 7, 1976

2003-04 CAL	44	7	22	29	4
NHL Totals	269	59	103	162	56

–signed September 28, 2004 by Mulhouse (French league)

REIRDEN, TODD
b. Deerfield, Illinois, June 25, 1971

2003-04 ANA/PHO	7	0	2	2	4
NHL Totals	183	11	35	46	181

–played 2004-05 with Houston Aeros (AHL)

RENBERG, MIKAEL
b. Pitea, Sweden, May 5, 1972

2003-04 TML	59	12	13	25	50
NHL Totals	661	190	274	464	372

–signed May 26, 2004 by Lulea (Swedish Elite League)

RHEAUME, PASCAL
b. Quebec City, Quebec, June 21, 1973

2003-04 NYR/STL	42	1	3	4	9
NHL Totals	305	39	52	91	140

–played 2004-05 with Albany River Rats, New Jersey's AHL affiliate, after signing with the Devils as a free agent in the summer of 2004

RIBEIRO, MIKE
b. Montreal, Quebec, February 10, 1980

2003-04 MON	81	20	45	65	34
NHL Totals	197	34	68	102	56

–signed January 17, 2005 by Espoo (SM-Liiga, Finland)

RICCI, MIKE
b. Scarborough (Toronto), Ontario, October 27, 1971

2003-04 SJ	71	7	19	26	40
NHL Totals	1,014	233	355	588	901

– did not play professionally in 2004-05

RICHARDS, BRAD
b. Murray Harbour, Prince Edward Island, May 2, 1980

2003-04 TB	82	26	53	79	12
NHL Totals	326	84	193	277	63

–signed November 8, 2004 by AK Bars Kazan (Super League, Russia); suffered abdominal injury and flew home on December 16, 2004

RICHARDSON, LUKE
b. Ottawa, Ontario, March 26, 1969

2003-04 CBJ	64	1	5	6	48
NHL Totals	1,247	32	147	179	1,925

–remained at home in Columbus for the balance of the season; did not play professionally in 2004-05

RISSMILLER, PAT
b. Belmont, Massachusetts, October 26, 1978

2003-04 SJ	4	0	0	0	0
NHL Totals	4	0	0	0	0

–played 2004-05 with Cleveland Barons, San Jose's AHL affiliate

RITA, JANI
b. Helsinki, Finland, July 25, 1981

2003-04 EDM	2	0	0	0	0
NHL Totals	15	3	1	4	0

–signed August 17, 2004 by HPK Hameenlinna (SM-Liiga, Finland)
–played for Finland at 2005 World Championship

RITCHIE, BYRON
b. Burnaby, British Columbia, April 24, 1977

2003-04 FLO	50	5	6	11	84
NHL Totals	144	10	17	27	156

–signed September 25, 2004 by Rogle (Swedish league, Division 2)

RIVERS, JAMIE
b. Ottawa, Ontario, March 16, 1975

2003-04 DET	50	3	4	7	41
NHL Totals	390	16	40	56	311

–began 2004-05 playing with Detroit in Original Stars Hockey League
–played 2004-05 with Hershey Bears (AHL)

RIVET, CRAIG
b. North Bay, Ontario, September 13, 1974

2003-04 MON	80	4	8	12	98
NHL Totals	517	26	75	101	629

–signed January 11, 2005 by TPS Turku (SM-Liiga, Finland)

ROBERTS, GARY
b. North York (Toronto), Ontario, May 23, 1966

2003-04 TML	72	28	20	48	84
NHL Totals	1,029	397	409	806	2,345

–did not play professionally in 2004-05; remained at home in Toronto running his fitness centre, Station 7

ROBIDAS, STEPHANE
b. Sherbrooke, Quebec, March 3, 1977

2003-04 DAL/CHI	59	3	10	13	41
NHL Totals	257	13	33	46	104

–signed September 17, 2004 by Frankfurt (Deutsche Eishockey Liga, Germany)

ROBINSON, NATHAN
b. Scarborough (Toronto), Ontario, December 31, 1981

2003-04 DET	5	0	0	0	2
NHL Totals	5	0	0	0	2

–played 2004-05 with Grand Rapids Griffins, Detroit's AHL affiliate, as well as Syracuse Crunch (AHL)

ROBITAILLE, LUC
b. Montreal, Quebec, February 17, 1966

2003-04 LA	80	22	29	51	56
NHL Totals	1,366	653	717	370	1,125

–played for IMG WorldStars team that toured Europe in December 2004

ROBITAILLE, RANDY
b. Ottawa, Ontario, October 12, 1975

2003-04 ATL	69	11	26	37	20
NHL Totals	318	51	96	147	85

–signed April 26, 2004 by Zurich (Swiss league)
–played for Canada at Deutschland Cup in November 2004

ROCHE, TRAVIS
b. Grand Cache, Alberta, June 17, 1978

2003-04 MIN	5	0	1	1	0
NHL Totals	10	0	1	1	2

–played 2004-05 with Chicago Wolves, Atlanta's AHL affiliate

ROENICK, JEREMY
b. Boston, Massachusetts, January 17, 1970

2003-04 PHI	62	19	28	47	62
NHL Totals	1,124	475	645	1,120	1,345

–suffered from post-concussion syndrome and did not play in 2004-05

ROHLOFF, TODD
b. Grand Rapids, Illinois, January 16, 1974

2003-04 CBJ/WAS	59	0	5	5	26
NHL Totals	75	0	6	6	40

–played 2004-05 with Rochester Americans (AHL)

ROLOSON, DWAYNE
b. Simcoe, Ontario, October 12, 1969

2003-04 MIN	48	19-18-11	2,847	89	5	1.88
NHL Totals	245	83-99-42	13,709	561	16	2.46

–signed October 18, 2004 by Lukko Rauma (SM-Liiga, Finland)

ROLSTON, BRIAN
b. Flint, Michigan, February 21, 1973

2003-04 BOS	82	19	29	48	40
NHL Totals	736	190	242	432	223

–did not play professionally in 2004-05

RONNING, CLIFF
b. Burnaby, British Columbia, October 1, 1965

2003-04 NYI	40	9	15	24	2
NHL Totals	1,137	306	563	869	453

–did not play professionally in 2004-05

ROSA, PAVEL
b. Most, Czechoslovakia (Czech Republic), June 7, 1977

2003-04 LA	2	1	1	2	0
NHL Totals	36	5	13	18	6

–signed May 4, 2004 by Moscow Dynamo (Super League, Russia)

ROSSITER, KYLE
b. Edmonton, Alberta, June 9, 1980

2003-04 FLO/ATL	6	0	1	1	7
NHL Totals	11	0	1	1	9

–played 2004-05 with Chicago Wolves, Atlanta's AHL affiliate, as well as Wilkes-Barre/Scranton (AHL)

ROURKE, ALLAN
b. Mississauga, Ontario, March 6, 1980

2003-04 CAR	25	1	2	3	22
NHL Totals	25	1	2	3	22

–played 2004-05 with Lowell Lock Monsters, Carolina's AHL affiliate

ROY, ANDRE
b. Port Chester, New York, February 8, 1975

2003-04 TB	33	1	1	2	78
NHL Totals	310	25	27	52	734

–remained at home in Montreal; did not play professionally in 2004-05

ROY, DEREK
b. Ottawa, Ontario, May 4, 1983

2003-04 BUF	49	9	10	19	12
NHL Totals	49	9	10	19	12

–played 2004-05 with Rochester Americans, Buffalo's AHL affiliate

RUCCHIN, STEVE
b. Thunder Bay, Ontario, July 4, 1971

2003-04 ANA	82	20	23	43	12
NHL Totals	616	153	279	432	140

–began 2004-05 skating with the University of Western Ontario Mustangs in London, Ontario
–signed December 29, 2004 by Cortina (Serie A, Italy)

RUCINSKY, MARTIN
b. Most, Czechoslovakia (Czech Republic), March 11, 1971

2003-04 NYR/VAN	82	14	31	45	72
NHL Totals	817	208	300	508	677

–signed August 20, 2004 by Litvinov (Extraleague, Czech Republic)
–played for Czech Republic at 2005 World Championship (gold medal)

RUMBLE, DARREN
b. Barrie, Ontario, January 23, 1969

2003-04 TB	5	0	0	0	2
NHL Totals	193	10	26	36	216

–started 2004-05 with Springfield Falcons, Tampa Bay's AHL affiliate, but officially retired on December 18, 2004

RUPP, MIKE
b. Cleveland, Ohio, January 13, 1980

2003-04 NJ/PHO	57	6	6	12	47
NHL Totals	83	11	9	20	68

–played part of 2004-05 with Danbury Trashers (UHL)

RUUTU, JARKKO
b. Vantaa, Finland, August 23, 1975

2003-04 VAN	71	6	8	14	133
NHL Totals	185	13	21	34	311

–signed September 23, 2004 by HIFK Helsinki (SM-Liiga, Finland); played for Helsinki at 2005 Spengler Cup (December 26-31, 2004)
–played for Finland at 2005 World Championship

RUUTU, TUOMO
b. Vantaa, Finland, February 16, 1983

2003-04 CHI	82	23	21	44	58
NHL Totals	82	23	21	44	58

–underwent surgery in October to repair his left shoulder which he dislocated during World Cup of Hockey 2004
–upon recovery, played 2004-05 with Norfolk Admirals, Chicago's AHL affiliate

RYCROFT, MARK
b. Penticton, British Columbia, July 12, 1978

2003-04 STL	71	9	12	21	32
NHL Totals	80	9	15	24	36

–played 2004-05 with Briancon (French league)

RYDER, MICHAEL
b. St. John's, Newfoundland, March 31, 1980

2003-04 MON	81	25	38	63	26
NHL Totals	81	25	38	63	26

–signed September 19, 2004 by Leksand (Swedish league, Division 2)

SABOURIN, DANY
b. Val d'Or, Quebec, September 2, 1980

2003-04 CAL	4	0-3-0	169	10	0	3.55	
NHL Totals	4	0-3-0	169	10	0	3.55	

–split 2004-05 between Wheeling Nailers (ECHL) and Wilkes-Barre/Scranton Penguins (AHL)

SAKIC, JOE
b. Burnaby, British Columbia, July 7, 1969

2003-04 COL	81	33	54	87	42
NHL Totals	1,155	542	860	1,402	482

–did not play professionally in 2004-05

SALEI, RUSLAN
b. Minsk, Soviet Union (Belarus), November 2, 1974

2003-04 ANA	82	4	11	15	110
NHL Totals	516	25	61	86	621

–signed October 20, 2004 by AK Bars Kazan (Super League, Russia)
–played for Belarus at final Olympic qualifying tournament in February 2005

SALMELAINEN, TONY
b. Espoo, Finland, August 8, 1981

2003-04 EDM	13	0	1	1	4
NHL Totals	13	0	1	1	4

–played 2004-05 with Edmonton Road Runners, Edmonton Oilers' AHL affiliate

SALO, SAMI
b. Turku, Finland, September 2, 1974

2003-04 VAN	74	7	19	26	22
NHL Totals	348	35	90	125	82

–played 2004-05 with Frolunda (Swedish Elite League)

SALO, TOMMY
b. Surahammar, Sweden, February 1, 1971

2003-04 EDM/COL	49	18-21-7	2,791	119	3	2.30	
NHL Totals	526	210-225-73	30,436	1,296	37	2.55	

–signed June 3, 2004 by MoDo (Swedish Elite League); at season's end, he announced his retirement (though later signed in Sweden)

SALVADOR, BRYCE
b. Brandon, Manitoba, February 11, 1976

2003-04 STL	69	3	5	8	47
NHL Totals	281	12	28	40	289

–started 2004-05 playing rec. hockey in Brentwood Hockey League in St. Louis
–finished the season playing for Missouri River Otters (UHL)

SAMSONOV, SERGEI
b. Moscow, Soviet Union (Russia), October 27, 1978

2003-04 BOS	58	17	23	40	4
NHL Totals	459	146	193	339	81

–signed February 2, 2005 by Moscow Dynamo (Super League, Russia)

SAMUELSSON, MARTIN
b. Upplands Vasby, Sweden, January 25, 1982

2003-04 BOS	6	0	0	0	0
NHL Totals	14	0	1	1	2

–played 2004-05 with Providence Bruins, Boston's AHL affiliate

SAMUELSSON, MIKAEL
b. Mariefred, Sweden, December 23, 1976

2003-04 FLO	37	3	6	9	35
NHL Totals	188	19	30	49	98

–signed September 8, 2004 by Geneve-Servette (Swiss league)
–signed October 26, 2004 by Sodertalje (Swedish Elite League)
–played for Sweden at 2005 World Championship

SANDERSON, GEOFF
b. Hay River, Northwest Territories, February 1, 1972

2003-04 CBJ/VAN	80	16	20	36	38
NHL Totals	928	316	296	612	393

–signed January 5, 2005 by Geneve-Servette (Swiss league)

SANTALA, TOMMI
b. Helsinki, Finland, June 27, 1979

2003-04 ATL	33	1	2	3	22
NHL Totals	33	1	2	3	22

–played 2004-05 with Chicago Wolves, Atlanta's AHL affiliate

SAPRYKIN, OLEG
b. Moscow, Soviet Union (Russia), February 12, 1981

2003-04 CAL	69	12	17	29	41
NHL Totals	187	29	47	76	132

–signed September 25, 2004 by CSKA Moscow (Super League, Russia)

SARICH, CORY
b. Saskatoon, Saskatchewan, August 16, 1978

2003-04 TB	82	3	16	19	89
NHL Totals	372	9	50	59	440

–did not play professionally in 2004-05

SARNO, PETER
b. Toronto, Ontario, July 26, 1979

2003-04 EDM	6	1	0	1	2
NHL Totals	6	1	0	1	2

–played 2004-05 with Manitoba Moose, Vancouver's AHL affiliate, after signing with the Canucks as a free agent in the summer of 2004

SATAN, MIROSLAV
b. Topolcany, Czechoslovakia (Slovakia), October 22, 1974

2003-04 BUF	82	29	28	57	30
NHL Totals	704	259	260	519	277

–signed December 29, 2004 by Slovan Bratislava (Extraleague, Slovakia)
–played for Slovakia at 2005 World Championship

SAUER, KURT
b. St. Cloud, Minnesota, January 16, 1981

2003-04 ANA/COL	69	1	5	6	51
NHL Totals	149	2	7	9	125

–did not play professionally in 2004-05

SAUVE, PHILIPPE
b. Buffalo, New York, February 27, 1980

2003-04 COL	17	7-7-3	986	50	0	3.04	
NHL Totals	17	7-7-3	986	50	0	3.04	

–played part of 2004-05 with Mississippi Sea Wolves (ECHL)

SAVAGE, BRIAN
b. Sudbury, Ontario, February 24, 1971

2003-04 PHO/STL	74	16	16	32	38
NHL Totals	608	183	162	345	293

–did not play professionally in 2004-05

SAVARD, MARC
b. Ottawa, Ontario, July 17, 1977

2003-04 ATL	45	19	33	52	85
NHL Totals	421	105	199	304	362

–signed October 11, 2004 by Thurgau (Swiss league, B Division)
–signed November 23, 2004 by SC Bern (Swiss league); released
  December 9, 2004 by Bern because of poor conditioning
–played part of 2004-05 with Milano Vipers (Serie A, Italy)
–in late February 2005, Savard went to Florida to try to qualify for
  the Canadian Tour (golf) but failed after rounds of 78-79-78

SCATCHARD, DAVE
b. Hinton, Alberta, February 20, 1976

2003-04 NYI	61	9	16	25	78
NHL Totals	526	107	115	222	833

–remained at home on Long Island, where he got married during
  the season; did not play professionally in 2004-05

SCHAEFER, PETER
b. Yellow Grass, Saskatchewan, July 12, 1977

2003-04 OTT	81	15	24	39	26
NHL Totals	334	57	80	137	108

–signed November 30, 2004 by Bolzano (Serie A, Italy)

SCHASTLIVY, PETR
b. Angarsk, Soviet Union (Russia), April 18, 1979

2003-04 OTT/ANA	65	4	4	8	18
NHL Totals	129	18	22	40	30

–signed September 25, 2004 by Lokomotiv Yaroslavl (Super
  League, Russia)

SCHNABEL, ROBERT
b. Prague, Czechoslovakia (Czech Republic), November 10, 1978

2003-04 NAS	20	0	3	3	34
NHL Totals	22	0	3	3	34

–signed May 19, 2004 by Sparta Praha (Extraleague, Czech
  Republic)

SCHNEIDER, MATHIEU
b. New York, New York, June 12, 1969

2003-04 DET	78	14	32	46	56
NHL Totals	992	168	384	552	963

– did not play professionally in 2004-05

SCHULTZ, NICK
b. Strasbourg, Saskatchewan, August 25, 1982

2003-04 MIN	79	6	10	16	16
NHL Totals	209	13	23	36	53

–signed September 24, 2004 by Kassel (Deutsche Eishockey Liga,
  Germany)

SCHWAB, COREY
b. North Battleford, Saskatchewan, November 4, 1970

2003-04 NJ	3	2-0-1	187	2	1	0.64
NHL Totals	147	42-63-13	7,476	360	6	2.89

–did not play professionally in 2004-05

SCOTT, RICHARD
b. Hawkstone, Ontario, August 1, 1978

2003-04 NYR	5	0	0	0	23
NHL Totals	10	0	0	0	28

–did not play professionally in 2004-05

SCOVILLE, DARREL
b. Swift Current, Saskatchewan, October 13, 1975

2003-04 CBJ	8	0	1	1	6
NHL Totals	16	0	1	1	12

–split 2004-05 between Providence Bruins (AHL) and Hershey
  Bears (AHL)

SCUDERI, ROB
b. Syosset, New York, December 30, 1978

2003-04 PIT	13	1	2	3	4
NHL Totals	13	1	2	3	4

–played 2004-05 with Wilkes-Barre/Scranton Penguins, Pittsburgh's
  AHL affiliate

SEDIN, DANIEL
b. Ornskoldsvik, Sweden, September 26, 1980

2003-04 VAN	82	18	36	54	18
NHL Totals	315	61	90	151	108

–signed September 18, 2004 by MoDo (Swedish Elite League)
–played for Sweden at 2005 World Championship

SEDIN, HENRIK
b. Ornskoldsvik, Sweden, September 26, 1980

2003-04 VAN	76	11	31	42	32
NHL Totals	318	44	102	146	144

–signed September 18, 2004 by MoDo (Swedish Elite League)
–played for Sweden at 2005 World Championship

SEIDENBERG, DENNIS
b. Schwenningen, West Germany (Germany), July 18, 1981

2003-04 PHI	5	0	0	0	2
NHL Totals	63	4	9	13	22

–played 2004-05 with Philadelphia Phantoms, Philadelphia Flyers'
  AHL affiliate

SEJNA, PETER
b. Liptovski Mikulas, Czechoslovakia (Slovakia), October 5, 1979

2003-04 STL	20	2	2	4	4
NHL Totals	21	3	2	5	4

–played 2004-05 with Worcester IceCats, St. Louis's AHL affiliate

SEKERAS, LUBOMIR
b. Trencin, Czechoslovakia (Slovakia), November 18, 1968

2003-04 DAL	4	1	1	2	2
NHL Totals	213	18	53	71	122

–signed July 8, 2004 by Nurnberg (Deutsche Eishockey Liga,
  Germany)

SELANNE, TEEMU
b. Helsinki, Finland, July 3, 1970

2003-04 COL	78	16	16	32	32
NHL Totals	879	452	499	951	335

–signed December 21, 2004 by Jokerit Helsinki (SM-Liiga,
  Finland)

SEMENOV, ALEXEI
b. Murmansk, Soviet Union (Russia), April 10, 1981

2003-04 EDM	46	2	3	5	32
NHL Totals	92	3	9	12	90

–signed July 30, 2004 by SKA St. Petersburg (Super League,
  Russia)

SEMIN, ALEXANDER
b. Krasjonarsk, Soviet Union (Russia), March 3, 1984

2003-04 WAS	52	10	12	22	36
NHL Totals	52	10	12	22	36

–signed September 25, 2004 by Lada Togliatti (Super League,
  Russia)
–played for Russia at 2005 World Championship (bronze medal)

Defenceman Sheldon Souray (left) played in Sweden with Farjestad and was one of the most impressive North Americans in Europe.

SEVERSON, CAM
b. Canora, Saskatchewan, January 15, 1978

2003-04 ANA	31	3	0	3	50
NHL Totals	33	3	0	3	58

–played 2004-05 with Milwaukee Admirals, Nashville's AHL affiliate, after signing with the Predators as a free agent in the summer of 2004

SHANAHAN, BRENDAN
b. Mimico, Ontario, January 23, 1969

2003-04 DET	2	25	28	53	117
NHL Totals	1,268	558	593	1,151	2,273

–did not play professionally during 2004-05
–organized hockey summit December 7-8, 2004 in Toronto to try to solve hockey's most important on-ice problems

SHARP, PATRICK
b. Thunder Bay, Ontario, December 27, 1981

2003-04 PHI	41	5	2	7	55
NHL Totals	44	5	2	7	57

–played 2004-05 with Philadelphia Phantoms, Philadelphia Flyers' AHL affiliate

SHELLEY, JODY
b. Thompson, Manitoba, February 7, 1976

2003-04 CBJ	76	3	3	6	228
NHL Totals	197	7	10	17	693

–signed January 17, 2005 by Jyvaskyla (SM-Liiga, Finland)

SHIELDS, STEVE
b. Toronto, Ontario, July 19, 1972

2003-04 FLO	16		3-6-1	732	42	0	3.44
NHL Totals	241		79-102-39	13,364	587	10	2.64

–did not play professionally in 2004-05

SHISHKANOV, TIMOFEI
b. Moscow, Soviet Union (Russia), June 10, 1983

2003-04 NAS	2	0	0	0	0
NHL Totals	2	0	0	0	0

–played 2004-05 with Milwaukee Admirals, Nashville's AHL affiliate

SHVIDKI, DENIS
b. Kharkov, Soviet Union (Ukraine), November 21, 1980

2003-04 FLO	2	0	0	0	0
NHL Totals	76	11	14	25	30

–signed July 7, 2004 by Lokomotiv Yaroslavl (Super League, Russia)

SIKLENKA, MIKE
b. Meadow Lake, Saskatchewan, December 18, 1979

2003-04 NYR	1	0	0	0	0
NHL Totals	2	0	0	0	0

–signed October 8, 2004 by Klagenfurt AC (Austrian league)

SILLINGER, MIKE
b. Regina, Saskatchewan, June 29, 1971

2003-04 PHO/STL	76	13	11	24	68
NHL Totals	829	166	232	398	507

– did not play professionally in 2004-05

SIM, JON
b. New Glasgow, Nova Scotia, September 29, 1977

2003-04 LA/PIT	63	8	10	18	33
NHL Totals	158	18	18	36	90

–split 2004-05 between Utah Grizzlies, Phoenix's AHL affiliate, after signing as a free agent with the Coyotes in the summer of 2004, and Philadelphia Phantoms (AHL, on loan)

SIMON, BEN
b. Shaker Heights, Ohio, June 14, 1978

2003-04 ATL	52	3	0	3	28
NHL Totals	68	3	1	4	43

–played 2004-05 with Chicago Wolves, Atlanta's AHL affiliate

SIMON, CHRIS
b. Wawa, Ontario, January 30, 1972

2003-04 NYR/CAL	78	17	11	28	250
NHL Totals	605	125	128	253	1,596

–remained at home in Wawa; did not play professionally in 2004-05

SIMPSON, REID
b. Flin Flon, Manitoba, May 21, 1969

2003-04 PIT	2	0	0	0	17
NHL Totals	301	18	18	36	838

–played part of 2004-05 with Rockford Ice Hogs (UHL)

SIMPSON, TODD
b. North Vancouver, British Columbia, May 28, 1973

2003-04 ANA/OTT	62	4	4	8	152
NHL Totals	529	14	60	74	1,227

–signed December 16, 2004 by Herning IK (Oddset Ligaen, Netherlands)

SJOSTROM, FREDRIK
b. Fargelanda, Sweden, May 6, 1983

2003-04 PHO	57	7	6	13	22
NHL Totals	57	7	6	13	22

–played 2004-05 with Utah Grizzlies, Phoenix's AHL affiliate

SKOULA, MARTIN
b. Litomerice, Czechoslovakia (Czech Republic), October 28, 1979

2003-04 COL/ANA	79	4	21	25	32
NHL Totals	404	29	93	122	200

–signed September 17, 2004 by Litvinov (Extraleague, Czech Republic)

SKRASTINS, KARLIS
b. Riga, Soviet Union (Latvia), July 9, 1974

2003-04 COL	82	5	8	13	26
NHL Totals	389	18	49	67	156

–signed September 25, 2004 by Riga 2000 (Latvian league); left team on February 16, 2005
–played part of 2004-05 with Novosibirsk (Super League, Russia)
–played for Latvia at final Olympic qualifying tournament in February 2005
–played for Latvia at 2005 World Championship

SKRLAC, ROB
b. Port McNeill, British Columbia, June 10, 1976

2003-04 NJ	8	1	0	1	22
NHL Totals	8	1	0	1	22

–played 2004-05 with Albany River Rats, New Jersey's AHL affiliate

SLANEY, JOHN
b. St. John's, Newfoundland, February 2, 1972

2003-04 PHI	4	0	2	2	0
NHL Totals	268	22	69	91	99

–played 2004-05 with Philadelphia Phantoms, Philadelphia Flyers' AHL affiliate

SLEGR, JIRI
b. Jihlava, Czechoslovakia (Czech Republic), May 29, 1971

2003-04 VAN/BOS	52	6	20	26	35
NHL Totals	590	51	182	233	782

–signed August 20, 2004 by Litvinov (Extraleague, Czech Republic)
–played for Czech Republic at 2005 World Championship (gold medal)

SLOAN, BLAKE
b. Park Ridge, Illinois, July 27, 1975

2003-04 DAL	28	0	0	0	7
NHL Totals	290	11	32	43	162

–played 2004-05 with Grand Rapids Griffins (AHL)

SMIRNOV, ALEXEI
b. Tver, Soviet Union (Russia), January 28, 1982

2003-04 ANA	8	0	1	1	2
NHL Totals	52	3	3	6	20

–played 2004-05 with Cincinnati Mighty Ducks, Anaheim's AHL affiliate

SMITH, JASON
b. Calgary, Alberta, November 2, 1973

2003-04 EDM	68	7	12	19	98
NHL Totals	710	33	97	130	779

–remained at home in Calgary; did not play professionally in 2004-05

SMITH, MARK
b. Edmonton, Alberta, October 24, 1977

2003-04 SJ	36	1	3	4	72
NHL Totals	202	10	19	29	259

–played part of 2004-05 with Victoria Salmon Kings (ECHL)

SMITH, NATHAN
b. Edmonton, Alberta, February 9, 1982

2003-04 VAN	2	0	0	0	0
NHL Totals	2	0	0	0	0

–played 2004-05 with Manitoba Moose, Vancouver's AHL affiliate

SMITH, WYATT
b. Thief River Falls, Minnesota, February 13, 1977

2003-04 NAS	18	3	1	4	2
NHL Totals	83	7	8	15	15

–played 2004-05 with Milwaukee Admirals, Nashville's AHL affiliate

SMITHSON, JERRED
b. Vernon, British Columbia, February 4, 1979

2003-04 LA	8	0	1	1	4
NHL Totals	30	0	3	3	25

–played 2004-05 with Milwaukee Admirals, Nashville's AHL affiliate, after signing with the Predators as a free agent in the summer of 2004

SMOLINSKI, BRYAN
b. Toledo, Ohio, December 27, 1971

2003-04 OTT	80	19	27	46	49
NHL Totals	829	231	303	534	503

–signed February 11, 2005 by Motor City Mechanics (UHL)

SMYTH, RYAN
b. Banff, Alberta, February 21, 1976

2003-04 EDM	82	23	36	59	70
NHL Totals	642	198	232	430	511

–signed with Bentley Generals (Alberta Senior hockey league) in order to play with his brothers, Kevyn and Jaret, to start 2004-05 but was soon considered ineligible because the league ruled it would bar current NHLers from becoming ringers
–later mounted the Ryan Smyth and Friends All-Star Charity Tour, a four-game series through Red Deer, Moose Jaw, Regina, and Winnipeg
–played for Canada at 2005 World Championship (silver medal)

SNOW, GARTH
b. Wrentham, Massachusetts, July 28, 1969

2003-04 NYI	39	14-15-5	2,015	94	1	2.80
NHL Totals	348	131-134-43	18,741	857	16	2.74

–signed August 17, 2004 by SKA St. Petersburg (Super League, Russia); left team on December 16, 2004

SOMIK, RADOVAN
b. Martin, Czechoslovakia (Slovakia), May 5, 1977

2003-04 PHI	53	4	10	14	17
NHL Totals	113	12	20	32	27

–signed October 2, 2004 by MHC Martin (Extraleague, Slovakia)
–signed October 7, 2004 by Vsetin (Extraleague, Czech Republic)
–signed January 28, 2005 by Malmo (Swedish Elite League)

SONNENBERG, MARTIN
b. Wetaskiwin, Alberta, January 23, 1978

2003-04 CAL	5	0	0	0	2
NHL Totals	63	2	3	5	21

–played 2004-05 with Utah Grizzlies, Phoenix's AHL affiliate, after signing with the Coyotes as a free agent in the summer of 2004

SOPEL, BRENT
b. Calgary, Alberta, January 7, 1977

2003-04 VAN	80	10	32	42	36
NHL Totals	302	32	93	125	129

–did not play professionally in 2004-05

SOURAY, SHELDON
b. Elk Point, Alberta, July 13, 1976

2003-04 MON	63	15	20	35	104
NHL Totals	350	28	55	83	570

–signed September 22, 2004 by Farjestad (Swedish Elite League)
–played for Canada at 2005 World Championship (silver medal)

SPACEK, JAROSLAV
b. Rokycany, Czechoslovakia (Czech Republic), February 11, 1974

2003-04 CBJ	58	5	17	22	45
NHL Totals	420	39	123	162	277

–signed September 17, 2004 by Plzen (Extraleague, Czech Republic)
–signed January 4, 2005 by Slavia Praha (Extraleague, Czech Republic)
–played for Czech Republic at 2005 World Championship (gold medal)

SPEZZA, JASON
b. Mississauga, Ontario, June 13, 1983

2003-04 OTT	78	22	33	55	71
NHL Totals	111	29	47	76	79

–played 2004-05 with Binghamton Senators, Ottawa's AHL affiliate; won Les Cunningham Award at season's end as AHL's most valuable player

Joe Thornton led HC Davos to the Swiss league championship. He was later named MVP while playing for Canada at the 2005 World Championship.

SPILLER, MATTHEW
b. Daysland, Alberta, February 7, 1983

2003-04 PHO	51	0	0	0	54
NHL Totals	51	0	0	0	54

–played 2004-05 with Utah Grizzlies, Phoenix's AHL affiliate

STAAL, ERIC
b. Thunder Bay, Ontario, October 29, 1984

2003-04 CAR	81	11	20	31	40
NHL Totals	81	11	20	31	40

–played 2004-05 with Lowell Lock Monsters, Carolina's AHL affiliate

STAIOS, STEVE
b. Hamilton, Ontario, July 28, 1973

2003-04 EDM	82	6	22	28	86
NHL Totals	537	33	84	117	776

–signed January 28, 2005 by Lulea (Swedish Elite League); left Lulea on February 27, 2005

STAJAN, MATT
b. Mississauga, Ontario, December 19, 1983

2003-04 TML	69	14	13	27	22
NHL Totals	70	15	13	28	22

–played 2004-05 with St. John's Maple Leafs, Toronto's AHL affiliate

STANA, RASTISLAV
b. Kosice, Czechoslovakia (Slovakia), January 10, 1980

2003-04 WAS	6	1-2-0	211	11	0	3.13
NHL Totals	6	1-2-0	211	11	0	3.13

–played part of 2004-05 with Sodertalje (Swedish Elite League)
–played for Slovakia at Deutschland Cup in November 2004
–played for Slovakia at 2005 World Championship

STEFAN, PATRIK
b. Pribram, Czechoslovakia (Czech Republic), September 16, 1980

2003-04 ATL	82	14	26	40	26
NHL Totals	350	49	104	153	112

–signed October 23, 2004 by Ilves Tampere (SM-Liiga, Finland)

STEPHENS, CHARLIE
b. London, Ontario, April 5, 1981

2003-04 COL	6	0	2	2	4
NHL Totals	8	0	2	2	4

–played 2004-05 with Binghamton Senators, Ottawa's AHL affiliate, after signing with Ottawa as a free agent in the summer of 2004

STEVENS, SCOTT
b. Kitchener, Ontario, April 1, 1964

2003-04 NJ	38	3	9	12	22
NHL Totals	1,635	196	712	908	2,785

–missed the last half of 2003-04 because of post-concussion syndrome and did not play professionally in 2004-05

STEVENSON, JEREMY
b. San Bernardino, California, July 28, 1974

2003-04 MIN/NAS	56	5	4	9	105
NHL Totals	156	14	16	30	356

–played part of 2004-05 with South Carolina Stingrays (ECHL)

STEVENSON, TURNER
b. Prince George, British Columbia, May 18, 1972

2003-04 NJ	61	14	13	27	76
NHL Totals	613	74	112	186	924

–did not play professionally in 2004-05

STEWART, KARL
b. Scarborough (Toronto), Ontario, June 30, 1983

2003-04 ATL	5	0	1	1	4
NHL Totals	5	0	1	1	4

–played 2004-05 with Chicago Wolves, Atlanta's AHL affiliate

STILLMAN, CORY
b. Peterborough, Ontario, December 20, 1973

2003-04 TB	81	25	55	80	36
NHL Totals	645	184	250	434	326

–lived in Florida and helped coach his son, Riley, and his team; did not play professionally in 2004-05

ST. JACQUES, BRUNO
b. Montreal, Quebec, August 22, 1980

2003-04 CAR	35	0	2	2	31
NHL Totals	66	2	7	9	47

–played 2004-05 with Lowell Lock Monsters, Carolina's AHL affiliate

ST. LOUIS, MARTIN
b. Laval, Quebec, June 18, 1975

2003-04 TB	82	38	56	94	24
NHL Totals	364	109	150	259	120

–signed November 4, 2004 by Lausanne (Swiss league); left team on February 22, 2005

STOCK, P.J.
b. Montreal, Quebec, May 26, 1975

2003-04 BOS	1	0	0	0	0
NHL Totals	235	5	21	26	523

–did not play professionally in 2004-05

STOLL, JARRET
b. Melville, Saskatchewan, June 25, 1982

2003-04 EDM	68	10	11	21	42
NHL Totals	72	10	12	22	42

–played 2004-05 with Edmonton Road Runners, Edmonton Oilers' AHL affiliate

STORR, JAMIE
b. Brampton, Ontario, December 28, 1975

2003-04 CAR	14	0-8-2	660	32	0	2.91
NHL Totals	219	85-86-23	11,512	488	16	2.54

–split 2004-05 between Springfield Falcons (AHL) and Utah Grizzlies (AHL)

STRAKA, MARTIN
b. Plzen, Czechoslovakia (Czech Republic), September 3, 1972

2003-04 PIT/LA	54	10	16	26	20
NHL Totals	730	192	338	530	272

–signed September 17, 2004 by CSKA Moscow (Super League, Russia)
–played for Czech Republic at 2005 World Championship (gold medal)

STRBAK, MARTIN
b. Presov, Czechoslovakia (Slovakia), January 15, 1975

2003-04 LA/PIT	49	5	11	16	46
NHL Totals	49	5	11	16	46

–signed October 2, 2004 by Kosice (Extraleague, Slovakia)
–played for Slovakia at Deutschland Cup in November 2004
–played for Slovakia at 2005 World Championship

STROSHEIN, GARRET
b. Edmonton, Alberta, April 4, 1980

2003-04 WAS	3	0	0	0	14
NHL Totals	3	0	0	0	14

–played 2004-05 with Portland Pirates, Washington's AHL affiliate

STRUDWICK, JASON
b. Edmonton, Alberta, July 17, 1975

2003-04 CHI	54	1	3	4	73
NHL Totals	363	7	22	29	570

–signed January 17, 2005 by Ferencvaros (Hungarian league)

STUART, BRAD
b. Rocky Mountain House, Alberta, November 6, 1979

2003-04 SJ	77	9	30	39	34
NHL Totals	354	34	107	141	207

–did not play professionally in 2004-05

STUART, MIKE
b. Chicago, Illinois, August 30, 1980

2003-04 STL	2	0	0	0	0
NHL Totals	2	0	0	0	0

–played 2004-05 with Worcester IceCats, St. Louis's AHL affiliate

STUMPEL, JOZEF
b. Nitra, Czechoslovakia (Slovakia), July 20, 1972

2003-04 LA	64	8	29	37	16
NHL Totals	758	151	397	548	187

–played 2004-05 with Slavia Praha (Extraleague, Czech Republic)
–played for Slovakia at 2005 World Championship

STURM, MARCO
b. Dingolfing, West Germany (Germany), September 8, 1978

2003-04 SJ	64	21	20	41	36
NHL Totals	530	122	135	257	226

–signed August 8, 2004 by Ingolstadt (Deutsche Eishockey Liga, Germany)

STUTZEL, MIKE
b. Victoria, British Columbia, February 28, 1979

2003-04 PHO	9	0	0	0	0
NHL Totals	9	0	0	0	0

–played 2004-05 with Utah Grizzlies, Phoenix's AHL affiliate

SUCHY, RADOSLAV
b. Kezmarok, Czechoslovakia (Slovakia), April 7, 1976

2003-04 PHO	82	7	14	21	8
NHL Total	372	12	51	63	74

–signed October 4, 2004 by HK Poprad (Extraleague, Slovakia)
–played for Slovakia at 2005 World Championship

SUGLOBOV, ALEKSANDER
b. Elektrostal, Soviet Union (Russia), January 15, 1982

2003-04 NJ	1	0	0	0	0
NHL Totals	1	0	0	0	0

–played 2004-05 with Albany River Rats, New Jersey's AHL affiliate

SULLIVAN, STEVE
b. Timmins, Ontario, July 6, 1974

2003-04 CHI/NAS	80	24	49	73	48
NHL Totals	597	175	274	449	380

–did not play professionally in 2004-05

SUNDIN, MATS
b. Bromma, Sweden, February 13, 1971

2003-04 TML	81	31	44	75	52
NHL Totals	1,086	465	624	1,089	869

–played for IMG WorldStars team that toured Europe in December 2004

SUNDSTROM, NIKLAS
b. Ornskoldsvik, Sweden, June 6, 1975

2003-04 MON	66	8	12	20	18
NHL Totals	695	111	223	334	226

–signed October 1, 2004 by Milano (Serie A, Italy)

SURMA, DAMIAN
b. Lincoln Park, Michigan, January 22, 1981

2003-04 CAR	1	0	1	1	0
NHL Totals	2	1	1	2	0

–played in 2004-05 with Florida Everblades (ECHL)

SUROVY, TOMAS
b. Banska Bystrica, Czechoslovakia (Slovakia), September 24, 1981

2003-04 PIT	47	11	12	23	16
NHL Totals	73	15	19	34	26

–played 2004-05 with Wilkes-Barre/Scranton Penguins, Pittsburgh's AHL affiliate

SUTHERBY, BRIAN
b. Edmonton, Alberta, March 1, 1982

2003-04 WAS	30	2	0	2	28
NHL Totals	109	4	9	13	123

–played 2004-05 with Portland Pirates, Washington's AHL affiliate

SUTTON, ANDY
b. Kingston, Ontario, March 10, 1975

2003-04 ATL	65	8	13	21	94
NHL Totals	301	17	47	64	565

–began 2004-05 playing with Detroit in Original Stars Hockey League
–signed September 24, 2004 by GCK Zurich (Swiss league, B Division)
–loaned February 22, 2005 to Zurich (Swiss league)

SVATOS, MAREK
b. Kosice, Czechoslovakia (Slovakia), July 17, 1982

2003-04 COL	4	2	0	2	0
NHL Totals	4	2	0	2	0

–missed majority of 2003-04 season after serious shoulder surgery
–played 2004-05 with Hershey Bears, Colorado's AHL affiliate

SVITOV, ALEXANDER
b. Omsk, Soviet Union (Russia), November 3, 1982

2003-04 TB/CBJ	40	2	9	11	20
NHL Totals	103	6	13	19	78

–played 2004-05 with Syracuse Crunch, Columbus's AHL affiliate

SVOBODA, JAROSLAV
b. Cervenka, Czechoslovakia (Czech Republic), June 1, 1980

2003-04 CAR	33	3	1	4	6
NHL Totals	91	8	14	22	40

–signed September 27, 2004 by Trinec (Extraleague, Czech Republic)

SWANSON, BRIAN
b. Eagle River, Alaska, March 24, 1976

2003-04 ATL	2	0	1	1	0
NHL Totals	70	4	13	17	16

–signed April 20, 2004 by Kassel (Deutsche Eishockey Liga, Germany)

SWEENEY, DON
b. St. Stephen, New Brunswick, August 17, 1966

2003-04 DAL	63	0	11	11	18
NHL Totals	1,115	52	221	273	681

–remained at home in Boston; did not play professionally in 2004-05

SYDOR, DARRYL
b. Edmonton, Alberta, May 13, 1972

2003-04 CBJ/TB	80	3	19	22	32
NHL Totals	943	85	342	427	630

–did not play professionally in 2004-05

Henrik Sedin (left) joined brother Daniel playing for their old club team MoDo in Sweden.

SYKORA, PETR
b. Plzen, Czechoslovakia (Czech Republic), November 19, 1976

	GP	G	A	PTS	PIM
2003-04 ANA	81	23	29	52	34
NHL Totals	608	202	259	461	240

–signed August 12, 2004 by Metallurg Magnitogorsk (Super League, Russia); played for Magnitogorsk at 2005 Spengler Cup (December 26-31, 2004)
–played for IMG WorldStars team that toured Europe in December 2004
–played for Czech Republic at 2005 World Championship (gold medal)

TAFFE, JEFF
b. Hastings, Minnesota, February 19, 1981

	GP	G	A	PTS	PIM
2003-04 PHO	59	8	10	18	20
NHL Totals	79	11	11	22	24

–played 2004-05 with Utah Grizzlies, Phoenix's AHL affiliate

TALLINDER, HENRIK
b. Stockholm, Sweden, January 10, 1979

	GP	G	A	PTS	PIM
2003-04 BUF	72	1	9	10	26
NHL Totals	120	4	19	23	54

–signed September 9, 2004 by Linkoping (Swedish Elite League); left Linkoping on February 14, 2005; suspended by Linkoping in early February for the rest of the season after he and two other Swedes, Andreas Lilja and Kristian Huselius, were charged with (and later acquitted of) rape
–signed February 23, 2005 by SC Bern (Swiss league), the same day Swedish police re-opened the case (which was later dropped)

TAMER, CHRIS
b. Dearborn, Michigan, November 17, 1970

	GP	G	A	PTS	PIM
2003-04 ATL	38	2	5	7	55
NHL Totals	644	21	64	85	1,183

–did not play professionally in 2004-05

TANABE, DAVID
b. White Bear Lake, Minnesota, July 19, 1980

	GP	G	A	PTS	PIM
2003-04 PHO	45	5	7	12	22
NHL Totals	296	20	54	74	137

–signed October 21, 2004 by Rapperswil-Jona (Swiss league)
–signed October 29, 2004 by Kloten (Swiss league)
–won gold medal with USA at Deutschland Cup in November 2004

TANGUAY, ALEX
b. Ste. Justine, Quebec, November 21, 1979

	GP	G	A	PTS	PIM
2003-04 COL	69	25	54	79	42
NHL Totals	379	108	214	322	173

–signed October 7, 2004 by Lugano (Swiss league); left during season because of injury

TARNSTROM, DICK
b. Sundbyberg, Sweden, January 20, 1975

	GP	G	A	PTS	PIM
2003-04 PIT	80	16	36	52	38
NHL Totals	203	26	86	112	126

–signed October 9, 2004 by Sodertalje (Swedish Elite League)

TAYLOR, CHRIS
b. Stratford, Ontario, March 6, 1972

	GP	G	A	PTS	PIM
2003-04 BUF	54	6	6	12	22
NHL Totals	144	11	21	32	48

–played 2004-05 with Rochester Americans, Buffalo's AHL affiliate

TAYLOR, TIM
b. Stratford, Ontario, February 6, 1969

	GP	G	A	PTS	PIM
2003-04 TB	82	7	15	22	25
NHL Totals	593	65	83	148	395

–did not play professionally in 2004-05

TELLQVIST, MIKAEL
b. Sundbyberg, Sweden, September 19, 1979

	GP	W-L-T	MIN	GA	SO	GAA
2003-04 TML	11	5-3-2	647	31	0	2.87
NHL Totals	14	6-4-2	733	35	0	2.86

–played 2004-05 with St. John's Maple Leafs, Toronto's AHL affiliate

TETARENKO, JOEY
b. Prince Albert, Saskatchewan, March 3, 1978

	GP	G	A	PTS	PIM
2003-04 CAR	2	0	0	0	0
NHL Totals	73	4	1	5	76

–split 2004-05 between Lowell Lock Monsters, Carolina's AHL affiliate, and Houston Aeros (AHL)

THEODORE, JOSE
b. Laval, Quebec, September 13, 1976

	GP	W-L-T	MIN	GA	SO	GAA
2003-04 MON	67	33-28-5	3,961	150	6	2.27
NHL Totals	315	124-143-30	17,940	754	23	2.52

–signed December 20, 2004 by Djurgarden (Swedish Elite League)

THERIEN, CHRIS
b. Ottawa, Ontario, December 14, 1971

	GP	G	A	PTS	PIM
2003-04 PHI/DAL	67	1	9	10	52
NHL Totals	717	29	126	155	551

–did not play professionally in 2004-05

THIBAULT, JOCELYN
b. Montreal, Quebec, January 12, 1975

	GP	W-L-T	MIN	GA	SO	GAA
2003-04 CHI	14	5-7-2	821	39	1	2.85
NHL Totals	536	227-217-68	30,477	1,368	36	2.69

–did not play professionally in 2004-05

THOMAS, STEVE
b. Stockport, England, July 15, 1963

	GP	G	A	PTS	PIM
2003-04 DET	44	10	12	22	25
NHL Totals	1,235	421	512	933	1,306

–did not play professionally in 2004-05

THORNTON, JOE
b. London, Ontario, July 2, 1979

	GP	G	A	PTS	PIM
2003-04 BOS	77	23	50	73	98
NHL Totals	509	160	261	421	611

–signed July 8, 2004 by Davos (Swiss league); won gold medal with Davos at 2005 Spengler Cup (December 26-31, 2004) and led playoffs in points en route to championship
–played for IMG WorldStars team that toured Europe in December 2004
–played for Canada at 2005 World Championship (silver medal); named tournament MVP

THORNTON, SCOTT
b. London, Ontario, January 9, 1971

	GP	G	A	PTS	PIM
2003-04 SJ	80	13	14	27	84
NHL Totals	765	122	121	243	1,251

–signed January 18, 2005 by Sodertalje (Swedish Elite League)

THORNTON, SHAWN
b. Oshawa, Ontario, July 23, 1977

	GP	G	A	PTS	PIM
2003-04 CHI	8	1	0	1	23
NHL Totals	21	2	1	3	54

–played 2004-05 with Norfolk Admirals, Chicago's AHL affiliate

TIMANDER, MATTIAS
b. Solleftea, Sweden, April 16, 1974

	GP	G	A	PTS	PIM
2003-04 NYI/PHI	39	2	5	7	21
NHL Totals	419	13	57	70	165

–played 2004-05 with MoDo (Swedish Elite League)

TIMONEN, KIMMO
b. Kuopio, Finland, March 18, 1975

2003-04 NAS	77	12	32	44	52
NHL Totals	414	55	141	196	232

–signed October 31, 2004 by Lugano (Swiss league)
–signed November 8, 2004 by Brynas (Swedish Elite League)
–signed January 3, 2005 by KalPa (Finnish league, Division 2)
–played for Finland at 2005 World Championship

TJARNQVIST, DANIEL
b. Umea, Sweden, October 14, 1976

2003-04 ATL	68	5	15	20	20
NHL Totals	218	10	43	53	60

–signed September 16, 2004 by Djurgarden (Swedish Elite League)

TJARNQVIST, MATHIAS
b. Umea, Sweden, April 15, 1979

2003-04 DAL	18	1	1	2	2
NHL Totals	18	1	1	2	2

–signed August 30, 2004 by HV 71 Jonkoping (Swedish Elite League)

TKACHUK, KEITH
b. Melrose, Massachusetts, March 28, 1972

2003-04 STL	75	33	38	71	83
NHL Totals	856	431	401	832	1,861

–started 2004-05 playing rec. hockey in Brentwood Hockey League in St. Louis

TOOTOO, JORDIN
b. Churchill, Manitoba, February 2, 1983

2003-04 NAS	70	4	4	8	137
NHL Totals	70	4	4	8	137

–played 2004-05 with Milwaukee Admirals, Nashville's AHL affiliate

TORRES, RAFFI
b. Toronto, Ontario, October 8, 1981

2003-04 EDM	80	20	14	34	65
NHL Totals	111	20	20	40	81

–played 2004-05 with Edmonton Road Runners, Edmonton Oilers' AHL affiliate

TOSKALA, VESA
b. Tampere, Finland, May 20, 1977

2003-04 SJ	28	12-8-4	1,541	53	1	2.06
NHL Totals	40	16-11-5	2,088	74	2	2.13

–started season on injured list, receiving pay, following hip surgery as a result of an injury sustained while playing for Team Finland at World Cup of Hockey 2004
–signed January 13, 2005 by HV 71 Jonkoping (Swedish Elite League)
–also played part of 2004-05 with Ilves Tampere (SM-Liiga, Finland)

TREMBLAY, YANNICK
b. Pointe-aux-Trembles, Quebec, November 15, 1975

2003-04 ATL	38	2	8	10	13
NHL Totals	378	37	85	122	166

–signed November 16, 2004 by Sherbrooke (NAHL, Quebec)
–signed January 13, 2005 by Adler Mannheim (Deutsche Eishockey Liga, Germany)
–also played part of 2004-05 with London Racers (Elite Ice Hockey League, UK)

TRIPP, JOHN
b. Kingston, Ontario, May 4, 1977

2003-04 LA	34	1	5	6	33
NHL Totals	43	2	7	9	35

–signed April 20, 2004 by Adler Mannheim (Deutsche Eishockey Liga, Germany)

TRNKA, PAVEL
b. Plzen, Czechoslovakia (Czech Republic), July 27, 1976

2003-04 FLO	67	3	13	16	51
NHL Totals	411	14	63	77	323

–signed August 2, 2004 by Plzen (Extraleague, Czech Republic)

TUCKER, DARCY
b. Castor, Alberta, March 15, 1975

2003-04 TML	69	21	11	32	68
NHL Totals	609	127	171	298	1,015

–did not play professionally in 2004-05

TUGNUTT, RON
b. Scarborough (Toronto), Ontario, October 22, 1967

2003-04 DAL	11		3-7-0	548	22	1	2.41
NHL Totals	537	186-239-62	29,486	1,497	26	3.05

–did not play professionally in 2004-05

TURCO, MARTY
b. Sault Ste. Marie, Ontario, August 13, 1975

2003-04 DAL	73	37-21-13	4,359	144	9	1.98
NHL Totals	185	96-43-26	10,347	329	21	1.91

–signed November 13, 2004 by Djurgarden (Swedish Elite League); left Djurgarden on December 9, 2004 because he couldn't make adequate arrangements for his family to join him

TUREK, ROMAN
b. Strakonice, Czechoslovakia (Czech Republic), May 21, 1970

2003-04 CAL	18	6-11-0	1,031	40	3	2.33
NHL Totals	328	159-115-43	19,095	734	27	2.31

–signed November 9, 2004 by Ceske Budejovice (Czech Republic, Division 2)

TURGEON, PIERRE
b. Rouyn, Quebec, August 28, 1969

2003-04 DAL	76	15	25	40	20
NHL Totals	1,215	495	779	1,274	410

–remained at home in Dallas with his family; did not play professionally in 2004-05

TVRDON, ROMAN
b. Trencin, Czechoslovakia (Slovakia), January 29, 1981

2003-04 WAS	9	0	1	1	2
NHL Totals	9	0	1	1	2

–signed July 12, 2004 by Nottingham (Elite Ice Hockey League, UK)

TYUTIN, FEDOR
b. Izhevsk, Soviet Union (Russia), July 19, 1983

2003-04 NYR	25	2	5	7	14
NHL Totals	25	2	5	7	14

–signed November 11, 2004 by SKA St. Petersburg (Super League, Russia)
–played part of 2004-05 with Hartford Wolf Pack, New York Rangers' AHL affiliate

ULANOV, IGOR
b. Krasnokamsk, Soviet Union (Russia), October 1, 1969

2003-04 EDM	42	5	13	18	28
NHL Totals	702	24	129	153	1,122

–remained at home in Toronto with his family; did not play professionally in 2004-05

ULMER, LAYNE
b. North Battleford, Saskatchewan, September 14, 1980

2003-04 NYR	1	0	0	0	0
NHL Totals	1	0	0	0	0

–played 2004-05 with Hartford Wolf Pack, New York Rangers' AHL affiliate

Goalie Marty Turco had an impressive 2004-05 season with Djurgarden in Sweden.

UNDERHILL, MATT
b. Merritt, British Columbia, September 16, 1979

2003-04 CHI	1	0-1-0	61	4	0	3.93
NHL Totals	1	0-1-0	61	4	0	3.93

–split 2004-05 between Mississippi Sea Wolves (ECHL), St. John's Maple Leafs (AHL), and Providence Bruins (AHL)

UPSHALL, SCOTTIE
b. Fort McMurray, Alberta, October 7, 1983

2003-04 NAS	7	0	1	1	0
NHL Totals	15	1	1	2	0

–played 2004-05 with Milwaukee Admirals, Nashville's AHL affiliate

VAANANEN, OSSI
b. Vantaa, Finland, August 18, 1980

2003-04 PHO/COL	79	2	4	6	89
NHL Totals	303	10	35	45	335

–signed December 1, 2004 by Jokerit Helsinki (SM-Liiga, Finland)
–played for Finland at 2005 World Championship

VALICEVIC, ROB
b. Detroit, Michigan, January 6, 1971

2003-04 DAL	7	0	0	0	2
NHL Totals	193	28	20	48	61

–started 2004-05 with TPS Turku (SM-Liiga, Finland)
–played 2004-05 with Flint Generals (UHL)

VALIQUETTE, STEVE
b. Etobicoke (Toronto), Ontario, August 20, 1977

2003-04 EDM/NYR	3	1-1-0	134	8	0	3.93
NHL Totals	9	3-1-0	327	14	0	2.57

–played 2004-05 with Hartford Wolf Pack, New York Rangers' AHL affiliate

VAN ALLEN, SHAUN
b. Calgary, Alberta, August 29, 1967

2003-04 OTT	73	2	10	12	80
NHL Totals	794	84	185	269	481

–did not play professionally in 2004-05

VANDENBUSSCHE, RYAN
b. Simcoe, Ontario, February 28, 1973

2003-04 CHI	65	4	1	5	120
NHL Totals	290	9	10	19	660

–began 2004-05 playing with Toronto and New York in Original Stars Hockey League
–played 2004-05 with Wilkes-Barre/Scranton Penguins, Pittsburgh's AHL affiliate, after signing with Pittsburgh as a free agent in the summer of 2004

VANDERMEER, JIM
b. Caroline, Alberta, February 21, 1980

2003-04 PHI/CHI	46	5	12	17	83
NHL Totals	70	7	13	20	110

–played 2004-05 with Norfolk Admirals, Chicago's AHL affiliate

VAN RYN, MIKE
b. London, Ontario, May 14, 1979

2003-04 FLO	79	13	24	37	52
NHL Totals	148	15	35	50	78

–remained at home in London, skating with London Knights (OHL)

VARADA, VACLAV
b. Vsetin, Czechoslovakia (Czech Republic), April 26, 1976

2003-04 OTT	30	5	5	10	26
NHL Totals	417	53	109	162	360

–signed September 17, 2004 by Vitkovice (Extraleague, Czech Republic)
–played for Czech Republic at 2005 World Championship (gold medal)

VASICEK, JOSEF
b. Havlickuv Brod, Czechoslovakia (Czech Republic), September 12, 1980

2003-04 CAR	82	19	26	45	60
NHL Totals	293	51	66	117	199

–signed September 17, 2004 by Slavia Praha (Extraleague, Czech Republic)

VAUCLAIR, JULIEN
b. Delemont, Switzerland, October 2, 1979

2003-04 OTT	1	0	0	0	2
NHL Totals	1	0	0	0	2

–signed May 12, 2004 by Lugano (Swiss league)
–played for Switzerland at 2005 World Championship

VEILLEUX, STEPHANE
b. Beaureville, Quebec, November 16, 1981

2003-04 MIN	19	2	8	10	20
NHL Totals	57	5	10	15	43

–played 2004-05 with Houston Aeros, Minnesota's AHL affiliate

VERMETTE, ANTOINE
b. St. Agapit, Quebec, July 20, 1982

2003-04 OTT	57	7	7	14	16
NHL Totals	57	7	7	14	16

–played 2004-05 with Binghamton Senators, Ottawa's AHL affiliate

VERNARSKY, KRIS
b. Detroit, Michigan, April 5, 1982

2003-04 BOS	3	0	0	0	0
NHL Totals	17	1	0	1	2

–split 2004-05 between Providence Bruins, Boston's AHL affiliate, and Florida Everblades (ECHL)

VEROT, DARCY
b. Radville, Saskatchewan, July 13, 1976

2003-04 WAS	37	0	2	2	135
NHL Totals	37	0	2	2	135

–played 2004-05 with Portland Pirates, Washington's AHL affiliate

VIGIER, J.P.
b. Notre Dame de Lourdes, Manitoba, September 11, 1976

2003-04 ATL	70	10	8	18	22
NHL Totals	100	14	9	23	30

–played 2004-05 with Chicago Wolves, Atlanta's AHL affiliate

VISHNEVSKI, VITALI
b. Kharkov, Soviet Union (Ukraine), March 18, 1980

2003-04 ANA	73	6	10	16	51
NHL Totals	334	10	30	40	312

–played 2004-05 with Khimik Voskresensk (Super League, Russia)

VISNOVSKY, LUBOMIR
b. Topolcany, Czechoslovakia (Slovakia), August 11, 1976

2003-04 LA	58	8	21	29	26
NHL Totals	268	27	86	113	104

–signed September 27, 2004 by Slovan Bratislava (Extraleague, Slovakia)
–played for Slovakia at 2005 World Championship

VOKOUN, TOMAS
b. Karlovy Vary, Czechoslovakia (Czech Republic), July 2, 1976

2003-04 NAS	73	34-29-10	4,221	178	3	2.53
NHL Totals	279	98-129-35	15,607	662	12	2.55

–signed September 6, 2004 by Znojemsti Orli (Extraleague, Czech Republic)

–signed December 20, 2004 by HIFK Helsinki (SM-Liiga, Finland); played for Helsinki at 2005 Spengler Cup (December 26-31, 2004)

–played for Czech Republic at 2005 World Championship (gold medal)

VOLCHENKOV, ANTON
b. Moscow, Soviet Union (Russia), February 25, 1982

2003-04 OTT	19	1	2	3	8
NHL Totals	76	4	15	19	48

–started 2004-05 with CSKA Moscow (Super League, Russia), but spent most of the season with Binghamton Senators, Ottawa's AHL affiliate

VOROBIEV, PAVEL
b. Karaganda, Soviet Union (Kazakhstan), May 5, 1982

2003-04 CHI	18	1	3	4	4
NHL Totals	18	1	3	4	4

–played 2004-05 with Norfolk Admirals, Chicago's AHL affiliate

VRBATA, RADIM
b. Mlada Boleslav, Czechoslovakia (Czech Republic), June 13, 1981

2003-04 CAR	80	12	13	25	24
NHL Totals	208	46	44	90	56

–signed September 4, 2004 by Liberec (Extraleague, Czech Republic)

–played for Czech Republic at 2005 World Championship (gold medal)

VYBORNY, DAVID
b. Jihlava, Czechoslovakia (Czech Republic), June 2, 1975

2003-04 CBJ	82	22	31	53	40
NHL Totals	315	68	94	162	84

–signed August 9, 2004 by Sparta Praha (Extraleague, Czech Republic); played for Sparta Praha at 2005 Spengler Cup (December 26-31, 2004)

–played for Czech Republic at 2005 World Championship (gold medal)

WALKER, MATT
b. Beaverlodge, Alberta, April 7, 1980

2003-04 STL	14	0	1	1	25
NHL Totals	30	0	2	2	63

–played part of 2004-05 with Worcester IceCats, St. Louis's AHL affiliate

WALKER, SCOTT
b. Cambridge, Ontario, July 19, 1973

2003-04 NAS	75	25	42	67	94
NHL Totals	574	101	174	275	895

–signed on October 21, 2004 by Cambridge Hornets (OHA Senior A)

–Nashville's player representative at NHLPA meetings

–played for Canada at 2005 World Championship (silver medal)

WALLIN, NICLAS
b. Boden, Sweden, February 20, 1975

2003-04 CAR	57	3	7	10	51
NHL Totals	223	8	20	28	179

–signed September 19, 2004 by Lulea (Swedish Elite League)

WALLIN, RICKARD
b. Stockholm, Sweden, April 19, 1980

2003-04 MIN	15	5	4	9	14
NHL Totals	19	6	4	10	14

–played 2004-05 with Houston Aeros, Minnesota's AHL affiliate

WALSER, DERRICK
b. New Glasgow, Nova Scotia, May 12, 1978

2003-04 CBJ	27	1	8	9	22
NHL Totals	82	6	21	27	56

–signed May 13, 2004 by Berlin (Deutsche Eishockey Liga, Germany)

–played for Canada at Deutschland Cup in November 2004

WALZ, WES
b. Calgary, Alberta, May 15, 1970

2003-04 MIN	57	12	13	25	32
NHL Totals	452	80	115	195	246

–remained at home in Minnesota; did not play professionally in 2004-05

WANVIG, KYLE
b. Calgary Alberta, January 29, 1981

2003-04 MIN	6	0	1	1	10
NHL Totals	13	1	1	2	23

–played 2004-05 with Houston Aeros, Minnesota's AHL affiliate

WARD, AARON
b. Windsor, Ontario, January 17, 1973

2003-04 CAR	49	3	5	8	37
NHL Totals	481	25	49	74	439

–signed February 15, 2005 by Ingolstadt (Deutsche Eishockey Liga, Germany)

WARD, JASON
b. Chapleau, Ontario, January 16, 1979

2003-04 MON	53	5	7	12	21
NHL Totals	105	10	10	20	43

–began 2004-05 playing for Toronto in Original Stars Hockey League

–played 2004-05 with Hamilton Bulldogs, Montreal's AHL affiliate

WARD, LANCE
b. Lloydminster, Alberta, June 2, 1978

2003-04 ANA	46	0	4	4	94
NHL Totals	201	4	12	16	391

–remained at home in Lloydminster; did not play professionally in 2004-05

WARRENER, RHETT
b. Shaunavon, Saskatchewan, January 27, 1976

2003-04 CAL	77	3	14	17	97
NHL Totals	560	16	70	86	757

–played for IMG WorldStars team that toured Europe in December 2004

WEAVER, MIKE
b. Bramalea, Ontario, May 2, 1978

2003-04 ATL	1	0	0	0	0
NHL Totals	57	0	6	6	30

–played 2004-05 with Manchester Monarchs (AHL)

WEBB, STEVE
b. Peterborough, Ontario, April 30, 1975

2003-04 PIT/NYI	10	0	0	0	4
NHL Totals	321	5	13	18	532

–did not play professionally in 2004-05

WEEKES, KEVIN
b. Toronto, Ontario, April 4, 1975

2003-04 CAR	66	23-30-11	3,765	146	6	2.33
NHL Totals	277	78-136-33	15,088	720	19	2.86

–did not play professionally in 2004-05; remained at home in Toronto and worked on Skillz Hockey, an organization that helps less-fortunate kids develop skills and acquire equipment to play the game

WEIGHT, DOUG
b. Warren, Michigan, January 21, 1971

2003-04 STL	75	14	51	65	37
NHL Totals	912	224	604	828	734

–started 2004-05 playing rec. hockey in Brentwood Hockey League in St. Louis
–signed February 11, 2005 by Frankfurt (Deutsche Eishockey Liga, Germany)
–played for USA at 2005 World Championship

WEINHANDL, MATTIAS
b. Ljungby, Sweden, June 1, 1980

2003-04 NYI	55	8	12	20	26
NHL Totals	102	14	29	43	36

–signed September 18, 2004 by MoDo (Swedish Elite League)
–played for Sweden at 2005 World Championship

WEINRICH, ERIC
b. Roanoke, Virginia, December 19, 1966

2003-04 PHI/STL	80	4	15	19	46
NHL Totals	1,082	69	302	371	773

–signed February 14, 2005 by Villach (Austrian league)

WEISS, STEPHEN
b. Toronto, Ontario, April 3, 1983

2003-04 FLO	50	12	17	29	10
NHL Totals	134	19	33	52	27

–played most of 2004-05 with San Antonio Rampage, Florida's AHL affiliate; loaned to Chicago Wolves (AHL) for last part of '04-'05

WELLWOOD, KYLE
b. Windsor, Ontario, May 16, 1983

2003-04 TML	1	0	0	0	0
NHL Totals	1	0	0	0	0

–played 2004-05 with St. John's Maple Leafs, Toronto's AHL affiliate

WESLEY, GLEN
b. Red Deer, Alberta, October 2, 1968

2003-04 CAR	74	0	6	6	32
NHL Totals	1,247	124	382	506	891

–remained at home in Raleigh; did not play professionally in 2004-05

WESTCOTT, DUVIE
b. Winnipeg, Manitoba, October 30, 1977

2003-04 CBJ	34	0	7	7	39
NHL Totals	77	0	14	14	118

–signed September 30, 2004 by Jyvaskyla (SM-Liiga, Finland)

WESTRUM, ERIK
b. Minneapolis, Minnesota, July 26, 1979

2003-04 PHO	15	1	1	2	20
NHL Totals	15	1	1	2	20

–played 2004-05 with Utah Grizzlies, Phoenix's AHL affiliate

WHITE, COLIN
b. New Glasgow, Nova Scotia, December 12, 1977

2003-04 NJ	75	2	11	13	96
NHL Totals	323	12	42	54	522

–remained at home in New Jersey; did not play professionally in 2004-05

WHITE, PETER
b. Montreal, Quebec, March 15, 1969

2003-04 PHI	3	0	0	0	2
NHL Totals	220	23	37	60	36

–split 2004-05 between Philadelphia Phantoms, Philadelphia Flyers' AHL affiliate, and Utah Grizzlies (AHL)

WHITE, TODD
b. Kanata, Ontario, May 21, 1975

2003-04 OTT	53	9	20	29	22
NHL Totals	276	65	94	159	100

–signed December 21, 2004 by Sodertalje (Swedish Elite League); left Sodertalje on December 28, 2004

WHITFIELD, TRENT
b. Estevan, Saskatchewan, June 17, 1977

2003-04 WAS	44	6	5	11	14
NHL Totals	144	9	11	20	83

–played 2004-05 with Portland Pirates, Washington's AHL affiliate

WHITNEY, RAY
b. Fort Saskatchewan, Alberta, May 8, 1972

2003-04 DET	67	14	29	43	22
NHL Totals	700	205	330	535	219

–played for IMG WorldStars team that toured Europe in December 2004

WIEMER, JASON
b. Kimberley, British Columbia, April 14, 1976

2003-04 NYI/MIN	75	8	14	22	130
NHL Totals	677	88	110	198	1,317

–did not play professionally in 2004-05

WILLIAMS, JASON
b. London, Ontario, August 11, 1980

2003-04 DET	49	6	7	13	15
NHL Totals	95	17	15	32	23

–signed October 18, 2004 by Assat Pori (SM-Liiga, Finland)

WILLIAMS, JUSTIN
b. Cobourg, Ontario, October 4, 1981

2003-04 PHI/CAR	79	11	33	44	64
NHL Totals	258	48	85	133	140

–signed September 21, 2004 by Lulea (Swedish Elite League)

WILLIS, SHANE
b. Edmonton, Alberta, June 13, 1977

2003-04 TB	12	0	6	6	2
NHL Totals	174	31	43	74	77

–played 2004-05 with Springfield Falcons, Tampa Bay's AHL affiliate

WILLSIE, BRIAN
b. London, Ontario, March 16, 1978

2003-04 WAS	49	10	5	15	18
NHL Totals	118	17	13	30	47

–began 2004-05 playing with Toronto in Original Stars Hockey League
–signed October 8, 2004 by ZM Olimpija (Slovenian league); left ZM Olimpija on December 14, 2004
–played rest of 2004-05 with Portland Pirates, Washington's AHL affiliate

WILM, CLARKE
b. Central Butte, Saskatchewan, October 24, 1976

2003-04 TML	10	0	0	0	7
NHL Totals	395	36	53	89	293

–played 2004-05 with St. John's Maple Leafs, Toronto's AHL affiliate

WILSON, LANDON
b. St. Louis, Missouri, March 13, 1975

2003-04 PHO/PIT	54	6	4	10	47
NHL Totals	348	51	60	111	331

–signed June 23, 2004 by Espoo (SM-Liiga, Finland)

WISEMAN, CHAD
b. Burlington, Ontario, March 25, 1981

2003-04 NYR	4	1	0	1	0
NHL Totals	8	1	0	1	4

–played 2004-05 with Hartford Wolf Pack, New York Rangers' AHL affiliate

WITT, BRENDAN
b. Humboldt, Saskatchewan, February 20, 1975

2003-04 WAS	72	2	10	12	123
NHL Totals	568	19	53	72	894

–signed December 21, 2004 with Bracknell Bees (British Ice Hockey League, UK); left Bracknell on January 25, 2005

WOOLLEY, JASON
b. Toronto, Ontario, July 27, 1969

2003-04 DET	55	4	15	19	28
NHL Totals	665	67	228	295	402

–began 2004-05 skating and helping coach at his alma mater, Michigan State University Spartans
–signed February 18, 2005 by Flint Generals (UHL)

WORRELL, PETER
b. Pierrefonds, Quebec, August 18, 1977

2003-04 COL	49	3	1	4	179
NHL Totals	391	19	27	46	1,554

–remained at home in Denver; did not play professionally in 2004-05

WRIGHT, TYLER
b. Kamsack, Saskatchewan, April 6, 1973

2003-04 CBJ	68	9	9	18	63
NHL Totals	570	77	64	141	803

–played 2004-05 with EHC-Biel (Swiss league, B Division)

YABLONSKI, JEREMY
b. Meadow Lake, Saskatchewan, March 21, 1980

2003-04 STL	1	0	0	0	5
NHL Totals	1	0	0	0	5

–played 2004-05 with Milwaukee Admirals, Nashville's farm team, after being claimed off waivers by the Predators in January 2004

YAKUBOV, MIKHAIL
b. Barnaul, Soviet Union (Russia), February 16, 1982

2003-04 CHI	30	1	7	8	8
NHL Totals	30	1	7	8	8

–played 2004-05 with Norfolk Admirals, Chicago's AHL affiliate

YASHIN, ALEXEI
b. Sverdlovsk, Soviet Union (Russia), November 5, 1973

2003-04 NYI	47	15	19	34	10
NHL Totals	710	291	374	665	289

–signed February 14, 2005 by Lokomotiv Yaroslavl (Super League, Russia)
–played for Russia at 2005 World Championship (bronze medal)

YEATS, MATTHEW
b. Montreal, Quebec, April 6, 1979

2003-04 WAS	5	1-3-0	258	13	0	3.02
NHL Totals	5	1-3-0	258	13	0	3.02

–split 2004-05 between Philadelphia Phantoms (AHL) and Reading Royals (ECHL)

YELLE, STEPHANE
b. Ottawa, Ontario, May 9, 1974

2003-04 CAL	53	4	13	17	24
NHL Totals	640	68	117	185	326

–remained at home in Denver; did not play professionally in 2004-05

YONKMAN, NOLAN
b. Punnichy, Saskatchewan, April 1, 1981

2003-04 WAS	1	0	0	0	0
NHL Totals	12	1	0	1	4

–played 2004-05 with Portland Pirates, Washington's AHL affiliate

YORK, JASON
b. Nepean, Ontario, May 20, 1970

2003-04 NAS	67	2	13	15	64
NHL Totals	708	41	180	221	589

–signed February 17, 2005 by Geneve-Servette (Swiss league)

YORK, MIKE
b. Pontiac, Michigan, January 3, 1978

2003-04 EDM	61	16	26	42	15
NHL Totals	379	98	137	235	79

–played 2004-05 with Iserlohn (Deutsche Eishockey Liga, Germany)
–won gold medal with USA at Deutschland Cup in November 2004
–played for USA at 2005 World Championship

YOUNG, SCOTT
b. Clinton, Massachusetts, October 1, 1967

2003-04 DAL	53	8	8	16	14
NHL Totals	1,102	324	384	708	396

–signed January 7, 2005 by Memphis River Kings (CHL)

YZERMAN, STEVE
b. Cranbrook, British Columbia, May 9, 1965

2003-04 DET	75	18	33	51	46
NHL Totals	1,453	678	1,043	1,721	906

–did not play in 2004-05; spent much of his free time at the driving range or playing golf at his home course, Oakland Hills, Michigan

ZALESAK, MIROSLAV
b. Skalica, Czechoslovakia (Czech Republic), January 2, 1980

2003-04 SJ	2	0	0	0	0
NHL Totals	12	1	2	3	0

–signed September 17, 2004 by Skalica (Extraleague, Slovakia)
–signed November 19, 2004 by Litvinov (Extraleague, Czech Republic)

ZAMUNER, ROB
b. Oakville, Ontario, September 17, 1969

2003-04 BOS	57	4	5	9	16
NHL Totals	798	139	172	311	467

–signed August 23, 2004 by Basel (Swiss league)
–played for Canada at Deutschland Cup in November 2004

ZEDNIK, RICHARD
b. Bystrica, Czechoslovakia (Slovakia), January 6, 1976

2003-04 MON	81	26	24	50	63
NHL Totals	512	145	124	269	408

–signed October 7, 2004 by Zvolen (Extralegaue, Slovakia)
–played for Slovakia at 2005 World Championship

ZETTERBERG, HENRIK
b. Njurunda, Sweden, October 9, 1980

2003-04 DET	61	15	28	43	14
NHL Totals	140	37	50	87	22

–signed September 20, 2004 by Timra (Swedish Elite League)
–played for Sweden at 2005 World Championship

ZHAMNOV, ALEXEI
b. Moscow, Soviet Union (Russia), October 1, 1970

2003-04 CHI/PHI	43	11	25	36	28
NHL Totals	783	248	461	709	638

–signed November 15, 2004 by Vityaz Chekhov (Russian league, Division 2)

ZHERDEV, NIKOLAI
b. Kiev, Soviet Union (Ukraine), November 5, 1984

2003-04 CBJ	57	13	21	34	54
NHL Totals	57	13	21	34	54

–signed July 27, 2004 by CSKA Moscow (Super League, Russia)

ZHITNIK, ALEXEI
b. Kiev, Soviet Union (Ukraine), October 10, 1972

2003-04 BUF	68	4	24	28	102
NHL Totals	882	81	315	396	1,030

–signed December 6, 2004 by AK Bars Kazan (Super League, Russia)

ZHOLTOK, SERGEI
b. Riga, Soviet Union (Latvia), December 2, 1972

2003-04 MIN/NAS	70	14	17	31	19
NHL Totals	588	111	147	258	166

–signed October 2, 2004 by Riga 2000 (Latvian league)
–died November 3, 2004 while playing for Riga 2000, the result of cardiac arrythmia

ZIDLICKY, MAREK
b. Most, Czechoslovakia (Czech Republic), February 3, 1977

2003-04 NAS	82	14	39	53	82
NHL Totals	82	14	39	53	82

–signed September 17, 2004 by HIFK Helsinki (SM-Liiga, Finland); played for Helsinki at 2005 Spengler Cup (December 26-31, 2004)
–played for Czech Republic at 2005 World Championship (gold medal)

ZIGOMANIS, MIKE
b. North York (Toronto), Ontario, January 17, 1981

2003-04 CAR	17	0	3	3	2
NHL Totals	36	2	4	6	2

–played 2004-05 with Lowell Lock Monsters, Carolina's AHL affiliate

ZINGER, DWAYNE
b. Coronation, Alberta, July 5, 1976

2003-04 WAS	7	0	1	1	9
NHL Totals	7	0	1	1	9

–played 2004-05 with Portland Pirates, Washington's AHL affiliate

ZINOVJEV, SERGEI
b. Novokuznetsk, Soviet Union (Russia), March 4, 1980

2003-04 BOS	10	0	1	1	2
NHL Totals	10	0	1	1	2

–played part of 2003-04 and all of 2004-05 with AK Bars Kazan (Super League, Russia)
–played for Russia at 2005 World Championship (bronze medal)

ZIZKA, TOMAS
b. Sternberk, Czechoslovakia (Czech Republic), October 10, 1979

2003-04 LA	15	2	3	5	12
NHL Totals	25	2	6	8	16

–signed August 31, 2004 by Spartak Moscow (Super League, Russia)

ZUBOV, SERGEI
b. Moscow, Soviet Union (Russia), July 22, 1970

2003-04 DAL	77	7	35	42	20
NHL Totals	856	123	484	607	253

–remained at home in Dallas; did not play professionally in 2004-05

ZUBRUS, DAINIUS
b. Eelektrenai, Soviet Union (Lithuania), June 16, 1978

2003-04 WAS	54	12	15	27	38
NHL Totals	539	91	152	243	303

–signed July 1, 2004 by Lada Togliatti (Super League, Russia)
–played for Lithuania at 2005 World Championship, Division I

ZYUZIN, ANDREI
b. Ufa, Soviet Union (Russia), January 21, 1978

2003-04 MIN	65	8	13	21	48
NHL Totals	358	28	63	91	328

–signed September 25, 2004 by Salavat Ulaev Ufa (Super League, Russia)
–signed December 20, 2004 by Severstal Cherepovets (Super League, Russia)

69th World Championship

INNSBRUCK/VIENNA, AUSTRIA

APRIL 30 – MAY 15, 2005

Canada failed in its bid to win a third successive World Championship gold, losing the final game of the tournament to the Czech Republic, 3-0. Although the Canadians had a better lineup on paper than they had from 2003 and 2004 when they won gold, it was also a lineup replete with NHLers who hadn't played during the 2004-05 season, notably goalie Martin Brodeur. In fact, the team's most dominant players were Joe Thornton and Rick Nash, teammates during the year with Swiss champions HC Davos. Along with linemate Simon Gagne, this was the most explosive trio in Austria, but in the finals they were shut down by the Czechs. Tomas Vokoun, the tournament's top goalie, recorded the shutout. The Czechs scored once in the first and again in the second, adding a final goal into the empty net in the final minute. Canada went through the tournament looking impressive in some games (a 6-4 win over Latvia, a 3-1 win over USA) and wobbly in others (a 2-1 win over Ukraine, a 5-4 loss to Sweden). While they were the top team offensively, they also showed surprising weakness defensively, and this, in the end, caused their demise. The Czechs, on the other hand, didn't score much, but they allowed a mere nine goals in as many games, recording three shutouts along the way. Their only loss of the tournament was a 2-1 decision to Russia in the Qualifying Round. Russia, with an impressive 6-3 win over Sweden, claimed the bronze medal with a lineup that featured some of their best young stars: Ilya Kovalchuk, Alexander Ovechkin, and Pavel Datsyuk.

FINAL PLACINGS   GOLD CZECH REPUBLIC   SILVER CANADA   BRONZE RUSSIA

4th Sweden	11th Ukraine
5th Slovakia	12th Kazakhstan
6th USA	13th Slovenia
7th Finland	14th Denmark
8th Switzerland	15th Germany
9th Latvia	16th Austria
10th Belarus	

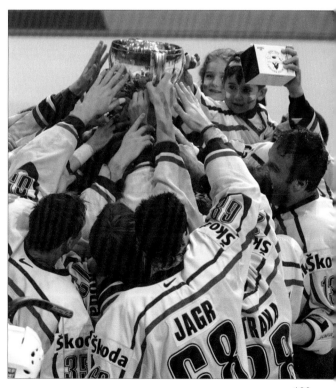

Tournament MVP: Joe Thornton (Canada)

MEDIA ALL-STAR TEAM

Goal:	Tomas Vokoun (CZE)
Defence:	Niklas Kronvall (SWE)
	Marek Zidlicky (CZE)
Forward:	Joe Thornton (CAN)
	Rick Nash (CAN)
	Jaromir Jagr (CZE)

IIHF DIRECTORATE AWARDS

Best Goalie: Tomas Vokoun (CZE)
Best Defenceman: Wade Redden (CAN)
Best Forward: Alexei Kovalev (RUS)

Members of the Czech Republic hold high the World Championship trophy following their 3-0 win over Canada in the gold medal game in Vienna on May 15, 2005.

TOP SCORERS

	GP	G	A	P	Pim
Joe Thornton (CAN)	9	6	10	16	4
Rick Nash (CAN)	9	9	6	15	8
Simon Gagne (CAN)	9	3	7	10	0
Ziggy Palffy (SVK)	7	5	4	9	10
Daniel Sedin (SWE)	9	5	4	9	2
Daniel Alfredsson (SWE)	9	3	6	9	6
Jaromir Jagr (CZE)	8	2	7	9	2
Alexander Ovechkin (RUS)	8	5	3	8	4
Vaclav Prospal (CZE)	9	2	6	8	4
Lubomir Visnovsky (SVK)	7	2	6	8	0

Petr Cajanek of the Czech Republic beats Swedish goalie Henrik Lundqvist during the semi-final game on May 14, 2005, won by the Czechs, 3-2.

SCORES & FINAL STANDINGS

PRELIMINARY ROUND

GROUP A (VIENNA)

	GP	W	L	T	GF	GA	P
Slovakia	3	2	0	1	13	5	5
Russia	3	2	0	1	9	5	5
Belarus	3	1	2	0	6	4	2
Austria	3	0	3	0	3	17	0

April 30	Russia 4	Austria 2
April 30	Slovakia 2	Belarus 1
May 2	Slovakia 3	Russia 3
May 2	Belarus 5	Austria 0
May 4	Russia 2	Belarus 0
May 4	Slovakia 8	Austria 1

GROUP B (INNSBRUCK)

	GP	W	L	T	GF	GA	P
Canada	3	3	0	0	17	5	6
USA	3	2	1	0	11	4	4
Latvia	3	1	2	0	8	10	2
Slovenia	3	0	3	0	1	18	0

April 30	Canada 6	Latvia 4
May 1	USA 7	Slovenia 0
May 3	Canada 8	Slovenia 0
May 3	USA 3	Latvia 1
May 5	Latvia 3	Slovenia 1
May 5	Canada 3	USA 1

GROUP C (INNSBRUCK)

	GP	W	L	T	GF	GA	P
Sweden	3	3	0	0	15	3	6
Finland	3	2	1	0	7	7	4
Ukraine	3	1	2	0	5	8	2
Denmark	3	0	3	0	2	11	0

April 30	Finland 2	Denmark 1
May 1	Sweden 3	Ukraine 2
May 2	Finland 4	Ukraine 1
May 2	Sweden 7	Denmark 0
May 4	Ukraine 2	Denmark 1
May 4	Sweden 5	Finland 1

GROUP D (VIENNA)

Czech Republic	3	3	0	0	6	1	6
Switzerland	3	2	1	0	8	5	4
Kazakhstan	3	1	2	0	3	4	2
Germany	3	0	3	0	2	9	0

May 1	Czech Republic 3	Switzerland 1
May 1	Kazakhstan 2	Germany 1
May 3	Switzerland 2	Kazakhstan 1
May 3	Czech Republic 2	Germany 0
May 5	Czech Republic 1	Kazakhstan 0
May 5	Switzerland 5	Germany 1

QUALIFYING ROUND

GROUP E (VIENNA)

Russia	5	3	0	2	13	8	8
Czech Republic	5	4	1	0	15	5	8
Slovakia	5	3	1	1	12	11	7
Switzerland	5	2	2	1	9	10	5
Belarus	5	1	4	0	4	11	2
Kazakhstan	5	0	5	0	3	11	0

May 6	Russia 3	Switzerland 3
May 7	Belarus 2	Kazakhstan 0
May 7	Czech Republic 5	Slovakia 1
May 8	Slovakia 3	Switzerland 1
May 8	Russia 2	Czech Republic 1
May 9	Russia 3	Kazakhstan 1
May 9	Switzerland 2	Belarus 0
May 10	Slovakia 3	Kazakhstan 1
May 10	Czech Republic 5	Belarus 1

GROUP F (INNSBRUCK)

Sweden	5	4	1	0	23	13	8
Canada	5	3	1	1	18	14	7
USA	5	2	1	2	14	10	6
Finland	5	1	1	3	12	13	5
Latvia	5	1	3	1	9	18	3
Ukraine	5	0	4	1	5	13	1

May 6	USA 4	Finland 4
May 7	Latvia 3	Ukraine 0
May 7	Sweden 5	Canada 4
May 8	Canada 3	Finland 3
May 8	USA 5	Sweden 1
May 9	USA 1	Ukraine 1

May 9	Finland 0	Latvia 0
May 10	Canada 2	Ukraine 1
May 10	Sweden 9	Latvia 1

RELEGATION ROUND
GROUP G

Slovenia	3	2	1	0	11	14	4
Denmark	3	2	1	0	10	9	4
Germany	3	1	1	1	13	6	3
Austria	3	0	2	1	7	12	1

May 6	Vienna	Germany 2	Austria 2
May 6	Innsbruck	Slovenia 4	Denmark 3
May 8	Innsbruck	Denmark 4	Austria 3
May 9	Innsbruck	Germany 9	Slovenia 1
May 10	Innsbruck	Denmark 3	Germany 2
May 11	Innsbruck	Slovenia 6	Austria 2

PLAYOFFS
QUARTER-FINALS

May 12	Vienna	Czech Republic 3	USA 2 (OT & SO)
May 12	Innsbruck	Canada 5	Slovakia 4
May 12	Vienna	Russia 4	Finland 3
May 12	Innsbruck	Sweden 2	Switzerland 1

SEMI-FINALS

| May 14 | Vienna | Canada 4 | Russia 3 |
| May 14 | Vienna | Czech Republic 3 | Sweden 2 |

BRONZE MEDAL GAME

| May 15 | Vienna | Russia 6 | Sweden 3 |

GOLD MEDAL GAME

| May 15 | Vienna | Czech Republic 3 | Canada 0 |

(left) Canadian goalie Martin Brodeur stops Slovakia's Ziggy Palffy on a penalty shot during Canada's 5-4 victory in the quarter-finals; (right) Canada's Rick Nash is stopped from in close by Czech goalie Tomas Vokoun during action from the gold medal game.

Hockey's Champions, 2004-05

INTERNATIONAL

2004 World Cup of Hockey—Canada
2005 World Championship, Men—Czech Republic
2005 World Championship, Women—USA
2005 World Junior Championship—Canada

2005 IIHF European Champions Cup—Avangard Omsk (Russia)
2005 IIHF Continental Cup—HKm Zvolen (Slovakia)
2005 IIHF European Women Champions Cup—AIK Solna (Sweden)

2004 Deutschland Cup—USA
2004 Karjala Cup—Finland
2004 Rosno Cup—Russia
2004 Spengler Cup—HC Davos

NORTH AMERICA—MINOR PRO

American Hockey League (Calder Cup)—Philadelphia Phantoms
Central Hockey League (Ray Miron Cup)—Colorado Eagles
East Coast Hockey League (Kelly Cup)—Trenton Titans
SPHL (President's Cup)—Columbus Cottonmouths
United Hockey League (Colonial Cup)—Muskegon Fury

CANADIAN SENIOR

Allan Cup—Thunder Bay Bombers

CANADIAN JUNIOR

Canadian Hockey League (Memorial Cup)—London Knights
Ontario Hockey League (John Ross Robertson Cup)—London Knights
Quebec Major Junior Hockey League (President's Cup)—Rimouski Oceanic
Western Hockey League (President's Cup)—Kelowna Rockets
Canadian Junior A Hockey League (Royal Bank Cup)—Weyburn Red Wings

CANADIAN UNIVERSITY

CIS, Men (University Cup)—Alberta Golden Bears
CIS, Women (Golden Path Trophy)—Wilfred Laurier Golden Hawks

CANADIAN WOMEN

Canadian Women's Championship (Abby Hoffman Cup)—Toronto Aeros
National Women's Hockey League (Championship Cup)—Toronto Aeros
Western Women's Hockey League (Championship Cup)—Calgary Oval X-Treme

U.S. COLLEGE

NCAA, Men—Denver Pioneers
Beanpot Tournament—Boston University Terriers
NCAA, Women—University of Minnesota Golden Gophers

EUROPE

Austria—Vienna Capitals
Belarus—Junost Minsk
Czech Republic (Extraleague)—HC Pardubice
Denmark—Herning Blue Fox
Finland (SM-Liiga)—Karpat Oulu
France—Mulhouse
Germany (Deutsche Eishockey League)—Eisbaren Berlin
Great Britain (British Ice Hockey League)—Bracknell Bees
Great Britain (Elite Ice Hockey League)—Coventry Blaze
Hungary—Alba Vlan Fevita
Italy (Serie A)—Milano Vipers
Latvia—Riga 2000
The Netherlands (Oddset Ligaen)—Amsterdam Bulldogs
Norway—Valerenga Oslo
Poland—GKS Tychy
Russia (Super League)—Dynamo Moscow
Slovakia (Extraleague)—Slovan Bratislava
Slovenia—HK Jesenice
Sweden (Swedish Elite League)—Frolunda
Switzerland—HC Davos

(left to right) Niklas Hagman, Rick Nash, and Joe Thornton wear their gold medals on April 7, 2005, following HC Davos's 3-2 win over ZSC Zurich in game five of the Swiss league finals. It was Davos's 27th league championship.